D1169619

Published by Straight Talk Books
P.O. Box 301, Milwaukee, WI 53201
800.661.3311 • timeofgrace.org

Cover image: Prixel Creative/Lightstock

Printed in the United States of America

ISBN: 978-1-942107-74-3

FEARLESS FAITH

DEVOTIONS FOR
COLLEGE STUDENTS

FOREWORD

It's with great pleasure that I greet this set of devotions, unique in that they arose from the Wisconsin Lutheran College academic community. I will always have a heart for this place, not only because of my 12 years as a regent, but because Time of Grace's media ministry really arose out of WLC.

If you want to have a conversation with agnostics and atheists, you'll find them in a university. I've heard people say that they went into college a believer and came out without their faith. Some of my friends aren't very religious either. And yet I've heard a few of them say that they wished they could believe.

Where does faith come from? How does no faith become some faith? How does a weak faith become a strong faith? The Bible tells us that "faith comes from hearing the message, and the message is heard through the word of Christ" (Romans 10:17). If you are interested in growing your faith, you can expedite the process by increasing your exposure to God's words. It's that simple.

These devotions are a tool for you. Each day this school year you'll find a story or insight from our human story, a word from the Word, and a suggestion of what to do with it. If your idea of Bible study is to wait until you find large blocks of time each week for it, you may never get started. Here's another way: read a little bit every day until it becomes a treasured habit, your best time of the day.

May God grow your faith through these devotions, and may they help you be inspiration and light for others in your life.

Pastor Mark Jeske

INTRODUCTION

"It's a dangerous business, Frodo, going out your door. You step onto the road, and if you don't keep your feet, there's no knowing where you might be swept off to." ~ J.R.R. Tolkien

I love this quote from the *Lord of the Rings*, and I believe it is fitting for the life of a college student. College is an adventure. If you are reading this book, you are either stepping into the unknown for the first time, are in the midst of your journey, or perhaps you are approaching a new adventure of life after college. The purpose of this devotion book is to help you not lose your way as you battle the doubts, fears, and temptations of college.

These devotions were written by college students and others who truly understand the struggles that a college student goes through. Beginning in August and ending in May, all of these devotions are brief and to the point, for as a college student, I truly understand the busy lifestyle. It is my hope that through their stories and God's Word you are able to stand firm and strong in your faith throughout college.

This project has certainly been an adventure for me! It was an adventure that began at the end of my junior year of college when I received a scholarship that required a senior project. It is only right then that I thank Gary and Sandra Greenfield, as without their generous gift this project may have never been born. I would also like to thank the many authors, editors, advisors, and others who contributed to the project. Without their support and help, this project would never have existed. Finally, I would like to thank Time of Grace, for without their partnership this project might have never been published.

To God be the glory!
Jacob Werre
Wisconsin Lutheran College
Class of 2015

AUGUST
MAKE A GOOD BEGINNING

HAPPY NEW YEAR?

Colossians 4:5 *Be wise in the way you act toward outsiders; make the most of every opportunity.*

Most people think that the new year starts in January. That's when most people get a new calendar, make resolutions, and look toward the future. For the average college student, however, the new year starts in August. For four or more years, this is the time when everything is in transition and there's opportunity to make changes. Daily routines include new people and a new schedule. Students are also challenged to step outside their comfort zones.

With the tumult of change happening everywhere at the start of a new school year, it's very important to remember our primary role as Christians: to love God and to love our neighbor. We always have a choice in how we interact with others, how we spend our time, and who we spend it with.

As the new school year starts, let's evaluate to see if any adjustments are needed: Who are these outsiders that Colossians 4:5 talks about? I'm meeting many new people—are they outsiders? Am I an outsider?

The fact is that we all feel like outsiders at some point. We all struggle in our own way. However, as Christians, we can build each other up and support each other. Earlier in Colossians 4, St. Paul tells us to devote ourselves to prayer and to pray for each other so that we can clearly share God's message in our words and in how we live our lives.

PRAYER Dear heavenly Father, please watch over me, whether I'm an insider or outsider. Send your Holy Spirit to work in my heart so that I may live to serve you. Amen.

NO WORRIES

Philippians 4:19 *My God will meet all your needs according to the riches of his glory in Christ Jesus.*

What if people don't like me? Do I have the right schoolbooks? What if I can't find my classrooms? Did I pack everything? These are a few of the many anxieties that are present as the school year is about to start. I remember my freshman year, when I moved from Arkansas to Wisconsin and knew nobody at college. One of my worries was that no one would be my friend and I would sit alone at lunch or in the classroom.

I've learned that we don't need to worry about these things when entering a new year of college. The apostle Paul tells us in Philippians 4:19 that God will take care of all our needs. Paul wrote this to the Philippians, who had given him an abundance of gifts. Paul was reminding them that God would provide for them just as God had provided for him through their gifts. And the greatest gift that God has provided for us is the gift of his perfect Son, who was sent to die on a cross for us.

Once I came to college, I realized there was no need to worry about having friends. Yes, sometimes I sit alone at lunch or in the classroom, but God has provided me with plenty of friends. The next time you're worried at the start of a school year, whatever the worry may be, remember that God is always there providing for what you need.

PRAYER Dear God, thank you for providing me with all the things I need in life, especially your Son. Please help me to not worry as I get ready for the school year and to understand you are always there for me. Amen.

PUT IT ON!

Ephesians 6:10-12 *Be strong in the Lord and in his mighty power. Put on the full armor of God, so that you can take your stand against the devil's schemes. For our struggle is not against flesh and blood, but against the rulers, against the authorities, against the powers of this dark world and against the spiritual forces of evil in the heavenly realms.*

I've gone through a number of transitions these past few weeks. I moved to a new apartment, said good-bye to some friends, and looked for a new job. It's easy to worry about outcomes to these changes, but Paul's words in Ephesians urge us to hold on to God.

It's August. This means that summer is coming to a close and school is on the horizon. If you're like me, you know that the start of a new semester brings a new daily routine and a tremendous fear of walking in late to the wrong class. It also brings new opportunities to grow, as well as new temptations that can take us down the wrong path.

How will you defend yourself against temptation? At times you'll be on your own and you'll have to make your own decisions. Mankind is sinful and can't stand up against temptation alone. We must equip ourselves with the armor of God. It's not enough to simply know what the armor of God is; we must *put it on*. We do this by anchoring ourselves in God's Word on a regular basis.

As you start another semester, challenge yourself to grow spiritually. Pinpoint areas of weakness in your life and use God's Word as your guiding light through temptation.

PRAYER Dear God, I struggle daily with temptation, and you know my areas of weakness. Please help me grow closer to you each day so that I can do the right thing in the face of temptation. Thank you for sending your Son to atone for my shortcomings. Amen.

IT'S BEEN TAKEN CARE OF

Matthew 6:34 *Do not worry about tomorrow, for tomorrow will worry about itself. Each day has enough trouble of its own.*

The school year is around the corner. Whether you're a freshman or a senior, there's so much you can worry about. Grades, friends, sports, clubs, money, relationships, and jobs can all be sources or causes for worry. These are important, and they should be something we are concerned about. And yet Matthew is telling us not to worry!

How can that be? God has told us to be good stewards, and if I'm going to pass that test, then I have to study and worry about it.

There's a balance between being prepared and worrying, and it's wonderful when you find it. You're able to study for the last time the night before that test and go to sleep thinking, "It's in God's hands now." This is exactly the point that Matthew is making. Why cause yourself more grief by worrying when your almighty God is in charge?

The best part is that the one thing we needed to be worried about has already been taken care of. Christ has conquered sin, death, and the devil for us, so we no longer have to worry about whether we'll end up in hell or heaven. We instead have faith and confidence in his victory and in our salvation.

PRAYER Dear Lord, please help me trust in you and not worry so much. I know I will worry again, but help me look past that worry and see that there's no point because my God is in control. Amen.

ALWAYS WITH YOU

Matthew 10:19,20 *Do not worry about what to say or how to say it. At that time you will be given what to say, for it will not be you speaking, but the Spirit of your Father speaking through you.*

College means a lot of new experiences. You may be a small-town person going into the big city for college. You may be coming from a small school to a large university. You may be leaving a close community of believers for a community where you don't know who the believers are. There will be times when you're questioned about your faith and why you're not going to a particular party or why you're getting up for church every Sunday morning.

At some universities, professors may shoot down your faith in class lectures and make you doubt what you've believed for most of your life. It can be worrisome to think about those times. What will you say when asked if you are a Christian? What will you tell your friends as they ask you to go to that party for the tenth time?

Your Savior will be with you! While Jesus hasn't promised direct inspiration to us as he did to the apostles, he has promised to be with us always. Like the apostles, Jesus does not want us to be afraid of what others might do to us or think of us as we let our lights shine. He will save us; he will rescue us—for that is who he is: Jesus, "he who saves." When we live our lives focused on Christ and his promises, it will be reflected in what we say when we are questioned by others.

PRAYER Lord, help me always focus on you and your promises, no matter what situation I'm in. Let your promises matter to me, comfort me, and give me courage for every situation, including when I'm questioned by others. Remind me that you are always there, even when I worry and fret about the future. Amen.

August 6

WORRISOME "FIRSTS"

1 Peter 4:10 *Each of you should use whatever gift you have received to serve others, as faithful stewards of God's grace in its various forms.*

The first day of college classes, the first day of a new job, the first date with someone you want to know better—all bring feelings of anxiety, excitement, and preoccupation with the unknown. Often these thoughts are a major distraction. You want to enjoy these "firsts," so what can you do to ease the worry?

In this passage God commands us to use our God-given gifts faithfully. One of the simplest actions we can take is to go to God in prayer. God has given us all unique talents and abilities. If you're outgoing and personable, be a friend to the individual sitting alone in the classroom. If you're shy, simply walk around with a smile on your face and reflect God's unconditional love. Ask God to help you be a blessing to the company that just hired you. Use your gift of organization, your math abilities, or your problem-solving skills to help your workplace prosper. Before you go on your date, pray God will bless your time together and help you honor him in all you say and do.

When you ask God to help you be a blessing, the "firsts" that conjure up doubts and insecurities are more manageable. The worry and anxiety fade, and you can focus on being an instrument of God's grace and serve those around you with your entrusted gifts.

PRAYER God of generosity and grace, take away all the fear and doubt that so often distract me from enjoying the opportunities you have placed in my life. Help me use my talents to be a blessing to those around me. Grant me success in all my new endeavors, and may I always bring glory to you. Amen.

DECISIONS, DECISIONS

Isaiah 26:3,4 *You will keep in perfect peace those whose minds are steadfast, because they trust in you. Trust in the LORD forever, for the LORD, the LORD himself, is the Rock eternal.*

Is the anxiety of a major decision weighing heavily on your mind? Just weeks leading up to my senior year at college, I decided to make a change in my education course. I had been double majoring, but felt that one of my majors was not the right fit for me. Several family members, friends, and teachers thought it would be foolish for me to drop one and that I had wasted my time. After weighing my choices carefully, I took it to the Lord in prayer.

Choices can be difficult. Our feelings can deceive us. Our thoughts can be clouded by sinful motives. We could easily make decisions for merely self-serving reasons. It is good to ask God to keep us from such paths when we make life-changing decisions.

What if, looking back, we discover that we have made foolish, self-centered, or even unethical decisions? Decisions like these don't bring God's smile on us, but God's curse. What can we do? We can confess every wrong motive to the Lord Jesus. He is our Rock. By his death on the cross, he won for us God's forgiveness and mercy. He wipes away from God's memory every impure decision we've ever made.

Jesus is our Rock. As we trust in Jesus, we can be confident of God's mercy—confident that even as we struggle to make future decisions, we may do it NOT under God's frown, but under God's peace and blessing. As Isaiah points out, our minds may remain steadfast during such bumpy times because through faith in Jesus we enjoy God's peace.

PRAYER Dear Lord, help me always trust in you when I am worried and bring me peace, knowing that your hand will always guide me. Amen.

YOU AREN'T ALONE

Matthew 6:24 *No one can serve two masters. Either you will hate the one and love the other, or you will be devoted to the one and despise the other. You cannot serve both God and money.*

The car is packed, your room is cleaned out, and you're about to take the first step as a college student. You sit and wonder, "Am I ready?" At a moment like this, it's hard not to let the anxiety and worry get to you. The unknown can be scary. But what's comforting is that you will never be alone. God has promised to be with you every step of the way.

College will bring many new and exciting opportunities. As with everything we do, we want our lights to shine through and show others the love of Jesus with our words and actions. We want to serve him in everything we do, but with college tuition, grades, and our social lives, we may be tempted to put something else before God. Look again at Matthew 6:24.

Devote yourself to God. Don't allow yourself to be drawn away by earthly idols. Begin your college experience with the love of God in your heart, knowing that your heavenly Father will be your one true refuge and source of strength through the trials, temptations, and moments of weakness. After all, didn't Christ master sin, death, and hell for us? By his death and resurrection, we have the assurance that he has mastered the biggest things for us. We can be confident that he will master all the smaller things in life for us as well.

PRAYER Dear heavenly Father, thank you for always guarding and protecting me and providing a source of spiritual strength as I face each day. Please help me keep my eyes focused on you and always remember your mercy and love. Amen.

BEGIN WITH JESUS

Colossians 3:17 *Whatever you do, whether in word or deed, do it all in the name of the Lord Jesus, giving thanks to God the Father through him.*

So you're here! Your journey has been a unique one, no doubt. Whether you're the first in your family to go to college, or you're finally tasting the rewards of your years of hard work, your road to get here has not been perfectly straight. Looking at your life experiences up to this point, it would be silly to assume your journey will suddenly become easy.

As you begin this new venture, it would be easy to say, "This is going to be so hard I might fail, so why even start?" But that's not the conclusion Paul leads us to in Colossians 3:17. Notice that Paul doesn't say, "Thank God for awesome things, but when things get tough, you're on your own." Paul says to begin all of your tasks with Jesus and thank God for that. There are certainly no guarantees for the outcome, but the promise of God's protection is evident.

Begin this day, and all of your days, with a prayer of dedication and thanksgiving. Jesus will be with you as you go.

PRAYER Lord Jesus, as I begin today, be with me. Guide my steps to safely serve you, bless my efforts to glorify you, and let my life be an example of your unsurpassed love. Heavenly Father, thank you for blessing me with one more day to serve, glorify, and worship you in my life. Through your Son, my Savior. Amen.

GOD HOLDS YOUR HAND

Isaiah 41:13 *I am the LORD your God who takes hold of your right hand and says to you, Do not fear; I will help you.*

Each of my college years started the same way, with one particular image blazing in my mind when I felt lonely and homesick: the red taillights of a car driving away.

That car held my family, and I was left behind. I had decided to go to college across the country, and I would not see them for many months. No quick trips home, no holiday gatherings, and very little contact.

Those red taillights made me want to shout, "Wait! Don't leave me alone!" It felt like abandonment, although I was the one who chose to attend school far away. The hand at my side felt empty and alone, just like me.

Even before we feel abandoned, God claims us. When our hands feel empty, God takes hold and leads us. When we feel alone, God is right next to us. He wants to help us learn, move forward, and grow.

Loneliness can hit you at any stage. Perhaps you're just starting college, everything feels strange, and you're not sure what to expect. Maybe you're in the middle years, taking on new challenges and responsibilities. You could be in your last year, soon to enter the work force or pursue higher education.

Know that in the midst of it all, God is standing beside you, holding your hand, and helping you each step of the way.

PRAYER Gracious God, thank you for claiming me as your own. Teach me to let go of my fears of loneliness. Guide me to trust that you hold my hand and will always help me. Amen.

THE FRUIT OF THE SPIRIT

Galatians 5:22,23 *The fruit of the Spirit is love, joy, peace, forbearance, kindness, goodness, faithfulness, gentleness and self-control. Against such things there is no law.*

We've all been there before—the nerves and anxiety at the beginning of a new school year. So many thoughts occupy the mind: What do I wear? Will I make a lot of friends this year? Is this folder with the cute puppies on it too kiddish? By the end of the day, a whole other set of worries may take their place. We rarely need help coming up with a long list of concerns or "me" thoughts.

However, we do need the help of the Spirit in aspiring to those things that are most important for a child of God: those attributes that God wishes us to model in our everyday lives.

In this passage from Galatians, Paul addresses characteristics in the faith lives of those who call themselves children of God. Paul calls these the "fruit of the Spirit." These are attributes we receive from God that we cannot grow into on our own. "For what I want to do I do not do, but what I hate I do" (Romans 7:15).

As we move forward into the new school year, instead of focusing on the encroaching worries that bother us, why not concentrate on what our good God has done for us and what we can do as stewards of God? Through the fruit of the Spirit, may God's will be carried out in our words and actions. And may prideful thoughts and selfish worrying be pushed far from our minds as we live lives of service to God.

PRAYER Father in heaven, in this coming school year, be with me every step of the way. Be with me so that the fruit of the Spirit may be revealed in my words and actions. Thank you for redeeming me and keeping me as one of your very own. In your name I pray it, dear Lord Jesus. Amen.

WHEREVER YOU GO

Joshua 1:9 *Be strong and courageous. Do not be afraid; do not be discouraged, for the LORD your God will be with you wherever you go.*

I always felt a slight wave of anxiety at the start of each new school year. Even when I was a veteran heading into my senior year of college, I couldn't help worrying about the new year. Would my friends and I still be close? How hard would my classes be? What challenges would I face?

It's easy to skim through Bible passages like Joshua 1:9. Sure, sure, don't be afraid; God's got it. But when was the last time that you really meditated on this promise? Just take a moment to think. God is all-powerful and all-knowing. He knit us together in the womb, knows us better than we know ourselves, and has complete control over the course of our lives. Beyond all comprehension, he loves us, and we are his children. On top of all of this, he promises that "the LORD your God will be with you wherever you go." Wow! I can't even wrap my head around the amazing blessing of having the God of the universe always by my side.

As much as we would like to believe that we can control the outcome of our lives, we can't. And thank God for that! We have One who loves us, cares for us, and will be with us wherever we go. There is no need to worry. God is with us!

PRAYER Dear God, forgive me for worrying and not placing my trust fully in you. Thank you for the comfort and promise to never leave me. Amen.

August 13

GOD CAN HANDLE IT

Lamentations 3:22-24 *Because of the L*ORD*'s great love we are not consumed, for his compassions never fail. They are new every morning; great is your faithfulness. I say to myself, "The L*ORD *is my portion; therefore I will wait for him."*

Feeling overwhelmed? It's that time of year again. A brand-new school year will begin soon, bringing about many challenging classes, a full schedule, changes within friend groups, new living arrangements, or maybe even a completely different school. Life will once again transition from that carefree, school-free summer to a year filled with many unknowns, upcoming challenges, and uncertainties.

It can be so easy to become discouraged in the midst of all of this chaos. However, it is crucial to remember that all the chaos is meant to drive us to realize that we are not alone. In Lamentations 3:22-24 we are reminded of this in a beautiful way.

No matter what we find ourselves going through, we can be sure that our God and Savior is never going to leave our side. In fact, he has promised to hold our hands through it all and is always there to listen. Cast it all on him: your fears, anxieties, and worries. The one who has compassion on you, who loves you more than anything, so much that he would die for you—and did!—can handle it.

PRAYER Lord, please help me look to you for help and guidance not only during this school year but also throughout my entire life. Your love for me is great and awesome; help that love to shine in my heart so that others may see you living within me. Amen.

CHRISTIAN CHARACTER

1 Timothy 4:12 *Don't let anyone look down on you because you are young, but set an example for the believers in speech, in conduct, in love, in faith and in purity.*

Media drives culture in American society today. Media tells college students to let go of their studies, their families, and their relationship with Christ to live a party lifestyle because "you only live once." Because college culture is so enriched in the idea of partying, many people think every college student falls into this category. However, Paul reminds us in 1 Timothy 4:12 that this is not the truth.

As young adults, we are given the responsibility of being the next generation to "take the reins of the world," so to speak. Generations ahead of us and generations yet to come will look to us as the leaders of the world in the near future. Since one of the most important aspects of leadership is character, how important for us to be entrenched in our faith! How important to plumb the depths of scriptural realities about sin and grace, about morality and absolute truth, about heaven with Christ and hell apart from him. These truths will shape our Christian character by the power of the Holy Spirit, who works through the Word, so we are enabled to set an example for those who are looking to us for guidance.

PRAYER Dear God, please give me and my peers the courage it takes to throw away the ways of the world and continue to follow your teachings. Give us the strength to be leaders in Christ and to continue his work. Amen.

LET GOD BE THE BALANCE

Philippians 4:13 *I can do all this through him who gives me strength.*

"Worrying is like sitting in a rocking chair. It gives you something to do but doesn't get you anywhere." This English proverb is often a great reminder when we get caught up worrying about the upcoming school year and how we will juggle classes, homework, a job, and a social life. It's easy to exhaust our energy being anxious about all the tasks before us, when really we're missing the true balance in our lives that will prepare us to make a good beginning to the year. That balance factor is God. Spending time with God will give us strength to accomplish what needs to be done.

Paul wrote a powerful message for the Philippians and for us to hear in the passage above. Allow God to be the balance in your life that makes all things possible. When worry and anxiety creep into your mind, take a moment to reflect on the words of this passage, knowing that through God, you can do all things. Whether you're starting your first year of college, completing your last, or somewhere in between, it's natural to feel overwhelmed by the tasks before you at the beginning of a new school year. Prepare yourself spiritually by spending time in God's Word, and prepare yourself physically by using your time wisely to balance your busy schedule. Get off your rocking chair and leave your worries behind because God will give you strength to accomplish whatever may lie ahead of you.

PRAYER Dear Lord, when the worries and anxieties of this life become a burden too big to bear, help me remember the words of Philippians 4:13. Give me strength; help me keep a balance in my life and make time for you. Thank you for giving me another year to grow in your grace. Prepare me for the school year ahead, but more important, prepare me for heaven, where I will spend eternity with you. Amen.

ONLY IN ME

Deuteronomy 8:3 *He humbled you, causing you to hunger and then feeding you with manna, which neither you nor your ancestors had known, to teach you that man does not live on bread alone but on every word that comes from the mouth of the LORD.*

I want to be a better Christian. You know, more and more like a child of God. But like every other human, I find myself failing to reach my goal and vowing to "do better next time." Every *effort* on my part leads me back to God's truth: I need to trust in him for everything—especially for the perfection I need to be like him.

When I have a desire to improve a shortcoming, my sinful nature is so often *right there,* and I let my God down. "How will I *ever* be made 'right'? How will *I* overcome my flaws?"

"Only in ME," is God's daily word to me.

Humility. Humility before God. A necessity linking all humans. When we come before him admitting our mistakes, confessing our sin, he points us to Jesus, the Bread of Life, who satisfies our hunger through forgiveness much like the manna of God satisfied the physical hunger of Israel in the wilderness. God gave his perfect Son to make us whole . . . perfect . . . forgiven! That is his promise. We have his word!

We are not perfect Christians—by ourselves. But in the midst of our shortcomings, we know our perfect God freely dispenses grace to those who ask for it—for Jesus' sake.

That said, let us lean on our God and live for him!

PRAYER Heavenly Father, I am a sinner. Without you I can't make a new start. Use the consciousness of my sin and my forgiveness in Jesus to strengthen my faith in you as I rely on you for every aspect of life. Amen.

BE WISE

Ephesians 5:15,16 *Be very careful, then, how you live—not as unwise but as wise, making the most of every opportunity, because the days are evil.*

Have you ever made a "not-so-smart" choice? I think it's safe to say that we've all made choices that have slipped into this category at one point or another. For many, college brings about a newfound freedom as parents take a step back from the role of encouraging and reminding their children to make smart decisions. Our own sinful nature, peer pressure, and college norms make many ungodly activities seem very attractive. This is by no means, though, a license to sin.

Even though we have a Savior who never made bad choices and forgives us for our not-so-smart choices, we need to be cautious, as the passage above reminds us. These verses are not talking about being wise by studying for exams, making healthy choices, or getting plenty of sleep. *Wise* here means to grow in our faith by hearing God's powerful Word on a daily basis. There are many ways to do this: read a daily devotion, go to church, have a weekly Bible study, or just spend time reading and meditating on God's Word. The Holy Spirit is truly powerful; let him work in your heart and see what he can do for you.

PRAYER Lord, help me grow wise by making time for you on a daily basis. Thank you for the blessing of your Word, and help me make the most of it by using the opportunities that have been laid before me to grow stronger in my faith. Amen.

DRINK YOUR MILK!

1 Peter 2:2,3 *Like newborn babies, crave pure spiritual milk, so that by it you may grow up in your salvation, now that you have tasted that the Lord is good.*

Beginnings in life, whether a new school year, becoming an uncle, or learning how to drive a car, rarely happen exactly how we think they will. It's safe to say that, like newborn babies, we have no idea what will happen in an hour, next week, next semester, etc. We are totally reliant upon, and need to be totally trusting of, our heavenly Father if we want to survive.

Look at today's passage again. God tells us that his provisions are everything we need! Reading his Word, going to church, being in fellowship with other believers, and other faith-strengthening acts are not like vegetables—although they are good for us, we dislike the taste. No, God tells us that his teachings are as pure and wonderful tasting as milk is to infants.

As his children, our heavenly cravings never go away. But because we are sinful, neither does our desire for earthly cravings, which soon lead to sin and death. It's easy to give in to earthly cravings when overwhelmed and afraid of the thought of a new school year, but peace and comfort are found in the object of our faith: Jesus, who has delivered us from sin and death through his sacrifice on the cross.

PRAYER Father, strengthen my heavenly cravings so that I may continue to live fearlessly due to the assurance that you will provide for my every need. Amen.

August 19

BUILD YOURSELF UP

Jude 1:20,21 *Dear friends, by building yourselves up in your most holy faith and praying in the Holy Spirit, keep yourselves in God's love as you wait for the mercy of our Lord Jesus Christ to bring you to eternal life.*

We try lots of things to make us feel better about ourselves. Working out is a healthy way to do that; eating better or wearing something flattering are other ways. However, some people turn to eating disorders, alcohol, or even drugs to get instant gratification. Do any of these things actually make us feel better, though? Sure, for a little while we might look in the mirror in our new back-to-school outfit and think, "I'm ready to conquer the first day of classes," but what happens when you leave your room and your roommate gives you a once-over and smirks?

The Bible tells us to build ourselves up in our faith through the power of the Holy Spirit. He makes us feel really good about ourselves. Whether it's the first day of classes or ringing the doorbell on a first date, he will make us feel like we can take on anything that comes our way. All we have to do is arm ourselves with God's love and the Spirit will lead the way.

So next time you look in the mirror and think, "If I just worked out more," instead think, "God loves me because I am his child. I am perfect in his eyes because Christ died for all of my sins." Then you don't have to turn to earthly fixes to make yourself feel good.

PRAYER Dear Lord, you have told me that I am perfect in your eyes. You created me in your image. Remind me of that when I feel troubled or worried, because I know that you are more important than earthly things. Amen.

WATCHING OVER YOU

Psalm 121:7,8 *The Lord will keep you from all harm—he will watch over your life; the Lord will watch over your coming and going both now and forevermore.*

Have you ever felt your guardian angel at your side? It might have been when you just missed the other car coming around the turn. In that moment, you were acutely aware of the protection God provides you with on a daily basis.

These verses come at the end of Psalm 121. The earlier verses talk about looking to the mountains and seeing help coming from the Lord our Maker. He is the one who keeps us safe from all danger and harm. The psalms have an interesting way of repeating the same message in different ways. This psalm is no different. Each verse has a different way of sharing the wonderful comfort that God is always watching over us.

Reread the verses above.

What does that mean to you as you enter college?

Do you see the number of comings and goings that your future holds? I know from experience that college brings a number of moves, trips, and other adventures your way.

What comforts do you see in this psalm? I see the assurance that no matter where I go—home, school, on a mission trip, on a vacation—God will be there to watch over everything I do.

God is always there watching over the paths you take. Sometimes things may not go the way you planned, but he ensures your safety at every turn. Take heart and know that he is there.

PRAYER Dear Lord, thank you for always being there for me. Keep me safely in the palm of your hand. Forgive me for the times I forget your never-ending protection. Amen.

August 21

PREPARE YOURSELF

2 Timothy 4:2 *Preach the word; be prepared in season and out of season; correct, rebuke and encourage—with great patience and careful instruction.*

Have you ever been in a situation in which you felt anxious or lacked confidence? Maybe it was before a test or a presentation in class or a sporting or arts event, or maybe it was in an unfamiliar social situation. Regardless of the endeavor, that anxiety and lack of confidence is most likely rooted in two truths: 1) You were concerned with how you and others perceived your performance and 2) you felt ill-prepared to perform well.

The apostle Paul recognized this same anxiousness in his disciple Timothy. Paul gives Timothy several critical calls to action: to preach the gospel, to correct, to rebuke, and to encourage fellow Christians. To a man who lacked confidence, this could be an overwhelming task. When we are overwhelmed, we can often act with haste and without care. Paul recognizes these potential pitfalls when writing to Timothy and gives Timothy a strategy to act with patience and care: diligent preparation.

You may be thinking that that applied to a first-century preacher, but how does that apply to us now? As Romans 12 outlines, God has given us all different gifts and calls us to different passions. We recognize and practice this concept often in our worldly passions of academics, cocurriculars, social relationships, and more, but this is just as true and even more critical in our spiritual lives.

So the question is, How are you preparing? What is your game plan to be prepared for a situation in which you must act with patience and care? The answer lies in Paul's first instruction, "Preach the Word." In order to preach and share the Word with confidence, we must study and know the Word.

PRAYER Lord, give me the confidence to preach boldly. Amen.

JESUS BRINGS PEACE

Psalm 37:37 *Consider the blameless, observe the upright; a future awaits those who seek peace.*

How do I live as a person of peace in a world of chaos? Whenever we step onto a new campus, into a new job, or into a new year, that one question can be rather difficult to answer. The people and things surrounding us, whether at a Christian or secular school, *will* present temptations and challenges that we *will* have to face. The chaos of the sinful world is so alluring and so easy to become a part of that we find "peace" in things that only harm us in the end. How then do I live as a person of true peace?

King David, who battled the same temptations we battle, gives us simple instructions in today's passage. Actively search out people who have that same desire for peace as you do. Recognize where the "upright" and the "blameless" find their true peace. True peace comes from the knowledge you have that Christ has redeemed you from the chaos and the sin that plagues the world and our hearts. True peace is found only in Jesus. We live as people of peace by knowing the peace we have in Christ. We have a future because we have peace.

So live in that peace. Show people in your new surroundings why you have joy. Share that peace with others who don't know it. You have a future and you want others to have that same future. Tackle this new year, school, or job, relishing in the peace Jesus brings to you.

PRAYER Dear God, as I begin this new year, help me always recognize the peace you bring to me. Give me opportunities to share that peace with others, and guide me in all my endeavors. Amen.

BE READY!

Matthew 24:44 *You also must be ready, because the Son of Man will come at an hour when you do not expect him.*

When I was young, I was deathly afraid of kidnappers. I would wrap myself tightly in my blanket with my stuffed animals tucked under my arms. I figured that if anyone ever did break in, my blanket and stuffed animals would be with me and I wouldn't be alone. In my innocent, childish mind, I was prepared, but looking back on it now it sounds silly, because nothing could ever prepare me for that.

Jesus said that he will come when we least expect it, but what if we prepare for his coming so that when he does get here, we're ready to leave with him? What if we live our lives in a way so that when he does come, we're witnessing to someone who has never heard his Word or showing love to someone who has been cruel to us?

We don't know when Jesus is coming, but we can do our best to live lives of love, kindness, and patience. We can be dedicated to God so that when he does come, we are filled with his Word in our hearts. Of course, like the silly child that I was with my blanket, we may not be fully prepared. We are sinful, but we continue to be lights in this dark world. We do this out of thankfulness and love for the most amazing man who ever walked this earth and who will come again to take us home.

PRAYER Dear Lord, I know no matter how hard I try, I will never be able to live the way that you want me to live, but help me be filled with your Word so that your Holy Spirit works through me and that I may be prepared for your coming. Amen.

FINDING REAL COMFORT

Proverbs 3:5,6 *Trust in the Lord with all your heart and lean not on your own understanding; in all your ways submit to him, and he will make your paths straight.*

When I was a little boy, I used to sit on my momma's lap and she would read children's books to me. I have many happy memories of time spent with her. It seems like such a short time ago when I was that little guy on my momma's lap. Time has really flown by since then. Already I am starting my third year in college. My life seems so hectic now. Classes resuming, doing undergraduate research, balancing time at work, and having a social life leave me feeling drained. It seems like when I need time most is exactly when it moves the fastest.

It's so easy to get stressed out with all the things that need to be done. Worry and anxiety about classes and my future so easily get me down. Despite all of my efforts, life speeds by as I do my best to hang on and not let my worries get the best of me. However, all of my exertions are useless. When that happens, I'm reminded that I'm looking for comfort in the wrong place. True peace of mind cannot be found in any of my endeavors. Comfort—I mean *real* comfort—comes with the knowledge that Christ is our strength. This verse seems tailor-made to combat my worries. What a blessing to know that the Lord cares about me. He loves me so much that he wiped my sins away. True comfort can be found in him, trusting that all of my worries are small compared to his incredible love.

PRAYER Dear Lord, thank you for the incredible love that you show me daily. Please help me cast all my worries and anxiety on you with the full knowledge that you will not give me more than I can bear. I love you, Jesus; please help me show it. Amen.

EVERYDAY WORSHIP

John 4:23,24 *A time is coming and has now come when the true worshipers will worship the Father in the Spirit and in truth, for they are the kind of worshipers the Father seeks. God is spirit, and his worshipers must worship in the Spirit and in truth.*

Have you recently ended a relationship because you weren't all that into it? As you begin classes this fall, do you have a professor who seems to have that attitude about one of the courses he teaches? If the professor's not passionate about the class, then you're likely to put a halfhearted effort into it all semester too. And then there's your new roommate; already things aren't going as well as you had hoped, but you're really not interested in putting in any effort yourself to try to make things better.

Don't let that be your mind-set toward your relationship with your Savior. God's not interested in a halfhearted relationship with you; he wants you to worship him in Spirit and in truth. Worship is not just something you do in church. It's something you have an opportunity to do all the time. You either live your life worshiping the Lord or you don't. Get a good start to the school year by doing the things you want to do: honoring God in your life and thanking and praising him for the forgiveness he's given you through Jesus Christ. Be in contact with his Word regularly so that your worship of him is continually fueled, and avoid bad influences in your life so that your worship is not tainted. God sought you and made you his child. Now you can be the kind of worshiper who brings glory to him.

PRAYER Dear God, whatever this coming year may bring, help me truly worship you in all that I do. Amen.

PUT THE WEIGHT ON GOD

1 Peter 5:6,7 *Humble yourselves, therefore, under God's mighty hand, that he may lift you up in due time. Cast all your anxiety on him because he cares for you.*

During weight-lifting competitions, there is an event in which the athletes have to lift a bar stacked with the heaviest weights they can possibly stand. They only have to get it over their heads once before they drop it back down to the floor, exhausted.

Can you imagine lifting that much weight? Or even carrying a weight of any size above your head day after day? This is often what it feels like to be in college. There are so many assignments, responsibilities, relationships, and fears to hold above our heads that by the end of each day, it feels like we are carrying a bar loaded with weights of all sizes that we can never seem to drop.

We try to hand some of the weights to our friends or parents, but eventually their bars are full too. We feel guilty for not being able to bear the weight that God has given us, which makes the bar heavier and us weaker. That's when the apostle Peter tells us that God comes and tells us to give him the bar. We question at first: "I can carry this bar no matter how heavy it feels." But then we see our mighty God with his muscles that are forever fresh and his limbs that never tire. And remember, Christ has already lifted away the biggest burden of all—our guilt. Without any help from us, he removed it as far as the east is from the west. We are free.

PRAYER Dear almighty Comforter, help me remember that you want to lift my burdens. Give me the strength to know that you are there to catch every one of my worries and that I am not able to conquer them alone. Amen.

INVEST IN WHAT MATTERS

Psalm 1:1,2 *Blessed is the one . . . whose delight is in the law of the* LORD, *and who meditates on his law day and night.*

The schedule of a college student can be insane. At my busiest times, I went from class to work to basketball practice to the library until I collapsed into bed. Not only was my time for food and friends limited, but (more important) my time with God was practically nonexistent. I had convinced myself that the distractions of this world were more important than spending time in his Word.

It took me a long time to learn how ridiculously skewed my thinking was. How could an extra ten minutes of sleep or cramming for a math test possibly (and successfully) compete for my time with the God who created me, saved me, and loves me? It's true that God wants us to succeed and work hard on this earth. However, when the activities in our daily lives take the place of God, we lose sight of what really matters. Instead of living for the fleeting moments and successes of this earth, we need to invest our time in what *really* matters: eternal life with God.

In our busiest times, it's easy to push God to the side. However, I've found that in my busiest times, I need God even more. When I set aside time to be with God, I find joy and comfort that sustain me through this life.

PRAYER Dear God, help me always put you first by meditating on your Word day and night. Forgive me for forsaking you and becoming sidetracked by the distractions of this world. As I go through this busy time as a college student, comfort and sustain me with your Word. Amen.

SET ASIDE GOD TIME

Proverbs 16:3 *Commit to the LORD whatever you do, and he will establish your plans.*

With all that's going on in college and all the hustle and bustle of daily life, it's often hard to find time or energy to pray. It's incredibly important to set aside time for God, otherwise it's easy to fall away or lose track of God entirely. When that happens, temptations grow easier and easier to fall for. I have experienced this firsthand as I got too busy to attend chapel or any Bible studies last semester. Many things I never even thought to do before this year suddenly became temptations.

Solomon wrote the words of Proverbs 16:3, words that are applicable to every one of us. Reading these words, I gather that every action and thought should be with God in mind. It is sort of like pretending that your mom or dad is behind you watching everything you do. God sees everything you do. The nice part comes with the next words of that passage. God reminds us that he establishes our plans. College will be easier if we do two things: 1) pray to God daily; 2) hear his Word regularly. It's through his Word that we find out what his will is for our lives and by his Word that the Holy Spirit empowers us to live according to it. If we work with God's will in mind, everything will turn out for our eternal good.

PRAYER Lord, thank you for getting me to where I am today and for always having my best in mind. Lead me to understand your will and to always act in the best way for both me and my neighbor. Amen.

WORK AS FOR THE LORD

Colossians 3:23,24 *Whatever you do, work at it with all your heart, as working for the Lord, not for human masters, since you know that you will receive an inheritance from the Lord as a reward. It is the Lord Christ you are serving.*

"Sit down and relax. The boss isn't here. Considering how little we get paid, you work way too hard." This was the "wisdom" shared with me by a longtime employee of the pizza joint where I was working a summer job, slowly saving up money for college. I was taken aback and didn't quite know how to respond.

In Colossians 3, Paul examines the motivation for hard work. Paul was not speaking to minimum wage pizza cooks, but to slaves. He encourages them to work diligently even when their masters aren't carefully watching them or checking their work.

It must have been disheartening for the slaves to toil for their masters in exchange for minimal or no wages. However, Paul reminds them that they would "receive an inheritance from the Lord as a reward." Moreover, with their work they also had a chance to praise the Lord and act as a witness.

College, unlike slavery, is a challenging experience with a rich reward at the finish. However, similar to the slaves in Paul's letter, college students often work unsupervised. Parents and professors act in hands-off roles. Paul reminds us to work not for our human masters, but for the Lord.

With this in mind, we work each day with anticipation of both the earthly reward to our labor and the reward in heaven.

PRAYER Father God, refocus me on serving you. Let my work not be for myself, my parents, or my professors, but for the sake of your kingdom. Amen.

August 30
SET YOUR WORRY ASIDE

Philippians 4:6,7 *Do not be anxious about anything, but in every situation, by prayer and petition, with thanksgiving, present your requests to God. And the peace of God, which transcends all understanding, will guard your hearts and your minds in Christ Jesus.*

A night of procrastination. A paper that's not going to write itself. Three tests in the span of one week. All these scenarios lead to stress, anxieties, and worry. Worry is an insulting sin against God because it breaks the First Commandment. It's the opposite of faith, and without faith we can feel confused, even paralyzed. God tells us his grace is sufficient and to put worries to the wayside even when we feel like we're drowning in a multitude of troubles. The apostle Paul addresses this issue in today's passage. Read the verses again.

At times like these, it's easy to deny God's grace and be led astray from God's presence. Worry focuses us on what our problems are and crowds out what's good in our lives. Worry over the concerns of life becomes sinful when it prevents you from thinking about anything else, including God. We find rest in Christ. He took the blame for our worries and lack of faith and was punished for them on the cross. Give thanks to Jesus, who reconciled us with God and gave us peace.

PRAYER Dear Lord, grant me your guiding hand when I face life's struggles. In the heat of the moment, panic and fear seem to be the first things on my mind. When these stressful situations arise, Lord, empower me to overcome the scariest of days and embolden me with a sense of security and serenity. Through all things, Lord, you are the Rock that I can lean on day by day. Thank you for showing me how to stay calm in the most hectic times. In your Son's name, I pray. Amen.

NO FEAR

Psalm 46:1-3 *God is our refuge and strength, an ever-present help in trouble. Therefore we will not fear, though the earth give way and the mountains fall into the heart of the sea, though its waters roar and foam and the mountains quake with their surging.*

What do you fear? As a college student, I doubt your biggest worries involve the kinds of disasters the psalmist describes. Yet there's no denying that, in the moment, a crisis or challenge can feel as terrifying as an earthquake.

Earthquakes or not, I think this psalm writer's point is that no matter the magnitude of what happens to us, we don't have to fear. God is our refuge and strength. Did you notice that? *God.* You are not your source of strength. Your boyfriend or girlfriend is not your source of strength. Not even energy drinks are your source of strength, although they're great if you want a sugary boost.

As you read on through this section of Scripture, it gets better. Not only does God provide you strength and a place of refuge, but he's also an ever-present help in trouble. When you're a college student, that ever-present part is important. You never know when you'll find yourself pulling an all-nighter, dealing with a difficult roommate, or standing up for your values when a situation puts them to the test. Take comfort that God is always there; there's no need to fear.

What do you fear? Thanks to your strength from God, you can complete the following sentence with peace and confidence: "Therefore I will not fear, though . . ."

PRAYER God, I know you're my source of strength, but it's easy to forget that. Remind me that you are my refuge and that you are present in every moment and every situation. Amen.

SEPTEMBER
LIVING IN THE PEACE GOD GIVES

THE ULTIMATE DIRECTOR

Colossians 3:15 *Let the peace of Christ rule in your hearts, since as members of one body you were called to peace. And be thankful.*

Lights, camera, action! What does every successful movie have? It wouldn't be much of a movie without props, sets, and actors, but one of the most important people is the director. Without a director there would be no order to the movie, no plan at all. Thankfully, our lives have the ultimate director, our Father in heaven.

Knowing that God has a plan brings peace and comfort. We might not always know why things happen, but everything is in God's hands. The peace of Christ, mentioned in our verse, is the knowledge that he has redeemed us from all our sins.

In light of the comfort that we have in this passage, we can rest assured that through all the demands and hardships that we face in life, there is One who is in control of all things. We can put our trust in God and have peace in our hearts, knowing that we are part of God's plan of redemption.

What in your life might be causing you to not recognize that our heavenly Father is in control? Do you worry about studying, exams, career decisions, or living away from home? We sometimes let our earthly worries crowd out the one truth that exists. God loves us and Christ has redeemed us, and in Christ, our heavenly Father will ensure that everything works out for the good of those who love him.

PRAYER Dear Lord, as I face daily struggles, please grant me peace and contentment that comes through your Word. Allow me to find comfort through your promise that you love me and will take care of me and that you are always in control. Amen.

THE GREATEST PEACE

Romans 5:1,2 *Therefore, since we have been justified through faith, we have peace with God through our Lord Jesus Christ, through whom we have gained access by faith into this grace in which we now stand. And we boast in the hope of the glory of God.*

Peace. Where do you feel the most at peace? I usually say my uncle's cabin on a lake in northern Wisconsin. However, as I've spent more time away from home, traveling, working—basically growing up—I've found a new peace in spending time at my childhood home. As you go through your years of college and the times after, I'm sure you'll find your places and times of peace changing.

There is one peace, however, that never changes or leaves: the peace we have with God through Jesus. We are wretched sinners, but through the death of Christ, God does not see us as awful sinners. He sees men and women in white robes, standing before him at peace and in the glory of heaven.

Life can be hectic. From a freshman trying to figure out what college will be like to a senior worried about life after graduation to sophomores and juniors with their own worries, there are decisions to make, deadlines to meet, issues to solve, meetings to schedule. Through it all, though, we can know that one meeting will have no issues. Our final meeting with God will be glorious and marvelous! We can find peace in this knowledge of hope in God.

PRAYER Dear Lord, thank you for giving me the greatest peace possible, the peace of heaven waiting for me. When life gets busy and I worry too much, remind me that you have already given me the white robe of heaven. Amen.

WORK IS A BLESSING

1 Thessalonians 4:11,12 *Make it your ambition to lead a quiet life: You should mind your own business and work with your hands, just as we told you, so that your daily life may win the respect of outsiders and so that you will not be dependent on anybody.*

Work, work, work. Is there ever an end to it? By the time we enter college, many of us have realized that summer is our opportunity to earn money for school. The summer days of carefree playing are gone. Or as we enter the postgraduate life, we may pessimistically think of the long careers that await us: from a temporary job, to school, to a full-time job until retirement or death comes. Having these thoughts we might wonder, *What is the point to endless work?*

Since creation, God has given his people jobs. From the beginning, Adam was given the task of maintaining the Garden of Eden, and from there on out, each person has been expected to faithfully carry out his or her vocation. Seems like a pretty dull way to live, right? Yet there are many logical reasons to work. Through work, we provide for our families, we gain a sense of pride and identity, and we contribute to the progression of society. Besides these benefits of work, is there another motivation to strive to "mind your own business and work with your hands"?

The answer is found in the attitude with which we approach life, through the lens of Christianity. Why do we do anything that we do? To serve and honor God, of course! Let your light shine in your work so that you can give our God glory and thanks!

PRAYER "Brothers, sisters, let us gladly give to God our all, our best—service hearty, thorough, honest, with a living love impressed. All our duty, all our striving, all our time to him belong; praise him, then, with true devotion; come before him with a song." Amen. (*Christian Worship* hymnal [CW] 484:1)

GOD HAS A PURPOSE FOR YOU

Jeremiah 1:5 *Before I formed you in the womb I knew you, before you were born I set you apart; I appointed you as a prophet to the nations.*

The passage selected for this devotion is from a section titled "The Call of Jeremiah." In it, God is telling Jeremiah what his plan for his life is. When I started college, I thought I knew what I was going to do with my life. I had my major chosen, my career path set; I was even sure of who I was going to marry. Looking back now, I have a completely different life than what I thought I would have. And that's not a bad thing. It's actually a wonderful thing! Through my experiences in college, even though I didn't always realize it, God was guiding me to the path he planned out for me. It didn't matter what my plan was or what I thought I was meant to do. God knew—and still knows!—exactly what he wants me to be doing, and he knows what he wants you to be doing too.

As a child of God, you can also take this passage to heart and know that God has a plan for your life. You may or may not have some plans already. Maybe you're wondering what it is that God wants you to do. No matter your lot in life, God's ultimate purpose for you on earth is to be his own and live under him and serve him in righteousness. God always knows what his plan is for you. Trust that he will continue to use you for his purposes throughout your life.

PRAYER Lord, thank you for knowing what your plan is for my life. Help me always remember that my future is in your hands and trust that you will always guide me to fulfill your will. In Jesus' name, I pray. Amen.

September 5

PAY ATTENTION

John 1:29 *The next day John saw Jesus coming toward him and said, "Look, the Lamb of God, who takes away the sin of the world!"*

Look—a Bible verse! Look—a commercial! Look—a funny video! Look—a party, a meeting, a tweet, an internship, an application, a football game, a coffee shop, a nap!

What's competing for your attention? Do you get yanked around by whatever presents itself at the moment, or do you *choose* what gets your attention? And what do you choose? Things with deadlines, things you enjoy, things that provide stress relief, things that others press upon you?

What about the Baptizer's simple words? Does his call hold your attention? "Look!" Of *all* the things you attend to today, will this be one?

"The Lamb of God." Will you see the sacrifice—the silent Lamb who embodies divine power and purity? Will you see the necessity for God *in flesh*—walking down the road, pointed at in awe or derision, faith or accusation?

"Look." The sin of the world. Will you see your sin there? The minutes, hours, days of attention spent on silly, empty things . . . and NOT spent on the Lamb of God?

"Look, the Lamb of God, who takes away the sin of the world!" Will you see your redemption?

You are free! Be free from shame, from the guilt of misspent attention. Look with joy on the Lamb! He takes away your sin. He looks on you with love.

PRAYER Forgive my distracted and misdirected attention, Lord. Thank you for relieving me of my sin. Strengthen my vision to see the Lamb of God always before me. Amen.

BE CONTENT WITH GOD'S PLAN

Matthew 6:28,29 *Why do you worry about clothes? See how the flowers of the field grow. They do not labor or spin. Yet I tell you that not even Solomon in all his splendor was dressed like one of these.*

"I'm not sure if I want to be married to your dad anymore . . ."

Those are the words my mom said to me one August afternoon just before I was about to begin my junior year in college. In that moment my mind took off.

"Everything is different now."
"My whole life is changed."
"My whole life is *ruined*."

Do you know what God calls all of those things in his Word? *Worry.* I was given one piece of information and chose to assume that God was going to let the worst happen. But that's a lie that we as Christians *cannot* believe, as the Scriptures remind us in Matthew 6:28,29.

I spent days laboring and letting my mind spin over everything that was happening in my family. I had such a grand plan for my life, and now it was ruined—good thing God's plan was better. Allow me to explain myself. My parents staying married forever was part of the grand plan that I had for my life. What I've come to realize is that although God would love my parents to stay together, his plan for *my life* is much bigger and grander than how my parents' marriage turns out. His grand plan included sending Christ to die for my sins.

No more laboring, no more spinning. God has blessed all with the gift of Christ. So forget your plans for one second and be content with God's plan.

PRAYER Dear heavenly Father, I am sorry for those times when I labored and spun in the fields of my own worry. Please help me forever see the blessings you have put in my life and praise your plan above my plans. Amen.

WHY, GOD?

Ecclesiastes 3:1 *There is a time for everything, and a season for every activity under the heavens.*

One would be hard-pressed to find a college student who doesn't ask himself or herself why things happen. A few common phrases might be: "Why did this happen to me?" or "Why is life so difficult?" While it's true that positive and negative things happen to everyone, we must always keep in mind who is really in control—our Maker and Preserver.

Solomon writes in Ecclesiastes 3:1 about how to view everything that happens in our hectic and crazy lives. At first glance, this passage doesn't look like it's telling us how to view our lives. However, if we look a bit deeper, God is telling us that he has a plan. The fact that we know his greatest plan—the plan of our salvation in Christ—gives us reason to trust that he always has our best interests in mind. There will be times of good followed by times of bad. Therefore we can trust him because he will use the events in our lives for his purpose.

Let's apply this to our lives now. One example would be this: your boyfriend or girlfriend suddenly breaks up with you. You probably feel many emotions, including sadness and anger. What many people don't see in the situation is that God allowed it to happen. God let it happen even though we may not always understand why. God has our eternal interests in mind. That is why he sent his Son to die for us.

So how are we to view our hectic lives? God tells us that we can be at peace knowing that he is in control of everything.

PRAYER Dear Lord, please give me a sense of contentment and peace knowing that you have prepared a time for everything. In your name, I pray. Amen.

September 8

TRUE PEACE

Romans 12:18 *If it is possible, as far as it depends on you, live at peace with everyone.*

I've lived on this earth for a couple of years now, and one thing I've noticed is that there are different types of people. This becomes quite evident in friendships, work, and in the classroom. One individual may try to direct attention to herself while another may do his best to deflect it. Some people focus on giving to others while many more are intent on taking from them.

Of course, most people are very much the same in some areas. People want wealth. People want to be loved. People want power or leverage. People want the truth. The problem is that *want* is the opposite of *contentment*. Wanting something we can't have often causes conflict within ourselves and in our relationships with others. God wants us to be content and to live at peace with those who are not content.

Wow. How are we supposed to live at peace with others when their very existence threatens our chances at getting stuff, especially stuff that will (temporarily) make us happy?

Our dilemma is missing some important pieces of the puzzle, and those pieces are the peace, love, and forgiveness found in Jesus.

Unfortunately, sin will never go away. Thankfully, Jesus came and died for us; in him we have contentment. We maintain this lasting contentment by staying in his Word on a regular basis and living lives that are pleasing to him. True peace can be found no other way. Through him we can live at peace with others.

PRAYER Dear God, please help me regularly read your Word and live a life that pleases you. Life has a tendency to pull me in different directions; please help me find lasting peace in you. Amen.

GOD TOOK CARE OF IT

Psalm 103:11,12 *As high as the heavens are above the earth, so great is his love for those who fear him; as far as the east is from the west, so far has he removed our transgressions from us.*

Do you feel entrapped by sin? Don't worry. God took care of it.

Sin is everywhere—it's an unstoppable force that we can't escape. You sin once and tell yourself, *I'm never going to do that again. That was awful.* But there you are, one day later, one week later, one hour later, committing a similar sin, or a different sin. Is there a way out of this trap?

God provides us with reassurance in his Word. "As far as the east is from the west," God took away our sin. There is no end for east and west—they are eternal, just like God's love for us. God forgave *all* your sins because of his Son's death on a cross. Not just that one sin that you can't seem to escape, but even the sins that you don't realize are sins! There's no need to worry about that sin—God took care of it. How can you not be content when you think about that?

The next time you feel yourself being entrapped by sin, turn to God first. Think about how much he loves you—so much that he removed all your transgressions!

PRAYER Dear God, thank you for your wonderful, undeserved love! Help me turn to you every time I feel discontent with my life. Help me realize that I can be content, because you have forgiven my sin. In Jesus' name, I pray. Amen.

YOU ARE PERFECT!

Luke 15:7 *I tell you that in the same way there will be more rejoicing in heaven over one sinner who repents than over ninety-nine righteous persons who do not need to repent.*

Studying. Friends. Sports. Dates. Work. Phone calls home. This may look like a familiar to-do list for a college student. It seems there's always something going on. All these things constantly piling up can cause stress and make us feel lost.

Let's take a look at the context surrounding Luke 15:7. The Pharisees were giving Jesus a hard time because a crowd of sinners had gathered to listen to what he had to say. Like always, Jesus had the perfect response. Starting in Luke 15:4, he says, "Suppose one of you has a hundred sheep and loses one of them. Doesn't he leave the ninety-nine in the open country and go after the lost sheep until he finds it? And when he finds it, he joyfully puts it on his shoulders and goes home. Then he calls his friends and neighbors together and says, 'Rejoice with me; I have found my lost sheep.' "

To borrow a quote from a popular old-school hip-hop song by Vanilla Ice: "Anything less than the best is a felony." It may seem difficult to always give your best in everything you do. This can lead to frustration and exhaustion. Then you take a look at your sinfulness and come to the depressing realization that it actually is impossible to do the best that God demands. Thankfully Jesus did the best in our place. There's nothing we can do except look to our Savior for forgiveness. God the Father now rejoices in our perfection found through his Son and strengthens us to fight temptation.

PRAYER Dear Lord, I know I can never live up to the perfection you demand, yet I live in the peace that Jesus has earned in my place. Please forgive me through your Son. Amen.

HAVE A CONFESSION TO MAKE?

1 John 1:9 *If we confess our sins, he is faithful and just and will forgive us our sins and purify us from all unrighteousness.*

I have a confession to make: I wrote this devotion the day before it was due. You typically don't tell your professor or boss that you started and finished a project the day before it was due, but confession is exactly what God wants of us— especially when it comes to our sins.

First John 1 impresses on us the spiritual difference between us and God and how confession fits into addressing that vast difference. "God is light; in him there is no darkness at all" (verse 5). God is everything good. He is everything we cannot be on our own.

Think about your day and how you should have been better. Can you even *count* the sins? John is pretty frank about how we need to view ourselves: "If we claim to be without sin, we deceive ourselves and the truth is not in us" (1:8). More than that, if we pretend or claim to be without sin, "we make him out to be a liar and his word is not in us" (1:10). There's nothing worse than being without God.

But there is a solution to this separation from God. Confession is the first step. "But if we walk in the light, God himself being the light . . . the sacrificed blood of Jesus, God's Son, purges all our sin" (1:7 MSG). Our God is so faithful and just! *His* Son died so that *he* could forgive *you* . . . and me. Let us walk with him in that light.

PRAYER Dear Lord, I humbly come before you and confess that I have not been faithful. Please forgive me and help me walk with you. Amen.

ROOTED IN CHRIST

Jeremiah 17:7,8 *Blessed is the one who trusts in the LORD, whose confidence is in him. They will be like a tree planted by the water that sends out its roots by the stream. It does not fear when heat comes; its leaves are always green. It has no worries in a year of drought and never fails to bear fruit.*

A natural disaster leaves a home in ruins. A stock market crash puts a family in financial stress. A sudden illness or death of a loved one creates unwanted depression and anxiety. All these situations have something in common: lack of control. When we are faced with these situations, it's common to look with anger at God and ask *why.*

Jeremiah encourages us to place our trust and confidence in the Lord. Like a tree's roots that are planted firmly in the ground, we should plant our roots of faith in God's Word. Heat and drought are damaging conditions that leave us wondering how we will survive. However, God assures us that if we remain in him, our leaves will always be green and we'll continue to bear fruit. Blessed are those who trust in the Lord and whose confidence is in him!

Rather than asking *why,* the question that should come to mind is, What can I do about it? Since there's no way to change the past, we can go to God in prayer, asking him to help us sort out the future. While the road ahead may seem dusty, place your trust in the One who is in ultimate control and put your roots in the stream of forgiveness of sins and grace earned by Christ and his death on the cross.

PRAYER Dear Lord, thank you for being an ever-present source of trust and confidence. When life seems uncertain, remind me to look to you for guidance. Help me look to you in times of need, in times of thankfulness, and in times of praise. Amen.

YOUR PLANS OR GOD'S PLANS?

James 4:13-15 *Now listen, you who say, "Today or tomorrow we will go to this or that city, spend a year there, carry on business and make money." Why, you do not even know what will happen tomorrow. What is your life? You are a mist that appears for a little while and then vanishes. Instead, you ought to say, "If it is the Lord's will, we will live and do this or that."*

What are your plans? This seems to be near the top of the list of questions asked to college students. Whether you're trying to figure out your major or what you'll do after college, people want to know what your plan is.

With such pressure, it's easy to get sucked into the feeling that you need a carefully designed plan to follow. Perhaps you've heard the saying, "If you want to hear God laugh, tell him your plans." The meaning of this saying is that life throws you curveballs, and most plans will change or never even come to fruition.

We are not in control! For some this is hard to swallow, but for Christians it's a relief. We have an almighty God who's in control. All we have to do is trust in him. So by all means, keep making your plans, because it's good to have goals and to be organized. But remember that God's will is greater than our will and that even if our plans fail, God's plan for us will never fail.

In fact, his plan for us culminated nearly two thousand years ago when Jesus died for all of our sins and granted us access to heaven.

PRAYER Dear Lord, help me trust in you and know that you have a plan for me, even if I don't know what it is. As I make my temporary plans, help me follow your will and keep you at the forefront. Amen.

THE HEAVENLY BANQUET

Matthew 22:14 *Many are invited, but few are chosen.*

A few years ago, a young man was invited to a family gathering and the dinner to follow. He was excited to be there and to celebrate with his family, but his excitement quickly disappeared when dinner was served. He was seated at the opposite end of the table from his family, with friends and acquaintances in between! He was definitely not content with just being invited. He wanted to be there, but on his terms.

This real-life story is not far off from a story that Jesus tells in Matthew 22. He tells a story about a king who prepared a wedding banquet for his son. He had his servants invite anyone they could find until the banquet was filled. The invitation was for everyone, but there was a catch: you had to wear the wedding clothes the king gave you. If you did not, you could not get in. The king entered the banquet and saw a man without wedding clothes. The man was kicked out of the banquet. After telling the story, Jesus then says today's passage.

Seem harsh? It's only harsh when we aren't content with getting into heaven God's way. Heaven is God's home. Who are we to tell him how we should enter? The answer is that we have no right. Rather, we are to be content putting on God's "clothes." We put on the clothes that have been washed in the blood of Jesus' perfect life and innocent death. We need to put our trust and confidence in Jesus.

PRAYER Dear Lord, I am humbled by the invitation to your banquet in heaven. I ask that you help me enter on your terms. Help me put my trust and confidence in what Jesus has done for me that I may enter into your heavenly banquet. Amen.

OUR FINAL GOAL

Ecclesiastes 3:11 *He has made everything beautiful in its time. He has also set eternity in the human heart; yet no one can fathom what God has done from beginning to end.*

As someone who struggles with depression, it can be hard at times to see the good in life. I know that I'm not alone. I've talked with friends who struggle with eating disorders, suicidal thoughts, anxiety, battles with sin, etc. It's easy for people to narrowly focus on the negative things in life and forget all the good that God lavishes on us. It's interesting how we so eagerly pray to God in times of trouble or when we want something, but fail to pray when things go well in order to thank and praise him.

Ecclesiastes 3:11 and the preceding verses remind us that God has complete control in this world. And when we remember this, we can see the beauty in life, in the good and the bad. Romans 8:28 often seems overused, but it's most definitely true. God works for the Christian's good because of Christ's completed work.

It's good to be reminded that God's world is full of beauty. However, we also need to be reminded that this world is only temporary and believers have perfect eternity with Christ waiting for them. With that final goal in mind, we can find true peace and comfort. The apostle Paul understood these truths. He states in Philippians 1:23 that he desires to be in heaven with Christ because it "is better by far." Just as Paul knew that his ministry was not yet complete, we too should be devoted to our faith while on this earth. Our final rest comes in heaven with Jesus.

PRAYER Dear Lord, please help me faithfully and joyfully live for you while on this earth. Help me also keep the end goal of eternal life in mind to help me through the times of trouble in this life. Amen.

GOD'S PEACE IS OUR CONTENTMENT

John 14:27 *Peace I leave with you; my peace I give you. I do not give to you as the world gives. Do not let your hearts be troubled and do not be afraid.*

Balancing schoolwork, a job, extracurricular activities, friends, and family can be overwhelming, not to mention the problems within those areas: papers, tests, conflicts, relationship drama. It's easy to put Jesus on the back burner, but it's integral to go to God with all our troubles. In John 14:27, Jesus assures his disciples, and *us,* that he gives us his peace.

"Peace I leave with you" was a common Jewish salutation during Jesus' time. Just like today's greetings, it was often spoken superficially. Today when we say, "How are you?" we normally either a) don't wait for or b) don't care about the answer. This is how "the world gives"—it's empty and shallow. Likewise, Jesus could have just said, "Peace I leave with you" and then stopped right there. But he didn't. Instead, he adds "*My* peace I give you." He's not giving us the world's artificial peace. He gives us *his* genuine and sincere peace.

The world says, "If you do this, *then* you will have a peaceful life." Jesus tells us to come to him as we are, and he will bring us through to the very end of our troubles. He says, "Do not let your hearts be troubled and do not be afraid." We can calm our hearts and not live in fear because Christ died and rose again to give us spiritual peace. Have peace in God because God's peace is our contentment.

PRAYER Lord Jesus, thank you for giving me your sincere peace. Help me confide, trust, and come to you when things in my life get tough (and even when they aren't). I know that you genuinely care and that it is only through you that I can have true peace in this world. In your name, I pray. Amen.

WORK TOGETHER

Romans 12:4-6 *Just as each of us has one body with many members, and these members do not all have the same function, so in Christ we, though many, form one body, and each member belongs to all the others. We have different gifts, according to the grace given to each of us.*

Think about your most recent school day. How many people did you see or talk to? Did you have any meetings? What about sports practice or a music rehearsal? College life is filled with opportunities to keep busy and entertained.

In Romans 12, Paul teaches that every person has been given different strengths and abilities. God chose your gifts specifically for you! These gifts enable you to serve the Savior in your own personal way. They also allow you to work together with those around you to reach common goals and proclaim the name of Jesus in everything you do.

In my own life, I was blessed with musical and athletic abilities. Playing in band and on the basketball team has shown me firsthand that life is much easier when everyone uses their strengths together. Band rehearsal is weak and confusing when people are missing, but when everyone plays together, the result is beautiful music! On the basketball court, it's crucial that teammates work together. You may be a great athlete, but if you don't have teamwork, your team may never find success. You must play to each other's strengths and work together.

God designed us to use our gifts together to serve him in our daily lives. Throughout your college career, you will encounter countless opportunities to serve the Savior with your gifts. Whatever these gifts may be, the most important thing is that you use them to glorify God.

PRAYER Dear God, thank you for giving me a unique set of gifts. Help me use them to the best of my ability and work with others to bring glory to your name. Amen.

IN THE RIGHT PLACE FOR YOU

Acts 17:26-28 *From one man he made all the nations, that they should inhabit the whole earth; and he marked out their appointed times in history and the boundaries of their lands. God did this so that they would seek him and perhaps reach out for him and find him, though he is not far from any one of us. "For in him we live and move and have our being."*

I was reading through the book of Acts a while back when a few passages jumped off the page at me. It was one of those faith moments when God, through his Word, came to me right where I was, right when I needed him. Those passages are the focus for today. Please read them again.

I had been spending way too much mental energy wondering if I was in the place where I could be best serving God. Those thoughts were immediately halted when I read these verses. I gained peace as I began to grasp the fact that God has set each of us in our places for reasons beyond what we can comprehend. Consider where you are in your life: the city you live in, the people in your life, the place you work. Looking at all of these things, imagine the ways in which God has used you, or intends to use you for his purposes! How wonderful is our God that he has so intentionally placed all of us where we are, in order that, together, we can show the love of Jesus to a world that so desperately needs him.

PRAYER Dear Lord, I trust that the situation you've put me in is exactly where you want me to be. Help me live in a way that allows you to best use me as the vessel for your purposes. Amen.

THIS IS NOT OUR HOME

John 14:1-3 *Do not let your hearts be troubled. You believe in God; believe also in me. My Father's house has many rooms; if that were not so, would I have told you that I am going there to prepare a place for you? And if I go and prepare a place for you, I will come back and take you to be with me that you also may be where I am.*

Are there times that you simply feel like throwing your hands up in the air and just walking away from everything? Classes are more difficult than you thought they would be, your friends are not being supportive about the decisions you are making, and you don't know who or what you can trust. It's hard to understand at times, but that is the way life on earth is supposed to be.

We face hardships on earth so that we are pointed toward heaven. Read today's passage again. Jesus is speaking and right away he says, "Do not let your hearts be troubled." He understands that we face hardships, but he offers the great reassurance that we have a place in heaven waiting for us. He has gone ahead and is preparing our place.

When it seems like things are going in a million different directions and you don't know what is happening, remember that through it all, this is not where we will remain. Heaven is waiting for us, and what a great place that will be.

PRAYER "I'm but a stranger here; heaven is my home.
Earth is a desert drear; heaven is my home.
Danger and sorrow stand round me on every hand.
Heaven is my fatherland; heaven is my home"
(CW 417:1). Thank you, Lord, that heaven is where I will live one day. Amen.

September 20
TRUE HUMILITY

Psalm 149:4 *For the* Lord *takes delight in his people; he crowns the humble with victory.*

Author Ernest Hemingway once remarked, "There is nothing noble in being superior to your fellow man; true nobility is being superior to your former self." It seems as though we are always competing with other people for superiority. Students compete for grades or teacher approval, workers compete to produce the most marketable ideas, and even friends can compete to be the "best" friend. Yet according to Hemingway, true nobility is for you to become better than the person you used to be.

For Christians, this statement reminds us that we were born sinful but through Jesus we are made new. The great Reformer Martin Luther says in his Small Catechism, "Our Old Adam with his evil deeds and desires should be drowned by daily contrition and repentance, and die, and that day by day a new man should arise, as from the dead, to live in the presence of God." Daily contrition and repentance are necessary aspects of our lives since we continue to fall far short of God's law. We must humble ourselves and realize that we are the worst of sinners.

As Psalm 149:4 reminds us, God does not leave us lying in sin, which is fortunate for us. Our greatest victory is not our own; Jesus has won it for us. On this earth, people will still compete for superiority, but where faith is concerned, we cannot improve our condition on our own. It is the saving work of the Holy Spirit that enables us to cast off our old sinful self and allows our new self to serve others in humility.

PRAYER My heavenly Father, I am sorry for the many ways in which I daily sin against you. Keep me humble as I keep you first in my life, remembering that I am your child. In Jesus' name, I pray. Amen.

DON'T LOSE SLEEP OVER GUILT

Proverbs 28:13 *Whoever conceals their sins does not prosper, but the one who confesses and renounces them finds mercy.*

Do you ever question your abilities and actions as a Christian leader? You might think you're being a good friend by avoiding confrontation, but deep down you wish you could speak up because you see your friends making bad choices. You see other students in leadership positions who seem to have their lives together, while you struggle with your own weaknesses and addictions that you could never admit to other Christians for fear of judgment. It seems like living a double life is the only option: being an advocate for Christ while nurturing shady relationships. Before you lose more sleep over your guilt, read Proverbs 28:13 again.

Being in denial about your own guilt will only increase the pain it brings into your life. Rather than fighting it, God gives us friends and family to help guide us through our troubles. Read Psalm 32. David describes how unhealthy it is to internalize guilt. You can see how destructive it is for your health and relationships, in addition to being a distraction from your intense schedule.

Call up someone you trust as soon as guilt starts to spiral out of control. You might be surprised how just talking to someone can help. Even the people you would least expect often struggle silently and have their own stories to share. Pray for forgiveness. God showed David mercy and wants to show mercy to you, and the joy you feel from being forgiven will encourage you to help others.

PRAYER Dear Lord, always remind me that you never want guilt to distract me from serving others and appreciating those I love. Help me share with everyone the peace that is only found in you. Amen.

WHEN REALITY SETS IN

John 16:33 *I have told you these things, so that in me you may have peace. In this world you will have trouble. But take heart! I have overcome the world.*

It's happening. The reality of being back in the hectic and demanding schedule of a college student seems to hit hard just about this time each semester. The projects begin to pile up, the endless studying plays on *repeat* night after night, and multiple stressors sneak into our lives. We may begin to feel overwhelmed. And what of the temptations to sin and not be faithful to God? What of the challenges, the attacks on us and on our faith? How well do we cope? How well do we persevere?

In all of these times, though, we can find comfort knowing that the trials and ills that we face throughout this life are only temporary—and that they are worth facing through to the end.

Jesus conquered sin and death—our greatest challenge—so that someday we get to spend an eternity with him free from pain, sorrow, despair, and every other consequence of sin that you could possibly imagine. What an awesome victory to look forward to! So don't sweat the difficulties of this life. They won't last. And we do have one sure thing that *will* last—an everlasting home in heaven, safe in our Father's arms.

PRAYER Dear Lord, help me fix my eyes on the prize of my heavenly home and find peace. Help me realize that even when I am faced with what seems to be more than I can handle, these difficulties will not last. Help me persevere. Thank you for the sacrifice of your Son. Because of him, I get to spend forever in your holy presence! Amen.

September 23

GOD WILL DELIVER US

Psalm 31:14,15 *I trust in you, Lord; I say, "You are my God." My times are in your hands; deliver me from the hands of my enemies, from those who pursue me.*

I admit that I once touched a sick friend's contaminated possessions in the hopes of contracting the stomach flu! I wanted the benefit of a day of watching movies on the couch, not doing any of my mounting work. It is sad that the overwhelming lifestyle of the college student can make a day with a high fever and a garbage can near the couch seem appealing!

With ever-present papers, career development opportunities, and interpersonal relationship obligations, you probably also feel as though you'll never rest again. Just as you finally sit down for 15 minutes of solitude and a snack, your phone buzzes, your computer rings with e-mail notifications, and you hear knocking on the door. You might not call these responsibilities "enemies," but they definitely seem hostile at times as they affect your health and challenge your morale.

But there is good news! Our God is in control. With him on our side, we can handle anything that comes our way.

However, this doesn't happen magically. It happens through contact with him and with his promises. How many hours a day do we spend on social media or working on homework? How much time do we spend with our God? Try spending just five minutes today in his Word and two minutes today in prayer. The peace that comes from tapping into our perfect Creator who is in control of our lives is such a blessing!

PRAYER Dear Lord, sometimes I feel overwhelmed with responsibilities, hardships, and other "enemies" in my life. Please give me the courage to focus on you and your promises—to trust you . . . and then to share you with my world. Amen.

TRUE CONTENTMENT

1 Timothy 6:6,7 *Godliness with contentment is great gain. For we brought nothing into the world, and we can take nothing out of it.*

"Once I can travel, then I will really be happy." "If I could just earn a little bit more money, then I could finally upgrade my beater!" "I wish I were pretty like she is." Do any of these sentiments sound familiar? They certainly do for me. We often don't realize how much of our lives are spent coveting others' lives and chasing meaningless pursuits.

Don't get me wrong—striving for success in this life is definitely not wrong. God wants us to pursue our dreams through hard work and dedication. However, something very dangerous can happen when we believe that things like money or beauty will lead to happiness. As Paul wisely writes in the passage for today, "We brought nothing into the world, and we can take nothing out of it."

The key to happiness is found not in the things of this world, but through godliness with contentment. Sometimes the word *contentment* has a negative connotation of laziness, complacency, or stagnation. This is far from true, though. Contentment is not a situation or a circumstance. It is a state of mind: absolute trust in God and knowing that we lack nothing when we abide in him. It means being happy with what we have and where we are. It's not easy to live a life of contentment, but pray that God will help and enable you to live a life of contentment today.

PRAYER Dear God, forgive me for my constant dissatisfaction, covetousness, and desire for more. Help me be content with what I have and desire you above the things of this world. Thank you for fulfilling my every want and desire. Amen.

A POWERFUL DEMONSTRATION

1 Corinthians 2:4,5 *My message and my preaching were not with wise and persuasive words, but with a demonstration of the Spirit's power, so that your faith might not rest on human wisdom, but on God's power.*

"Hi, it's Vince from ShamWow! You'll be saying 'wow' every time you use this towel. This works wet or dry. Why do you wanna work twice as hard?"

If you're in the habit of watching infomercials (and I'm not, I promise), you may find yourself persuaded by their salesmanship. Do you hear the way that Vince guy talks? He's got confidence, he makes sense (of course you don't want to work twice as hard!), and above all, he just soaked up 8 gallons of orange juice with one ShamWow!

When the apostle Paul came to the Corinthian congregation, they were expecting someone like Vince. The Christians there wanted him to speak with confidence and to persuade them with talk that made sense. But he didn't do those things. Instead, he came with the only type of powerful demonstration that matters—the powerful demonstration that when the message of Christ crucified is preached, the Holy Spirit creates unshakeable faith.

God doesn't want to sell himself to you, and he doesn't try to make himself so small that he makes sense to our little human brains. A faith based on man's wisdom will fall away at the first sign of trouble. So be content with what God tells you in his Word, because those words lay a better foundation for your faith than any human salesmanship ever could.

PRAYER Dear Holy Spirit, help me appreciate God's Word, even when it doesn't seem relevant or persuasive. Use it to create in me an unshakable faith in Jesus. Amen.

DIFFERENT GIFTS, SAME SAVIOR

1 Corinthians 12:4-6 *There are different kinds of gifts, but the same Spirit distributes them. There are different kinds of service, but the same Lord. There are different kinds of working, but in all of them and in everyone it is the same God at work.*

I graduated from college, having found a job just a few weeks prior to graduation. Stepping into this job, I was prepared to be as professional as possible. This had been part of my training all through college. I was slightly surprised when I walked into an office that was far less professional than I expected. I work mostly with customers who have less professional training and education than I do. Due to this, I often find myself frustrated.

Sometimes I have to remind myself that these customers are people like me. They are God's children, and they have the gifts to do jobs that I cannot do. God has given them their own sets of gifts, just as he has given me mine.

Everyone on this earth has been given his or her own place in life. All people have their own gifts and talents, all given by God. If he puts the CEOs in their positions and also puts the homeless on the side of the street, then we know that he made that decision for a reason. All people should be treated as equals, and more important, as children of God. Christ died for all, not just the talented and rich.

PRAYER Dear Lord, sometimes I forget that I am not in charge of my life and that the blessings that I have are only because of your hand. Please remind me of that and help me to show love to all of your children. Amen.

LIVING WITH LOSS

Romans 6:23 *The wages of sin is death, but the gift of God is eternal life in Christ Jesus our Lord.*

Everyone has experienced or been affected by death. For many, including me, there has been a death in their family. With death come sadness, pain, loneliness, and uncertainty. Looking at death, I feel the most difficult part to face is the loss of that person in your life, the loss of his or her influence on your future, and the loss of memories shared.

Even if you haven't lost a loved one, I'm sure you've lost something. Whether it's your keys or something deeper—a relationship, your dream job, your reputation due to poor choices—loss is a feeling we all can relate to and understand.

These sufferings in our lives are directly related to our sin as stated in Roman 6:23. The sin that fills our world is the initial source of all the loss that we face in our lives. But the one thing we never lose is the hope we have in our God. The second half of this well-known verse is the most important information we could need. This reassurance of God's grace is constant. No matter what losses we have in our lives, God's love is the one thing we can fall back on. Our salvation through Jesus' death and resurrection is one thing we will never lose; his love is forever and his mercy never fails. It is a free gift.

PRAYER Dear God, thank you for the amazing, infallible gift that you have given me through the death of your Son, Jesus. Please give me your hand to help guide me through hard times and help reassure me through your Word. Thank you for all of your blessings, Lord. In your name, I pray. Amen.

GOD IS USING YOU

1 Corinthians 7:17 *Each person should live as a believer in whatever situation the Lord has assigned to them, just as God has called them. This is the rule I lay down in all the churches.*

"When I'm finally out in the world dealing with real issues and exploring new places, then I'll actually be doing something with my life." I can't even count the times I thought this throughout my years of being in school.

Having finally finished school, I look back and it's easy to see how wrong I was. While I was walking through those halls, studying in the library, and hanging out with friends, I was right where I needed to be. God had called me to learn. God had called me to listen. God had called me to be a missionary to everyone around me.

At every stage in life, from cradle to grave, God is using you to be his servant. Even in a boring class, he is teaching you patience and commitment. Even in the normal steps to the classroom, he is teaching you dedication and endurance. Even with your friends, he is training you to listen, love, and encourage.

Jesus calls us to walk with him every day of our lives. He gives purpose to our daily grind. Each day, we grow closer to him and we help others do the same. That is a mighty calling at every stage in life.

PRAYER Dear Lord, you give my life purpose by the life you lived, gave, and shared with me. Help me see my studies, my work, and my time with friends as an opportunity right now to serve you, grow in you, and share you with others. Amen.

HOW ARE YOU?

Philippians 4:11,12 *I am not saying this because I am in need, for I have learned to be content whatever the circumstances. I know what it is to be in need, and I know what it is to have plenty. I have learned the secret of being content in any and every situation, whether well fed or hungry, whether living in plenty or in want.*

"How are you?" Today I've learned that John, Mandy, Jenna, Katy, and Steven are all "good." This phrase that was established to invite two people into a conversation has become short for "hello."

In passing an acquaintance last week, he greeted me with a hello, paused, and then said, "Good." I hadn't even asked, "How are you?" He was following along with the norm and didn't wait for a response. He "jumped the gun" and got straight to the point—a characteristic of our cold-climate culture. What good is the phrase "How are you?" if it is brushed aside as a normality, only to be responded to with the answer, "Good"? What relevance does good have in one's life? You're good? Good at what? Good at life?

Philippians 4:11,12 tells us that we ought to strive for contentment. Contentment is not a reaction to life's circumstances; it is a proactive decision to immerse oneself in God's grace with the knowledge that he will bless us and deliver us (Psalm 68:19).

Choose to be content because God's work in Jesus provides peace. Choose to be content because we have a God who is bigger than our needs. Choose to be content because our lives are his. He will use us to carry out his will. What greater blessing could we have on earth? And so, I ask you, how are you today?

PRAYER Dear Father, in my daily walk with you, I pray that you will help me be content, because I know that you are my source of everything "good." Amen.

September 30
TRUE HAPPINESS

Proverbs 11:28 *Those who trust in their riches will fall, but the righteous will thrive like a green leaf.*

Get rich or die tryin'. The desire to get rich is highly prevalent in our society. Many people think money, fancy cars, and big houses will help them fill a void and find an ever-elusive happiness. Advertisers take advantage of this and entice people into thinking that buying Product X will make them happy: "Look at all the people smiling and having a great time because of our product!"

There are many passages throughout God's Word warning us of the dangers of chasing after earthly wealth or the risk of relying on money instead of God. The book of Proverbs is full of contrasts between the wicked and the righteous, and one of these strong dichotomies comes from our passage today. This proverb doesn't leave much room for interpretation or gray area. Trusting in wealth instead of God will not lead to a happy eternal outcome. But the second half of this verse brings to mind the words of Jesus in John 15:5: "I am the vine; you are the branches. If you remain in me and I in you, you will bear much fruit; apart from me you can do nothing." In Jesus and his forgiveness, we have true spiritual wealth.

As Christians, we know that money can't buy happiness. It may make life a little easier in the short term, or it may bring new problems and struggles. We know that true riches are rooted in the love of Jesus Christ. When we remain in him and follow his will for us, he promises we will thrive like a green leaf and bear much fruit.

PRAYER Dear Lord, please help me focus on you as my source of ultimate happiness. Amen.

OCTOBER
FIGHT THE GOOD FIGHT

FIGHT THE GOOD FIGHT

1 Timothy 6:12 *Fight the good fight of the faith. Take hold of the eternal life to which you were called when you made your good confession in the presence of many witnesses.*

"Never give up" is a common expression thrown around today. When directed at a sports team, the phrase can inspire vigilance and dedication. When a loved one is struggling with illness, it can give hope. Scenarios like this highlight an important fact about tasks: they are rarely easy and more often a battle. However, that does not mean they are impossible.

Paul, in his first letter to Timothy, is giving some valuable advice for Timothy to guide the church in Ephesus. There were concerns of false teaching being spread by some members of the church, and Paul urges Timothy to deal with the issue. Quite a daunting task for someone so young! However, Paul reassures Timothy that he is more than capable, by the grace of God.

Our struggles in life may be difficult, whether it's wrestling with temptation, workloads, or a family crisis, but God reminds us through Paul's letter of the victory that we already have in Christ. The more we learn to lean on God and "take hold" of our faith, the better equipped we are to face our struggles. Paul's advice is ultimately a reminder of who we are: warriors of faith, but more important, saved children of God.

"Never give up" is all well and good, but "fight the good fight" sounds better. Our battle is not hopelessly clinging to what strength we have left, waiting for everything to end. On the contrary, it's realizing the battle is already won.

PRAYER Dear Father, thank you for reminding me of the victory I have in your Son's sacrifice. Help me remember my gift of faith and use it as my true source of strength, so I may face every task in life, all to your glory. Amen.

October 2

SEEING OTHERS

Luke 10:33,34 *A Samaritan, as he traveled, came where the man was; and when he saw him, he took pity on him. He went to him and bandaged his wounds, pouring on oil and wine. Then he put the man on his own donkey, brought him to an inn and took care of him.*

Jesus saw people. Seeing led to compassion. In the parable of the good Samaritan, the Samaritan sees a person; the priest and the Levite see a problem.

It's easy to get too distracted, preoccupied, or agenda-driven to "see" others. It's easy to simply avoid needy people. But we *can* look at them. We *can* listen. Love begins with looking.

Why do we look away? Is it the hassle? the dirt? the commitment? We might have to pay if we look too closely and care too deeply. Loving means we might lose control of our schedule, our money, and our time.

When I was a little girl, I would get dressed up and strut around the house. I didn't ask to be looked at, but I silently craved to be seen.

All of us long to know that someone notices and cares. When I've messed up, I've usually failed in some way to see someone. Instead, I'm focused on my agenda, my thoughts, and my feelings. To truly love people, we must see them.

God sees us. His eyes are always upon us with love and compassion. He saw our need and acted by sending his Son to die for our sins. God cares. God sees. God loves—us.

Do you believe when you move toward God he sees you coming and runs toward you to kiss you? Share that love.

PRAYER God, when I watch Jesus loving others in the Bible, I am watching you love. I want to be rooted and grounded in that love so that what flows from you flows through me to others. Thank you for your love. Amen.

SLOW DOWN

2 Thessalonians 3:11-13 *We hear that some among you are idle and disruptive. They are not busy; they are busybodies. Such people we command and urge in the Lord Jesus Christ to settle down and earn the food they eat. And as for you, brothers and sisters, never tire of doing what is good.*

Slow down. God has already found you.

Join this club! Lead this team! Do this activity! One of the best things about college is that it's designed to be a social setting where you can do lots of STUFF. And while doing all of this stuff, you're told that college is a time to "find yourself." Where do you fit in?

Think of all the activities you do in college. Do you have a job? Do you play sports? Maybe you're part of a club. And on top of that, you have your studies. Have you found yourself yet?

The passage in this devotion reminds us that it's okay to slow down. Take comfort and know that God has already found you. He loved all of us enough to send his Son to die on a cross to take away all of our sins. We deserved nothing, and yet he took care of us. You can find yourself in the undeserved love of Christ.

It's easy to get caught up in the busyness of college, and it's okay to want to find yourself, but never forget him who found you first.

PRAYER Gracious Father, thank you for finding me first. As I continue in college and life, please help me slow down and strive to live in thanks to you. Amen.

AT THE TOP OF GOD'S LIST

Mark 12:30 *Love the Lord your God with all your heart and with all your soul and with all your mind and with all your strength.*

What do you love most? Is it hanging out with friends? playing video games? playing a sport or instrument? Is it money? How about your family, boyfriend, or girlfriend—are they on the top of your list? Is God on the top of that list?

God should be at the top of that list. Our actions and thoughts often do not show that he is at the top. We fail on a daily basis to let God know that we love him with all our heart, soul, mind, and strength. We skip church on Sunday and neglect daily devotion and prayer. We let foul words slip from our mouths. We cheat, lie, and gossip.

Yet Jesus has shown us time and again that we are at the top of his list. He has given promises such as "he will never leave you nor forsake you" (Deuteronomy 31:8) and he will "strengthen you and help you" (Isaiah 41:10). God ultimately shows us that we are on the top of his list through his perfect life, death, and resurrection. Even though we have sinned and have failed to show our love for our God and Savior, we can be assured of God's everlasting love.

PRAYER Dear heavenly Father, thank you for loving me and sending your Son, Jesus, to take away my sins. Help me show my love for you in all I do. Amen.

October 5

GOD'S WAYS, NOT OUR WAYS

Philippians 4:9 *Whatever you have learned or received or heard from me, or seen in me—put it into practice. And the God of peace will be with you.*

What can you control? That's a loaded question, but it's intended to be. As Christians, we know that ultimately God is in control of all things. Does that mean that you don't control anything? No! God gave you a free will. He didn't want you to be a robot that simply obeyed every command.

The bad news is that by nature the only commands we can obey are from our sinful hearts. Even when we are able to control our outward actions and words, our motives are sinful. Sin keeps us separated from God and makes hell a certainty. So we are not really, truly free, are we?

When we are brought to faith in Christ and receive his forgiveness, we also are brought into the freedom to live in a right relationship with God. Now, while you can't control what other people do or how they treat you, you can control what YOU do. You can say to yourself, "I'm not going to do things because I expect certain results or praise; I will do them because it is right."

How do you know what's right? Don't trust your own judgment, which can easily deceive you. How do we know what the Philippians learned and received and heard from Paul? He wrote it down for us!

Don't spend your time worrying about how people in this world react to what you do . . . think about how your God reacts. "The God of peace will be with you," precisely because he is at peace with us because of Christ.

PRAYER Dear Lord, help me do what is right in your sight and follow your ways, not mine. Amen.

CHOICES

2 Timothy 2:22 *Flee the evil desires of youth and pursue righteousness, faith, love and peace, along with those who call on the Lord out of a pure heart.*

Choices. Why is it that growing up comes with the need to make so many choices? Have you ever felt or been told, perhaps multiple times, that the choices you make now can determine your future?

Paul's second letter to Timothy encourages us to "flee the evil desires of youth." Is he saying we need to lead lame and boring lives? How can my desire to have one more beer or shot be evil? It makes me feel good and isn't harming anyone. Indulging in pornographic images because my girlfriend/boyfriend can't fulfill my physical needs isn't evil, right? Paul's letter tells us to flee from these desires, but also gives criteria for the friends I ought to have—"those who call on the Lord out of a pure heart."

Is fighting our evil desires a good fight? As defective sheep, we are easily enticed away from our Shepherd and follow the desires that we think will lead us to greener pastures. This good fight will not be easy and is not always easily overcome, but there is hope.

God wants us to put off "evil desires of youth" and embrace a mature path of righteousness, faith, love, and peace—a path of hope designed for success. God watches over you and will bring you from your rented apartment to your heavenly mansion. The rent has been paid with Jesus' blood—are you willing to take the journey?

PRAYER Lord, give me the wisdom to flee the evil desires of my youth and follow you. Help me trust your promises of heaven and keep me steadfast in your Word to fight the good fight. Amen.

DON'T BE LED ASTRAY

Proverbs 20:1 *Wine is a mocker and beer a brawler; whoever is led astray by them is not wise.*

Hammered. Sloshed. Wasted. Plastered. All of these terms refer to getting drunk. Sadly, college today is known as party time rather than as an institution of higher learning. Our culture and the mass media portray college as the time when it's normal to have huge parties and get completely drunk. You're young and you just want to have fun, right?

The passage in this devotion describes the misuse of alcohol very well. It's "not wise" for a variety of reasons. First, it's dangerous physically. You can die from it. Second, it affects your decision making, which often results in regrettable actions. Many people get hurt because they decide it's a good idea to do some parkour while intoxicated or have unwanted sex. Third and most important, God tells us it's sinful. Thank God we have forgiveness in Jesus!

Alcohol in and of itself is not evil. Paul tells us in 1 Corinthians 10:23 that although we have the freedom to do anything, "not everything is beneficial." It's okay to drink alcohol. I drink alcohol and will continue to do so. What's not okay is to drink in excess, to drink around someone who struggles with it, or to drink if you're underage. We love the Lord and therefore love others. As Christians in college, we have the privilege and responsibility to live lives that let our light shine and cause people to ask why we don't participate. We have an easy answer . . . Jesus.

PRAYER Dear Lord, college is a difficult phase in life and the issue of drinking is always present. Please help me make good decisions, know my limits, and let my light shine. Alcohol is a gift. I ask you to help me not misuse this gift. Amen.

AN AUDIENCE OF ONE

Exodus 23:2 *Do not follow the crowd in doing wrong. When you give testimony in a lawsuit, do not pervert justice by siding with the crowd.*

Hall-of-Fame basketball coach John Wooden once stated, "The true test of a man's character is what he does when no one is watching." Certainly, this quote illustrates a sound earthly principle: the image people seek to portray does not always align with what is going on behind the scenes. However, character is defined a bit differently for Christians than that quote suggests. Not a single moment passes in our lives when "no one is watching," because we have a loving God who is constantly watching over us. For us, the true test of our character is what we do when only God is watching.

I often consider how different my life would look if I truly lived for an audience of one—my heavenly Father. For encouragement, I love to look at Jesus' life as an example of perfect character. He showed us exactly what it means to have character.

I also find encouragement from Paul's words in 1 Timothy 6:12, as Paul was certainly no stranger to the fight of faith: "Fight the good fight of the faith. Take hold of the eternal life to which you were called." I love that he refers to this fight of faith as *good.* It is good! We get to live as Christians, and we get to fight this very good fight!

Furthermore, the encouragement to take hold of the eternal life to which we were called is so powerful, isn't it? God called each of us, through Christ's sacrifice on the cross, to eternal life. Seize every opportunity to thank him for that gift by living like his child!

PRAYER Heavenly Father, thank you for this good fight of faith! Help me always focus on living my life primarily for your glory. In your perfect name, I ask this. Amen.

GRACE, NOT JUSTICE

James 5:4 *Look! The wages you failed to pay the workers who mowed your fields are crying out against you. The cries of the harvesters have reached the ears of the Lord Almighty.*

Chris worked for a man who owned his own electrical business. After several years of working for the man, he simply stopped calling Chris. Chris tried reaching him for weeks, but never got a response. Chis then realized that this guy owed him thousands of dollars but was planning to never pay him. Chris finally gave up on ever getting his money.

We would all be pretty upset if that happened to us. If we work hard for it, we deserve to get what we are working hard for. If we are working hard in a class, we should deserve the A. If someone borrows something from us and loses it, we deserve to be reimbursed. In a world where the attitude of entitlement is everywhere, thank God that he hasn't given you what you deserve. Rather, he has given you such a great blessing: his Son, Jesus. Because of Jesus you now have forgiveness and eternal life. God has such a great love for you, and you didn't do anything to deserve it.

So next time something happens in your life that isn't fair or just, remember how God hasn't given you justice, but rather grace. Then reflect that grace to the ones who are unjust to you, knowing that you have blessings from God that are far more valuable than anything in this world.

PRAYER Dear Lord, I praise you for the blessings you have showered upon me, specifically your grace. As I live in a world of injustice, I ask you to help me not get caught up in the earthly things that I haven't received but feel I deserve. Help me remember that you have graciously given me something far greater in heaven. Amen.

TURN FROM TEMPTATION

Proverbs 1:10 *My son, if sinful men entice you, do not give in to them.*

Life is full of temptations. Solomon recognized it is inevitable that we will confront evil. Likewise, the great Reformation theologian Martin Luther reportedly said, "You can't stop birds from flying over your head, but you can keep them from building a nest in your hair."

In this fallen world, we are bound to be tempted. Sometimes, we may need to resist with tact and respect like Daniel (Daniel 1:8-16); other times we may have to flee like Joseph (Genesis 39:11,12). Regardless of what the temptation is and how we deal with it, it all goes back to the instruction of the wise king: "Do not give in to them."

God is serious about temptations and sins. He tells us that if we follow the path of temptations and sins, the end result will be eternal separation from God (James 1:13-15). Rather than resisting temptations out of fear, we Christians live morally to give God thanks and praise. We follow the example of Jesus by being well-versed in Scripture to meet the devil's temptations.

While others may entice us, God understands our weaknesses and gives us strength to live according to his will (Matthew 26:41). In 1 Corinthians 10:13, the apostle Paul tells us that God will not allow us to be tempted beyond what we can bear and that God will provide a way for us to resist temptations. When we do fail to resist temptation, Jesus invites us to repent and receive the forgiveness of our sins. We never face these battles alone. By using his Word, the sword of the Spirit, we will win the victory. With that promise and comfort, let us humbly ask him to strengthen us.

PRAYER Dear heavenly Father, grant me your Spirit and lead me not into temptation, but deliver me from evil. Amen.

A FRIENDSHIP WITH JESUS

James 4:4 *You adulterous people, don't you know that friendship with the world means enmity against God? Therefore, anyone who chooses to be a friend of the world becomes an enemy of God.*

The struggling alcoholic is wise to avoid regularly associating with her circle of friends who are frequent patrons at the trendy wine bar nearby. The obese man knows better than to join two of his coworkers at the all-you-can-eat buffet for lunch. Alcoholism and obesity are difficult enough battles to fight on their own without inviting those who would undoubtedly raise the intensity of the battle even more.

As we fight the good fight against Satan and our sly, sinful self, the last thing we want to do is befriend the world and provide the devil and our own sinful nature with another ally. Surely they do not need any reinforcements to oppose the new self dwelling in each of us through faith in Christ! James warned of this danger when he wrote today's verse. To be deceived into thinking that friendship with the world guarantees a spot with the "in crowd" is to confuse our enemies with our friends. Also, it underestimates how much deadly damage the wicked world can inflict.

Instead, let us be content to let our friendship rest with the One who not only says, "I have called you friends" (John 15:15), but who proved it by establishing our friendship at the cost of his own life. He has already overcome the world (John 16:33)! Take a pass on the world's "friend" request and instead foster your friendship with Jesus. He doesn't make the battle more difficult to fight than it already is; rather, he makes it easier, because his friendship is the foundation of our forgiveness.

PRAYER Lord Jesus, lead me to be wary of the world's friendship. Instead, help me see that in you I have the greatest friendship possible. Strengthen our friendship through your Word and sacrament. Amen.

YOUR GREATEST VICTORY

James 1:12 *Blessed is the one who perseveres under trial because, having stood the test, that person will receive the crown of life that the Lord has promised to those who love him.*

Whether at a Christian or public college, temptations abound; the devil works exceedingly hard to cause God's people to stumble. Peer pressure may surround you, and worldly decisions might be appealing: "Just this once. It won't hurt me. I know what I'm doing, and I'm in control." But once can turn into twice, which can turn into every time. Falling into a spiral never happens all at once. It's the accumulation of a series of small decisions made over time. Perseverance in making the right, godly choices time and time again will not be easy. Trust God's promises, that even though the right decision may not be popular, he will be with you and bless you.

I've heard it said that your greatest struggle will be your greatest victory. Whatever that struggle is for you—because it's different for every person—it will be your greatest victory with God's help. Without that struggle, there is no victory, because there is nothing to overcome. Embrace those temptations you overcome, because through your faith God has the greatest reward of all waiting for you—eternity with him in heaven!

PRAYER Heavenly Father, there are times in my life that temptation looms before me, and I struggle. I falter and lose sight of who I am through you. Help me remember my true identity because of your Son, Jesus, and bless my decisions that I may always do your will. Amen.

A LIGHT IN THE DARKNESS

Ephesians 5:11 *Have nothing to do with the fruitless deeds of darkness, but rather expose them.*

Have you ever ventured down inside a cave? It is cold, wet, and incredibly dark without the light from the sun. Without a light, exploring a cave is impossible for humans. It is dangerous due to the slippery rocks and the perils of an unexplored cavern with holes, bats, and who knows what else that might be lurking out of sight.

Our sinful world is like that dark cave. Sin plunges us into the deepest darkness, and we blunder around in life, not knowing which way is safe. God saw our condition and knew exactly what we needed: a light. God's Word guides our lives through the hazardous twists and turns of this world. God instructs his believers to not participate in the sins of the world, but we continuously disobey him. When this happens we are ashamed, and like Adam and Eve in the Garden of Eden, we are tempted to hide in the dark to cover up our sin. However, God's law is like a floodlight pointed directly on us to expose our faults and shortcomings. At the same time, though, the gospel is like lights along a path that lead us right to Jesus, the Savior who forgives all our sins.

In our thankfulness to Christ, we now live in the light of God's Word. Our lives of thankful service to Jesus should show our faith shining brightly so others may see and be drawn out of darkness and into Christ's wonderful light.

PRAYER Dear heavenly Father, thank you for the faith you have given me. Remind me that what I do in life should always demonstrate that faith and, when I am faced with the darkness of temptation, help me focus on the light of your Word. In Jesus' name, I pray. Amen.

HANGING TOUGH

Hebrews 4:15 *We do not have a high priest who is unable to sympathize with our weaknesses, but we have one who has been tempted in every way, just as we are—yet he did not sin.*

While at college I decided my limited finances were preventing me from experiencing the fun things I wanted to do. I purchased a clunker car for $300 and got myself three part-time jobs—against the advice of my parents and college staffers. I thought this would allow me to live the college lifestyle that I envisioned.

Four months later, I was exhausted from working long hours. I had less money than ever, my grades tanked, and I had lost my academic scholarship. The car broke down one last time, and as I watched the tow truck haul it away, I was overwhelmed by a feeling of failure.

I remember that moment vividly. I wish I could rewind life and listen to the advice that I had ignored. But that's not how it works. Bad choices have real consequences.

Today's Scripture reading reminds us that we don't endure the challenges of life alone. Jesus walked this earth and was "tempted in every way." Our Savior was attacked by jealous religious leaders; badgered by selfish crowds; and mocked, humiliated, and tortured to death by a corrupt government. And he never made the wrong choice. Not even once.

Bad choices are a fact of life. We make mistakes and deserve the consequences. But thanks to Jesus, those consequences are temporal. Like that clunker car being towed away, they will disappear forever when this life ends— only this time, we'll be overwhelmed by the feeling of victory!

PRAYER Heavenly Father, my sins and human limitations can mess things up, but I know that your power is made perfect in my weakness. Keep me firm through temptation, and use my limitations to highlight your limitless grace. Amen.

THE VICTORY IS OURS

Ephesians 6:13 *Therefore put on the full armor of God, so that when the day of evil comes, you may be able to stand your ground, and after you have done everything, to stand.*

When it's a bitterly cold winter day, it's wise to bundle up with thick layers. When a big project is due, it's wise to use time productively and plan accordingly. When interviewing for a new job, it's wise to dress professionally and exude confidence. These are all examples of preparing for what can be seen and is somewhat expected, but how does one prepare to fight against "authorities, against the powers of this dark world and against the spiritual forces of evil in the heavenly realms" (Ephesians 6:12)?

We live in a sinful world, surrounded by evil. Every day we are attacked by doubts and deceptions that threaten our faith. Life is full of choices that tempt us to follow what is contrary to God's will.

However, we must remember that the victory is ours through Christ. God's strength becomes our strength, and with his help we can fight our daily battles.

Paul's final advice is that we be alert and pray. Pray for wisdom, discernment, and endurance. Prepare yourself with continual Bible study; be on guard with the sword of the Spirit. Peter warns: "Be alert and of sober mind. Your enemy the devil prowls around like a roaring lion looking for someone to devour" (1 Peter 5:8). Prepare accordingly and stand firm.

PRAYER Heavenly Father, I pray for daily strength to fight the good fight. Thank you for the victory that is mine through Christ. Help me fight temptation confidently and stand firm in your truth. Amen.

STAND FIRM

Ephesians 6:14,15 *Stand firm then, with the belt of truth buckled around your waist, with the breastplate of righteousness in place, and with your feet fitted with the readiness that comes from the gospel of peace.*

I remember the first time I went to the beach. I ran into the ocean only to get knocked down by the waves. I'd get up, and as the water receded, I would get tripped up again. It was hard for me to stand my ground against the relentlessness of the waves.

Sometimes my life feels like my first trip to the beach. I go out with my friends, meet new people, and try new things, but I get pushed or pulled to do things that I don't want to do or know that I shouldn't do. Sometimes these temptations are coming straight at me and I can brace for them (like the waves I saw on the beach), but often they sneak up on me like a rip current pulling me out to sea. My strength was no match for the awesome power of the ocean, and my strength alone is no match for the devil and his temptations.

In his letter to the Ephesians that is the focus of this devotion, Paul has good advice on how I can ready myself to stand firm in the face of temptation. The battle against Satan is not won with swords and spears, but with character, courage, and Christ.

PRAYER Lord, when life's temptations seek to pull me away from you, help me stand solidly on you as my Rock. Thank you for giving me your Word as my source of encouragement and strength to stand firm against all temptations. Amen.

October 17

PROTECT YOURSELF

Ephesians 6:16,17 *In addition to all this, take up the shield of faith, with which you can extinguish all the flaming arrows of the evil one. Take the helmet of salvation and the sword of the Spirit, which is the word of God.*

Have you ever gone paintballing? I saw a crazy YouTube video once of a paintball hitting someone's bare leg in slow motion. The victim (who lost a bet) was pretty injured—after all, it hit bare, unprotected skin.

Most people who paintball wear a layer of clothing to protect themselves. They know they're entering a "war zone" and attack is imminent. They'd be foolish showing up without ample clothing to shield them from the sting of the paintballs.

Do you actively, consciously protect yourself from the devil's attacks? Or do you venture into life's war zone each day without considering how you'll handle his "flaming arrows"? You *know* his attacks are coming, so there's no reason not to be prepared. Ephesians urges us to go to battle with "the shield of faith . . . the helmet of salvation and the sword of the Spirit."

What exactly is the protection that softens the blow of the devil's arrows? God's Word, a strong prayer life, and supportive Christian friends, to name a few.

Just like a day spent on a paintball battlefield, you're sure to face attacks throughout your college life. You will never be able to avoid Satan altogether, but you can prevent or at least minimize the impact of his attacks. Don't forget who and what will protect you.

PRAYER Lord, you know as well as I do that Satan is out to get me every single day. His attempted attacks are unavoidable. Remind me to approach each day as a battle, with you and your truth by my side. Amen.

BE ALERT

1 Peter 5:8,9 *Be alert and of sober mind. Your enemy the devil prowls around like a roaring lion looking for someone to devour. Resist him, standing firm in the faith, because you know that the family of believers throughout the world is undergoing the same kind of sufferings.*

As citizens in a country with a solid judicial system and religious freedom, it's easy to become complacent in our mission as Christians. Since we rarely face physical persecution for our beliefs, the need to spread God's Word doesn't seem to be as urgent. All it takes are a few stories from Christians in countries where persecution occurs to remind us how hard Satan works.

In America, we are privileged to attend church, wear crosses, and talk about God without breaking any laws. Although we don't suffer for our faith, we are in a toxic environment that fosters complacency. Society's values are slowly eroding, forcing officials in public positions to agree with modern beliefs that clearly go against God's will. Oversensitivity toward not being "judgmental" has resulted in Christians becoming increasingly countercultural.

Instead of choosing to agree with what is popular, pray for the strength to share God's truth with a gentle, clear explanation. Not only does Satan work through secular institutions, but he also can work within the Christian church on earth. If conflict occurs within the church, it has less strength to proclaim God's Word. You don't have to be a missionary or minister to help spread God's Word. Speak up when Christians distort God's Word to please others. Don't be complacent in your mission, and encourage others to share their faith. Stand firm in your faith by cherishing the forgiveness you have in Jesus and by being in his Word.

PRAYER Help me remember that sharing the gospel is my biggest priority in all the work I do, O Lord. Amen.

SOW FOR THE SPIRIT

Galatians 6:8,9 *Whoever sows to please their flesh, from the flesh will reap destruction; whoever sows to please the Spirit, from the Spirit will reap eternal life. Let us not become weary in doing good, for at the proper time we will reap a harvest if we do not give up.*

Gardeners plant seeds because they know they'll harvest more of the same. The Bible says the same thing about making choices.

When Paul says "the Spirit," he means the Holy Spirit's work, through which God made you his child. Sowing "to please the Spirit" means making choices that reflect your status as God's child. In your life that means making choices that result in love, joy, peace, patience, kindness, goodness, faithfulness, gentleness, and self-control. You'll study instead of cheat, befriend instead of gossip, empathize instead of antagonize.

But there's a problem. You want to choose easy, gratifying things for yourself. It's a foreign concept for us to make decisions to please the Spirit. So how can you do it? Before you can sow for the Spirit, look at his blessings.

You know that in the past you've sown to please your sinful nature. Did you feel good about that in the end? Never. But do you believe that Jesus' life, death, and resurrection actually cover all your shortcomings? Because they do. Still not convinced? Read Galatians 3:26,27. Read it again. God sees the choices you make as if Jesus himself were making them. They're perfect. So you can forget about your guilt. You've got nothing to prove to God. That's the Spirit's blessing.

Now, how will you sow this time around? Choose actions filled with love, patience, and self-control, because you see a heavenly harvest of unending love and peace. Don't stop when your sinful nature fights back.

PRAYER Holy Spirit, make me sure of my status as God's child, and help me sow your love on earth. Amen.

REMEMBER WHO YOU ARE

Ephesians 4:14,15 *Then we will no longer be infants, tossed back and forth by the waves, and blown here and there by every wind of teaching and by the cunning and craftiness of people in their deceitful scheming. Instead, speaking the truth in love, we will grow to become in every respect the mature body of him who is the head, that is, Christ.*

Scenario 1: *Beep beep* goes your alarm on Sunday morning. Do you hit snooze or get up and get ready for church?

Scenario 2: "Hey! I heard there's a raging party going on. Want to go and get hammered?" Do you go or not?

Scenario 3: "Do you think I could get lucky with that hot guy tonight?" Do you do it or not?

Scenario 4: You're taking a test and can't remember an answer. Do you glance at your peer's test or not?

College is a time when many students can fall into temptations. Our parents no longer remind us to go to church, to study more, or to not get drunk at a party. Now is the time we put our faith to the test.

Paul says in Ephesians to no longer be tossed around by the deceitful scheming, cunning, and craftiness of people. It is through the work of the Holy Spirit, who creates and strengthens our faith, that we're able to fight off these temptations. Through Christ, we have the forgiveness of sins. We need to mature in Christ and read his Word.

Next time don't hit the snooze button, get drunk, have sex, or cheat on a test. Instead serve and praise God in everything you do. Remember who you are and whose child you are.

PRAYER Dear heavenly Father, thank you for sending your Son to earth to die for me and to be the perfect example. Help me say no to temptation, and help me praise and serve you in everything I do. Amen.

REJOICE IN SUFFERINGS?

1 Peter 4:12,13 *Dear friends, do not be surprised at the fiery ordeal that has come on you to test you, as though something strange were happening to you. But rejoice inasmuch as you participate in the sufferings of Christ, so that you may be overjoyed when his glory is revealed.*

Imagine growing up as the youngest child of three. Your older siblings pick on you all the time. When you think you've done something great, they tear you down. They mock you at every turn. Do you turn the other cheek as Jesus said in his Sermon on the Mount? Do you fight back? Do you give up?

Fighting the good fight can be troublesome at times, especially with those who have no interest and loathe the good news that we share. We may be mocked or ridiculed. Our message means nothing to them, and we can feel worthless. However, our Scripture lesson gives us hope in such times.

Peter writes that these confrontations are tests for us. All Christians will face trials and tribulations due to their faith. We may be called closed-minded, ridiculous for believing in that which we cannot see. We must continue to fight the good fight, but how can we do this in trying times?

Peter reminds us to rejoice as we participate in the sufferings of Christ. Jesus had mockers; he was crucified for his preaching. All of this was done so that we might have eternal salvation. This is why we continue to fight, no matter how hard it may be. We receive strength from Word and sacrament. We fight the good fight of faith.

PRAYER Lord God, help me not to be discouraged when trials come to me. Remind me that you will never test me beyond what I can bear as I look forward to everlasting glory with you forever. Amen.

WASHED CLEAN

2 Corinthians 7:1 *Since we have these promises, dear friends, let us purify ourselves from everything that contaminates body and spirit, perfecting holiness out of reverence for God.*

When I was little, I loved jumping in puddles. Actually, I still love jumping in puddles. But doing it now makes me thankful for my mom, who had to wash me clean afterward. It takes a lot of work to get the mess out of everything!

Our God has washed us clean from the mud of our bad choices, our guilt, and our natural sinful filth. That washing had to be done with a special detergent, Jesus' holy and precious blood. He gave that willingly even though it meant he would have to die while donating it. He wanted to clean us that much!

Now, just like my mom, God urges us not to go running back into the mud puddle. Clearly it would be inconsiderate for us to go out and get dirty again so that our moms would have to rewash everything. In the same way, it doesn't seem right for us to return to the filth of our sin after God has spent so much to make us clean!

In love for our Savior, avoid those things that contaminate your body and spirit. They will only leave you feeling cold, alone, and guilty. Instead, listen to your Savior's voice. You know how warm and comfortable it is being clean and fresh in him.

PRAYER Dear Lord, help me resist the temptation to return to the sin you have washed from me. Help me grow in my love for you, that I may listen to your voice more and more. Amen.

APPROVED BY GOD

2 Timothy 2:15 *Do your best to present yourself to God as one approved, a worker who does not need to be ashamed and who correctly handles the word of truth.*

Imagine you and your roommate have been getting irritated with each other. He's been playing his music really loudly. You made popcorn and didn't know he hated the smell. You both are sick of the other person's mess. But then . . . you come back one day and the place is spotless and you see a new pair of headphones on your roommate's dresser. You think to yourself that he's trying to make this work, so you will too.

If only things were that simple with God. We screw up daily, but there's not a simple fix for a life of sin. So you won't go to that party? Great. You are going to stand up for someone? Good for you. But none of that will make us presentable to our heavenly Father. We can fight the good fight against temptation all we want, but we are still sinful since conception (Psalm 51:5).

We cannot do anything to be approved by God, but thankfully we also have to do nothing to be approved by God. Our Savior Jesus did all of the hard work for us. He took on the sin of the world and carried all bad things on his shoulders while he hung on the cross. On judgment day we will have to stand before God, but with no shame. God will see us as pure because of what Jesus did for us.

PRAYER Heavenly Father, I am forever grateful for your gift to me through your only Son. I don't have to be ashamed in your presence because I am cleansed through faith in Christ. I place all of my sins at the foot of the cross; please forgive me for all the wrongs I do. I will live joyously and eagerly await your return so I can rejoice with you in eternity! Amen.

BE PREPARED

1 Peter 3:15,16 *In your hearts revere Christ as Lord. Always be prepared to give an answer to everyone who asks you to give the reason for the hope that you have. But do this with gentleness and respect, keeping a clear conscience, so that those who speak maliciously against your good behavior in Christ may be ashamed of their slander.*

Have you ever had to "wing" something? Maybe there was a time you had to give a speech or take an exam but were not quite fully prepared for it. Being prepared means you have studied and that you can defend your answers.

We are to be prepared to give the reason for the hope that we have. Peter tells us to be ready to tell others why we live with God in our hearts, why we believe Christ saved us, and why we have hope in eternal life. He also tells us how we are to answer those who have questions. Peter makes it clear we are not better than others because of our beliefs. Instead, we are to share the hope we have with gentleness and respect.

This leads to this question: Are you prepared? If someone asks you at your new internship, at a football game, or even on campus why you believe in God, are you prepared to give an answer? Furthermore, are you prepared to share God's Word with gentleness, respect, and patience? Christ died for our sins, which is not a subject for us to wing. Therefore, prepare to defend your faith and God by studying God's Word.

PRAYER Dear Lord, lead me to be prepared to give the reason for the hope I have so that I may use my life to share your wonderful love. Amen.

October 25

BE FILLED WITH THE SPIRIT

Ephesians 5:18,19 *Do not get drunk on wine, which leads to debauchery. Instead, be filled with the Spirit, speaking to one another with psalms, hymns, and songs from the Spirit. Sing and make music from your heart to the Lord.*

Mike was at a party. Beer in hand, he felt more confident speaking to women. As he approached a group of ladies, he thought, *I'm not too drunk. I'm loose but in control.* Moments later he staggered away, reeling from a slap. Mike didn't think much of it. After all, who was she to turn down his advances? The following Tuesday, Mike met his new chemistry lab partner. It was the woman he had made an inappropriate remark to! What would he do?

Paul, inspired by God, gives great instruction to the Ephesians. We recognize that our sinful nature likes to bump Jesus out of our hearts and take control. It's easy to make selfish decisions, have sinful sexual thoughts, and say rude things. How much more so will this happen if we are under the influence of excessive amounts of alcohol, medication, or other mind-altering substances!

The slope is a slippery one. Through the writings of Paul, God speaks to us and encourages us. He instructs us to encourage one another with his Word and to praise him with our thoughts and actions. After all, look what he has done for us through Christ's sacrifice! God blesses us when we read, discuss, and apply his Word to our lives. We learn more about Jesus and his love for us and how to cope with our sinfulness and the world's temptations. Regular participation in Bible study and worship pays eternal dividends.

PRAYER Dear God, please forgive me when I put myself and other worldly things before you. Bring me to repentance when I fail, and encourage me with the good news of your Son, Jesus, reminding me of the forgiveness I receive from you through him. All glory to Jesus. Amen.

October 26
BE ON YOUR GUARD

2 Peter 3:17 *Therefore, dear friends, since you have been forewarned, be on your guard so that you may not be carried away by the error of the lawless and fall from your secure position.*

Peter writes his second letter to warn Christians to not fall away from God. When he wrote the book, many people were concerned because the second coming of Christ had not yet happened. Peter warns Christians to stand firm in their faith.

Everybody faces temptations every day. Whether it's cheating on a test or stealing food from the cafeteria, or cheating on your significant other or skipping classes due to laziness, everyone has the opportunity to make good choices, as well as bad choices. As disciples of God, Christians face many temptations from "the lawless," through whom the devil works. Peter warns believers to "be on your guard" and to be ready for the temptations of man and fight through them with the help of God. We are in a "secure position" because God is on our side and we have faith through him. We cannot let the devil's temptations defeat us and win.

As college students, we face these problems every day, but God is the best protector, advisor, and anchor we have. He has given us his Word to read when we need clarification and help understanding a problem in life. He has given us family and friends to turn to and to lean on in times of need. God will never leave us and make us face temptations on our own. We will never be carried away by temptations as long as we stand secure in his name and keep God as the focal point in our lives.

PRAYER Lord, please help me fend off "the lawless" that I face daily and stay connected to you, living through you and thriving in you and your Word. Please give me the guidance I need to make God-pleasing choices in my life, the decisions that glorify your name. Amen.

HOLD FAST TO GOD'S WORD

2 Thessalonians 2:14,15 *He called you to this [salvation] through our gospel, that you might share in the glory of our Lord Jesus Christ. So then, brothers and sisters, stand firm and hold fast to the teachings we passed on to you, whether by word of mouth or by letter.*

Every day of his life, Jesus fought to save all people from death because of God's love. Like him, we live in a warzone between good and evil—life versus death—with no choice but to participate. Through Jesus' death and resurrection, the war has already been won for all believers, but that does not mean we stop fighting. To give up fighting would be to give up on the gift of life, which in turn leads to death.

Our choices determine what side we are fighting for. By making choices that go against God's will, we are fighting for the devil's schemes to bring all people to death. Thank God that he brings us back to him over and over again through his grace and mercy, because he has a plan for us.

In today's verse, we are taught by God how to fight the good fight of faith: by standing firm and holding fast to the teachings of his Word. How essential it is for us to study the Bible's teachings so that we are able to follow the path God has made for us. This path has an ultimate goal of bringing all people to eternal life through the love Christ revealed on the cross.

PRAYER Father, remind me of your love and fuel my heart with it so that I may not fall into the devil's traps. Help me make choices that will lead me and others to share in eternal glory. Amen.

A WAY OUT

1 Corinthians 10:13 *No temptation has overtaken you except what is common to mankind. And God is faithful; he will not let you be tempted beyond what you can bear. But when you are tempted, he will also provide a way out so that you can endure it.*

I'm being tempted. I'm being tempted all day. I'm being tempted to drink too much, to watch an inappropriate movie, to gossip, to do things that I'd be ashamed of if Jesus were next to me. This is why I need a Savior. No matter what I do or how well I behave, I am always being tempted. Since I am a sinful human, I give in to those temptations more often than I care to admit.

God says he will not let us be tempted beyond what we can bear but will also provide a way out. He gave us his Son so that even when we do fall into temptation, we are saved. God is so good. He continues to dig us out of the hole that we create for ourselves. I am saved even though I don't deserve it. I am saved even when I fall into temptation, when I know what is right but I choose wrong, and when I make mistakes. I am saved because Jesus loves me. I am saved.

PRAYER Dear Lord, I know that you never promised this life would be easy. You even told me that life would be challenging, but you promised that you would be with me every step of the way. Please stand by my side in the face of temptation and give me the strength to honor you in every decision I make. Thank you for sending your Son to die for me so that I may be with you in heaven someday. Amen.

October 29
THE COMPARISON TRAP

Galatians 6:4,5 *Each one should test their own actions. Then they can take pride in themselves alone, without comparing themselves to someone else, for each one should carry their own load.*

Ours is a world of comparison. We are exposed to standardized testing; we participate in competition and athletics. We also pride ourselves on working harder; making more money; and being smarter, more attractive, or kinder than others. It should not be surprising that this tendency toward comparison also creeps into our spiritual introspection and our relationship with God and our fellow brothers and sisters in Christ.

Yet it is the warning of the writer to the Galatians to avoid such action. What danger could this seemingly natural activity of comparison pose? There are two: First, we may become like the Pharisees, thanking God that we are not like other people. We must not become "confident in our righteousness" in the way the Pharisees were—that is, thinking that our good actions bring about our righteousness. Second, we must not be like the brother of the prodigal son, or the workers in the vineyard whose pay was the same as those who worked just an hour. These individuals were not satisfied with what they were given—not because what they received was inherently unfair, but because they compared themselves to others and became jealous.

God has blessed us all with diverse and unique talents, but we all struggle with our own personal sins. We are encouraged to evaluate our lives honestly rather than pit ourselves against others. We are reassured by God's promise that he will bless us all richly and guide our lives personally.

PRAYER Dear Lord, help me keep my eyes on you and your blessings, and help me avoid the temptation to compare myself to others. Amen.

BE JOYFUL, PATIENT, FAITHFUL

Romans 12:12 *Be joyful in hope, patient in affliction, faithful in prayer.*

These are such simple words and yet so difficult to carry out. In Romans 12 Paul writes about love and how we, as Christians, should interact with the world. This life is filled with difficulties, and it's easy to get swept away. Temptations lurk around every corner, and it often feels like there is no escape. College is a time when these difficulties seem to increase tenfold and numerous new temptations confront us. How do we react?

Be joyful in hope. Christ lived and died for the forgiveness of our sins. He rose again in victory over sin, death, and the devil. Our hope is more than a wish. It is the confident trust in salvation through Jesus.

Be patient in affliction. Life is not easy, but it is temporary. All of those difficulties and temptations will someday pass or will become foreign to you when you are enjoying eternal life in heaven. Grit your teeth, look to God, and persevere.

Be faithful in prayer. Prayer is powerful, but so often we set it aside. We get distracted and forget to talk to God. Communication is essential to relationships. How can we have a relationship with God if we don't pray? Whether you are in the best of times or the worst of times, pray—for your Father is listening. Make a prayer list and set aside a specific time for prayer. What better way to be faithful?

PRAYER Dear Lord, thank you for sending your Son to die on the cross so that I could be free from sin. Help me be joyful in the hope that that provides, patient in the affliction of this world, and faithful in the powerful tool of prayer. Amen.

UNDECIDED?

Psalm 27:1 *The LORD is my light and my salvation—whom shall I fear? The LORD is the stronghold of my life—of whom shall I be afraid?*

College students are asked countless times what their major is. For freshmen in college, the best answer is "Undecided." Colleges have done an unprecedented job at helping their students decide exactly what major they want to pursue. For upperclassmen, the question they cannot escape is this: What are your plans after graduation? Choosing to trust in the Lord and prayerfully relying on him to guide us through life is exactly what he wants from us.

Not having control over every second of our lives and future is very stressful to most people. However, God calls on us to trust in him. He does know every second of our lives and is completely in control. If we trust in him, we can have inner peace that he will take care of us. Redeemed by the blood of Christ, we move forward with confidence, knowing that God created us on purpose and for a purpose.

PRAYER Dear God, getting caught up in deadlines, résumé, exams, and all of the potential stressors that college life brings can make us forget who really is in control. Please set my paths straight and show me your will for my life. Give me peace in the knowledge that you know what the rest of my life entails. Amen.

NOVEMBER
TREASURES IN HEAVEN

INVISIBLE BLESSINGS

2 Corinthians 4:17,18 *Our light and momentary troubles are achieving for us an eternal glory that far outweighs them all. So we fix our eyes not on what is seen, but on what is unseen, since what is seen is temporary, but what is unseen is eternal.*

It's hard when everyone around you is happy and you're stressed out. The Bible acknowledges difficult situations, but there's still a reason to give thanks.

Like us, Paul faced stress. This passage is about being realistic in those stressful times and still being thankful. Dealing with temptations, living up to expectations, and repairing relationships is not easy. But even if those difficulties persist until death, eventually they are finished. You can give thanks because your glorious future will never end.

Eternal life with Jesus isn't just comfort for after you die. It's comforting because life with Jesus has already started. Even when everything goes wrong and you want to quit, God is your Father; Jesus is your Brother. Don't lose heart. Instead remember that even when you feel worthless, God loves you enough to die for you. No matter what other people say you are, God has made you a member of his family. Those invisible blessings made Paul thank God even in hard times. And then one day God will take away all the stress. Then he'll make your glory visible. In heaven you'll see perfectly just how glorious it is to be in God's family.

Want to be thankful even in tough times? Remember God's invisible blessings. Remember your baptism every time you take a shower. Spend time reading about how much God loves you and where you'll live forever. Your stress will pass, and glory is coming your way. It's already yours.

PRAYER Heavenly Father, when I'm stressed out, point me back to your promises. Give me joy in your blessings. Amen.

November 2

INVEST IN YOUR ETERNAL FUTURE

Matthew 6:19-21 *Do not store up for yourselves treasures on earth, where moths and vermin destroy, and where thieves break in and steal. But store up for yourselves treasures in heaven, where moths and vermin do not destroy, and where thieves do not break in and steal. For where your treasure is, there your heart will be also.*

You are an investor. Right now you are investing in your future by making the decision to attend college. There are many different ways we make investments, and you don't have to be a business major or stockbroker to learn how to invest wisely. You simply need to look at Jesus' Sermon on the Mount. Specifically, Matthew 6:19-21.

In these verses, Jesus warns against investing too much in our temporary, earthly lives. This doesn't mean we shouldn't plan for our earthly futures, but we need to be wary of letting our earthly pursuits get in the way of our heavenly ones.

While Jesus warns us not to overinvest in earthly treasures, he also tells us we should store up treasures in heaven. How do we invest in heaven? Any time or money we spend growing our faith or growing God's kingdom is an investment in our eternal futures: time spent in church or Bible study, love invested in Christian friendships, money given to support missions, and time spent witnessing to non-Christians.

God tells us in Isaiah 55:11 that his Word will never return to him empty. That means time spent in God's Word is an investment that will *always* have positive returns. It's the safest investment we can make. So, continue to invest in your earthly future, but remember that your eternal future is the one that really counts.

PRAYER Father, thank you for investing in me with the gift of your Son, Jesus. Help me follow his example and grow the investment you made in me by investing in your kingdom above my own. Amen.

LIVING A BALANCED LIFE

Matthew 16:26 *What good will it be for someone to gain the whole world, yet forfeit their soul? Or what can anyone give in exchange for their soul?*

It's the season of midterms. Be careful not to put your spiritual life on the back burner this time of year. We are warned about this in Matthew 16:26. Even though this is a warning, we can also take comfort in this passage. Through Matthew, God tells us that our souls are more important than any earthy treasures we could amass.

Surprise! Your devotion book has a few midterm questions too. This quiz is about time management and goals.

Question 1: How are you spending your time?
If my hunch is correct, you are pretty busy right now and balance may not exist. Your time is being spent on attending class and other academic commitments. You are also juggling your job, friends, clubs, and other activities. Don't forget about eating, sleeping, keeping up with social media, and exercising. Maybe it's been weeks since you've been to church or opened your Bible.

Question 2: What is important to you?
Take time to examine what is important to you and what goals you want to accomplish, both short-term and long-term. Your answer should always include living a balanced life. It's easy to get sidetracked, so setting boundaries with time and people will be necessary in order to accomplish your goals.

Even if your time management and goals are correlated, remember to live a balanced lifestyle with plenty of time for spiritual growth.

PRAYER Dear Jesus, thank you for every opportunity. Please enable me to focus on building your kingdom through the goals I set and the ways I manage my time. Help me prioritize spending time with you in the Word. Amen.

AMONG FAMILY

Ephesians 2:19 *You are no longer foreigners and strangers, but fellow citizens with God's people and also members of his household.*

Have you ever stayed with a stranger? Through my time as a travel choir member in high school and the mission trips I have been a part of, I have spent the night at several houses that belonged to people I knew nothing about.

Some were strange. One family only fed me vegetables for the week. Another had a black Lab that jumped onto me while I was on the *top bunk* of their bunk beds. Oh, and then I stayed with a family whose two young sons snuck their plastic snakes under my pillow while I was gone.

And then there was the Scheels family from Wyoming. I've never in my life felt so completely engulfed into a family before. They cooked for us. We played games every night. We threw a ball for their dog in the backyard. They made us never want to leave.

That's what it's like for Christians being in God's household. We become citizens with God's people through baptism. We are no longer strangers. Many of us cannot remember that moment of baptism, but I think that my experience with the Scheels family is an earthly representation of how God felt welcoming us into his family. He *engulfed* us into his family—after all, the price he paid in Christ to make us part of his family was *total*! Wouldn't it be foolish to leave God's household by neglecting his Word and sacraments? Being a member of God's family is being a citizen of the kingdom of heaven. And when you stay with God's people, you are never in the house of a stranger.

PRAYER Dear God, thank you for taking me into your household. I pray that those who are still foreigners and strangers will one day experience citizenship of your kingdom in heaven. Amen.

PRAY FOR THOSE IN AUTHORITY

1 Timothy 2:1,2 *I urge, then, first of all, that petitions, prayers, intercession and thanksgiving be made for all people—for kings and all those in authority, that we may live peaceful and quiet lives in all godliness and holiness.*

During elections, very few of us, if any, are thrilled when the candidate we didn't vote for gets into office. It's in times like these when this verse most resonates. God urges that prayers and thanksgiving be made for all people, even those who may not have earned our shortsighted, earthly stamp of approval.

God has placed people in their particular positions for a purpose. It may not make sense to us, but God calls us to be encouragers to those he placed in authority. He calls us to intercede for them, that we might have peace through his placements and live lives to his glory. God says that we will not understand everything that happens on this earth. That's hard for my small mind to come to terms with but also incredibly comforting to know that God's plan is infinitely bigger than I can imagine within my human judgments.

Let's make an intentional move to pray for those God placed in our lives, especially leaders. God doesn't promise that these leaders will be perfect, but he does reiterate time and again that he wants us to have peaceful lives in him. This starts with respecting those in authority and giving genuine thanksgiving for them as God's servants.

PRAYER Dear God of the nations, I pray that you open my heart to be able to find the good in those you have placed in my life here on earth. Bless these leaders and help them know your will. Amen.

STAY CLOSE TO YOUR SAVIOR

Colossians 2:6,7 *Just as you received Christ Jesus as Lord, continue to live your lives in him, rooted and built up in him, strengthened in the faith as you were taught, and overflowing with thankfulness.*

"What will happen when I graduate?"
"Are my prayers even being heard?"
"What is the point of all this?"

Maybe you've heard people make statements like these, or perhaps you've thought them at some point. With so much going on in a college student's life, where can one turn for strength and assurance?

Attending college is a great learning experience. You find out more about yourself every day. It is an exciting time, but it can be daunting and scary. Every day brings new problems to overcome and tough situations to weave through. Some things you encounter may cause you to question your faith. In today's Bible passage, Paul is speaking to the Colossians regarding their false teachings. Throughout the book he shows them that God is sufficient and that our human ideas cannot even come close to his wisdom. In the verse for today, Paul specifically reminds the Colossians of the importance of remaining close with their Savior and the blessings that come from doing so.

Maybe you're struggling with doubts about the future. Many times we worry about what will happen next and try to figure out our own plans. Today's verse reminds us to trust in God's plan and remain rooted in Jesus Christ. God's plans never fail. They are always perfect. What a blessing it is to have our perfect Savior guiding our path for us!

PRAYER Dear God, thank you for watching over me every day and working all things out for my good. Help me trust in your all-sufficient plans for my life and turn to you for strength and support. Amen.

November 7

IT'S ALL WORTH IT

2 Corinthians 5:7 *We live by faith, not by sight.*

Is it all worth it? The endless studying, the minimum wage job, the high expectations of being involved in a sport or student leadership role—is college really worth it? After all, others have gone on to successful careers without taking that four-year segue at a university and accumulating massive student loan debt. They have their nights free to do as they please instead of spending countless hours trying to make a chemistry equation balance. How can you know you made the right choice?

Faith—that's how you know. Faith that God has a plan for your life, even though you cannot presently see what his plan might be. Second Corinthians 5:7 perfectly illustrates how even though we may not see how our lives may end up, we can be comforted by the fact that God has it all planned out for us. Even obstacles that seem like massive detours in our lives are actually all part of his master plan.

So yes, it's all worth it. Even though the end result of your current efforts may be hidden from your sight, you can be certain that God led you to be in college for a reason. From the classes you take to the people you meet, God has created a unique path for you, and everything you experience in college will be a vital factor on your journey. As surely as he takes care of even the least of his creation, he will take care of you. Have faith in his plan.

PRAYER Dear Lord, thank you for the faith you have instilled in me to trust you and your plans for my life. Amen.

STRENGTH IN WEAKNESS

Romans 8:26 *The Spirit helps us in our weakness. We do not know what we ought to pray for, but the Spirit himself intercedes for us through wordless groans.*

We live in a world that hates weakness. In kindergarten, everyone raced to the door to be the line leader. In high school, you longed to go to homecoming with that cute senior football star or with the pretty, popular girl from homeroom. In college, you long to graduate and land that ideal job. At times, it seems like life is a 100-meter dash, and we're all sprinting to get ahead. But what happens when we trip and our high aspirations and lofty expectations are put to rest by tragedy, failure, broken promises, and disappointments? Our worldly strength is no match for a sinful world, constantly throwing stones in our path.

Whenever we face humbling experiences in life, God's Word is a constant source of strength and comfort. God's promises serve as a shining beacon of hope through the gloomy muck of this world. God empowers us with the strength of his Word. Even when the pain is greater than words can express, the Holy Spirit intercedes for us and lifts the burden onto his own shoulders. Sometimes we don't even know where to begin in our prayers. God promises that the Holy Spirit says it all for us—in groans.

Our God is the all-knowing, all-merciful, and all-loving deliverer from pain and sadness. He will stand by our side through every moment of weakness and rejoice with us in every moment of strength. The trials of this world don't stand a chance against our omnipotent God.

PRAYER Dear God, please comfort me in times of weakness, deliver me in times of sadness, and rejoice with me in times of joy. Thank you for the shining beacon of hope that is found in your Word. To you be all glory. In Jesus' name, I pray. Amen.

GENUINE JOY

Hebrews 11:1 *Faith is confidence in what we hope for and assurance about what we do not see.*

During a mission trip to Africa, I had the unique opportunity to attend a traditional African church service. The rural area surrounding the small, tin-roofed church was extremely poverty-stricken, and most of the members came from nearby villages comprised of huts. By the world's standards, these churchgoers had basically nothing. However, despite their circumstances, these people were absolutely rich with joy! The genuine joy that exuded from their hearts while worshiping was unlike anything I've ever seen.

What was the secret to their joy, their heartfelt worship of God in spite of their poverty? Hebrews 11:1 speaks of the type of faith that shone through those African people. Their joy undoubtedly did not come from this world; it was absolutely rooted in their hope for heaven. They did not have riches that a person could see, but their riches were unseen. They were confident of what Christ said is theirs: freedom from guilt; rescue from death; the status of saints before God; the glorious resurrection; God's gracious, good will; Christ as our brother; and God's promise that all things in heaven and on earth belong to his believers.

If we are ever tempted to be glum, let us remember the fine example of our African brothers and sisters and find our joy in Christ and his gifts. And, God willing, that joy will not go unnoticed by others. Our salvation—our hope for heaven—bought for us through God's precious sacrifice of his only Son is something to be truly cherished.

PRAYER Jesus, instill in my heart the joy and hope that can only come through the amazing salvation that you won for me. Let this joy and hope be a light to those around me, that they too may enjoy the incredible treasures of heaven! Amen.

NO OTHER NAME

Acts 4:12 *Salvation is found in no one else, for there is no other name under heaven given to mankind by which we must be saved.*

Tim Howard. Perhaps you know who he is. Most of America knew his name, at least temporarily, as Howard showed brilliance as the goalkeeper for the United States soccer team during the World Cup in June 2014. His instincts and athleticism allowed him to keep the ball out of the net as he made one incredible save after another.

Unless you are a die-hard soccer fan, I am guessing the name of Tim Howard was never on your radar or quickly fell off the radar after the tournament. That is what it is like with ordinary people: their time of popularity comes and goes and their names are forgotten. Tim Howard was able to make great saves for Team USA, but now he is out of sight and out of mind.

The words that the Holy Spirit inspired Peter to speak while under arrest and persecution are a reminder that there is only one name that stands forever: Jesus. And he makes the only true "save" that is necessary for us: he saved us from the punishment of sin. Only the name of Jesus has the power to change hearts and change lives. He thwarted every advance by our fiercest opponent, Satan. He batted down every shot of temptation that was taken at him and paid for our sins by dying on a cross. He rose from the dead so that now we can sing songs like crazy soccer fans, celebrating the victory that is ours through Christ.

Put your trust in the only name that truly is a "game changer"; Jesus is our best defense, and he has saved you!

PRAYER Dear Jesus, thank you for sharing your name with me in your Word so I can learn about your saving work. Amen.

CALL ON THE LORD

Psalm 4:1 *Answer me when I call to you, my righteous God. Give me relief from my distress; have mercy on me and hear my prayer.*

Have you ever had a tough conversation with your roommate, boyfriend/girlfriend, or coworker? You know, the one you absolutely dread. The type that's hard to address as well as receive. The type of conversation in which you didn't know what to say or what the outcome would be. Maybe you were thinking, *Will our relationship make it through this conversation?* or *Will we be stronger because of it?*

Where do you turn to find comfort in a time like this? Maybe to a parent or a close friend, but why not to the good Lord, the one who has all the answers?

I recently entered the human resources world, which very much matches my passion of helping others. However, this career field also consists of having tough conversations and letting people go. Within my first three months, I was faced with assisting with this exact challenge. It was horrible knowing beforehand that I was going to negatively impact someone's life. However, I was able to find comfort by calling on the Lord, which I did a lot. I called on him throughout the process: when I first heard, as I was preparing, during the actual delivery, and even afterward.

It's crazy because so often during tough times we feel we are going at it alone or that it's all on our shoulders. In reality we have the best possible weapon on our side! The next time you are faced with approaching the person you live with about changing roommates or talking to your significant other about how your long-distance relationship isn't hacking it—call on God. He will be merciful and hear your prayer!

PRAYER Lord, when I am faced with tough conversations, please remind me that I never need to go through these conversations alone—you are always by my side. Amen.

OVERCOME THE WORLD

1 John 5:4,5 *Everyone born of God overcomes the world. This is the victory that has overcome the world, even our faith. Who is it that overcomes the world? Only the one who believes that Jesus is the Son of God.*

We often take things for granted. Look at all the blessings God has provided! Just stop and smell the roses. Okay, we can do that, but then we need to get back to the "real world." How often do we take our faith for granted?

Prior to our reading, in verse 3, the author states: "This is love for God: to keep his commands. And his commands are not burdensome." If we love God, we see how much he has done for us every day. We see his ultimate love, which he showed us by sacrificing his only Son on a cross! Don't you want to serve him faithfully and obediently?

What a difficult thing it is to love and serve God our whole lives. Our human nature sees this as a burden, but it's not. Once you start serving God, you realize how easy it can be. Remember his love for you and all he has done for you! Human nature still gets in the way, but when that happens, pick yourself back up—go back to the Word of God to find reassurance and strength.

To "overcome the world" seems such a daunting task. But as the verse clearly states, when you believe that Jesus is the Son of God, you can overcome the world!

So stop and smell the roses. Realize that faith is a gift from God. This is a wonderful gift that leads to a lifetime in heaven with our Creator, our Savior, our Sanctifier!

PRAYER Dear Lord, thank you for the wonderful gift of faith. Help me realize the strength your Word gives, and help me share your Word with everyone I know so that they may overcome the world as well. Amen.

TREASURE THAT LASTS

1 John 2:17 *The world and its desires pass away, but whoever does the will of God lives forever.*

When I was a little boy, I loved to pretend I was a pirate. I was quite a ferocious sight wandering around my backyard with my little wooden sword. I was savage Blackbeard aboard his mighty warship *Queen Anne's Revenge.* I pretended to battle the English privateers that dared sail into my waters. However, most of all I searched for buried treasure. I dug in sandboxes and all over my backyard looking for loot and plunder. I smile now at those memories and think how I was looking for treasure in all the wrong places.

Any treasure that I would search for was an earthly treasure, with no value in heaven. Gold, jewels, and riches can be spent. They provide temporary enjoyment but eventually will be exhausted. The only treasure worth seeking is found through knowledge and faith in Christ. His blessings do not fade. Our passage for the day underlines this idea. His grace, mercy, and unending love for us are so much more precious than any treasure found buried in a chest.

PRAYER Dear Jesus, thank you so much for loving me and for giving me a treasure that lasts. Help me live to serve you and please you with my life. I love you, Jesus—please help me to show it. Amen.

PRAY BOLDLY

Genesis 18:32 *Then he said, "May the Lord not be angry, but let me speak just once more. What if only ten can be found there?" He answered, "For the sake of ten, I will not destroy it."*

Think back to the past few days, weeks, or months. Did you have a bad day or a series of bad days? Maybe you failed a class, had financial problems, or your friends have been ignoring you. The list could go on and on. Now think about when this day or time happened. What did you do?

In this Genesis account, God told Abraham he was going to destroy the city of Sodom because of its wickedness. This news was upsetting to Abraham because his nephew Lot would be destroyed along with any other righteous people who may be living in the city. Abraham immediately prayed to God, asking if he would spare the city if 50 righteous people were in it. He continued to boldly ask for mercy if 45, 40, 30, 20, and finally 10 righteous people were in the city.

Abraham was persistent. He prayed boldly and confidently. We may do the same thing. Look how boldly Abraham persisted, and how patiently God listened. When you had that bad day, did you pray boldly and confidently? Or did you pray with little hope? God answers all prayers; sometimes it is just not the answer we want.

In the end, God did destroy the city, but he saved Lot and his family. God answers our prayers knowing what's best for our faith. We can be confident that we have a God who will listen and answer our prayers because his Son, Jesus, atoned for all our sins. God has nothing but goodwill toward us now. You may not understand why things happen now, but know that our loving God died for you and has a plan for you and your life.

PRAYER Dear God, thank you for always listening and answering my prayers. Amen.

ASK JESUS

John 14:14 *You may ask me for anything in my name, and I will do it.*

Do you like to be disappointed? When's the last time you were totally let down? Maybe it was a group member failing to hold up his or her end of the project or parents who decided to end their marriage promises. Whatever the case may be, we've all been significantly let down.

Jesus' disciples were foolishly under the impression that the kingdom of God would be an earthly one. I'm sure in the back of their minds they were disappointed when they saw their Savior die in such a cruel fashion. They were undoubtedly praying that Jesus would peel himself off of that rugged cross and establish his kingdom. How, then, could Jesus have made this promise in John 14:14?

When we are met with apparent contradictions in Scripture, we simply let Scripture interpret Scripture. God answers ALL prayers. That's as simple and true as we can make it. Now, he may say "yes," "no," or "not right now." Regardless of which answer we get, it is a certainty that the answer is in our best interest. God has the big picture in mind when answering our prayers. Although he may say no to our earthly minded request, he knows what the final outcome will be.

So when you pray in Jesus' name, give thanks, for you know that your prayer *is* answered. What an awesome blessing it is to be so confident in your prayers.

PRAYER Heavenly Father, each prayer I send to you is an opportunity to learn trust. Guide my heart to accept whatever answer you give, even if that answer is contrary to my desires. In your Son's name, I pray. Amen.

FIX YOUR EYES ON JESUS

Hebrews 12:2 *[Let us fix] our eyes on Jesus, the pioneer and perfecter of faith. For the joy set before him he endured the cross, scorning its shame, and sat down at the right hand of the throne of God.*

Have you heard of "backwards planning"? This is an educational pedagogical concept in which the teacher constructs the end goal first and then works backward so that everything points to the final results. This sounds fairly logical, right?

This passage gives us a highly effective teaching technique—modeling. As children, our parents modeled for us what we needed to know to become adults. Christ is the model of our faith. He is described as the "pioneer and perfecter of our faith." He created faith and perfected it.

Is there any way that we too can perfect our faith? What does perfection look like? If we can't truly reach perfection, is there hope for us since God demands perfection?

What a treasure of heaven that Christ was perfect in our place. We can't be perfect, but spiritually we are transformed to perfection by Christ. Christ's sacrifice, planned from the very beginning, made us perfect and holy. We can show our thankfulness by fixing our eyes on him, the true model of perfection. Our end, heaven, has been prepared for us from the beginning.

How will you plan time with God in your schedule today? He plans each day with you in mind.

PRAYER Lord, thank you for being perfect in my place and enduring the cross for the joy that has been set before me. Help me fix my eyes on you until I reach my final home in heaven. Amen.

JESUS WILL CATCH YOU

Matthew 14:30,31 *When he saw the wind, he was afraid and, beginning to sink, cried out, "Lord, save me!" Immediately Jesus reached out his hand and caught him. "You of little faith," he said, "why did you doubt?"*

Faithfulness is a quality we expect in our friendships. When a friend says he will meet us for dinner, we expect he will be there. When a roommate says she will help us understand an assignment, we expect that she will be faithful to her word.

Unfortunately, sometimes our friends let us down because they don't always keep their word. If we are disappointed by a friend consistently, we begin to doubt the friendship and, as a result, we might lose that friend. Having doubts about a friendship can be challenging, but the most important relationship we have will never be lost. While he lived on earth as a man, Jesus experienced all the ups and downs of faithful and faithless friends. What's different about a friendship with Jesus, though, is that we never have cause to doubt.

One night on a lake, Peter demonstrated his belief in Jesus' power by stepping out onto the water to meet him. However, Peter lost faith in Jesus' ability when he saw the power of nature. Jesus' reaction is a message for all believers when they lose sight of their most faithful friend. Though we become distracted by problems in life, we have no cause to doubt that Jesus is working for our good—after all, that is what he has promised (Romans 8:28), and he is faithful. He always keeps his word! May we remember that the Jesus who died for us so we never sink into hell will catch us whenever we feel we are sinking during life. He will never let us down.

PRAYER Dear Jesus, my friend and Savior, strengthen me when I have doubts in life. Catch me when I fall, and may I ever trust in you. Amen.

NO WAITING

Psalm 145:18 *The LORD is near to all who call on him, to all who call on him in truth.*

I recently interviewed for several teaching jobs. After receiving three job offers, I finally came to interview for the job I deeply wanted. I waited and waited for what felt like a week. During those long, thought-provoking days, having received offers yet longing for just one more, I was so tempted to pick up the phone and contact the principal.

"Am I still in the running?" I would ask. "You know, I do have other offers on the table," I would add, just to make the point crystal clear. I thought feverishly about what I could have said differently during the interview that might have sealed the deal.

I felt I had to wait. God never wants us to feel that way. Psalm 145:18 tells us clearly that our heavenly Father is near to us when we need to call on him. He delights in us, his children, when we have a request to make, no matter how trivial it may seem. He is our heavenly principal, waiting to answer our call.

My sweaty palms and worry-filled days were the results of earthly concerns. The thing about our Savior is that he can hear these cries of our heart and he does not want us to waste a moment pondering whether or not to whisper them in his direction.

I received the job. More important, I learned the only call that can truly make a difference is the one I make to my Great Deliverer. He hears it. He answers it. He loves it. No wait time necessary.

PRAYER Heavenly Father, you hear the longings of every heart. Although I deserve way less, you shower me with attention. Forgive me for the times I forget that. Hear my call and answer me. Amen.

AM I GOOD ENOUGH?

Matthew 19:21 *Jesus answered, "If you want to be perfect, go, sell your possessions and give to the poor, and you will have treasure in heaven. Then come, follow me."*

Am I a good enough Christian? Alex could not get that question out of his head . . . for *two* reasons!

First, Amy. Wow! The most intriguing girl ever! But her comment in Psychology 201 was troubling. "I want a good Christian guy to date and marry. No settling for this girl!"

Am I a 'good enough' Christian? The self-analyzing was killing Alex! Amy was new to campus . . . what did she know? His reputation wasn't stellar. What were people telling her? Would his friends be kind and not say too much? He *really* wanted a chance with Amy—but did he measure up?

And now this "rich man" from the Bible reading for Philosophy 100! The professor was demonstrating the thinking of Christians who actually believe the Bible. A true Christian would acknowledge that to be *worthy of heaven* was to be ready to give up *all* things and be 100% devoted to God. "Perfection," some would say.

Wow! First Amy and now God! *Am I good enough for either of them?* Alex wondered.

If only the rich man had trusted Jesus. He would've walked with God's Son and heard his words! "Worthiness" is not found in *me*. It's found in Jesus. He died for the world's sin— our unworthiness—and *made us* worthy before God through *his* perfection!

I trust that about Jesus, Alex thought. *I AM worthy in him! Maybe Amy understands that about Jesus too. He is all I have to offer.*

PRAYER Jesus, give me peace of heart and mind in you. Amen.

AN EVERLASTING INHERITANCE

1 Peter 1:3,4 *Praise be to the God and Father of our Lord Jesus Christ! In his great mercy he has given us new birth into a living hope through the resurrection of Jesus Christ from the dead, and into an inheritance that can never perish, spoil or fade. This inheritance is kept in heaven for you.*

A young man asked his billionaire father for his share of the inheritance. The young man basically said, "I wish you were dead so that I can have your money." It's not exactly the best approach, but amazingly it worked! The father gave the son his share, and the son went out and blew it all. He spent every dime until he was left with neither money nor a job to make money.

Could you imagine if that inheritance would have never run out? Think about what you would do if you had a bank account that was always stocked with a billion dollars. The truth is that it would not matter. We would have to leave that wealth behind when we died. The simple fact is this: money doesn't last.

As we approach this Thanksgiving, praise God that he has given us something far greater than money. In fact, he has given us an inheritance that will last for eternity: it will never spoil, perish, or fade away. It is an eternal inheritance that includes being with our Savior forever as we look with our own eyes at his glory. Money comes and goes, but living with our Savior will last forever. Give thanks to God for giving us such an inheritance that will never run out.

PRAYER Dear Father, thank you for calling me by your gospel and giving me a new birth into your family. I thank you for all of my blessings, but especially for the inheritance that awaits me—eternal life with you. Keep me clinging to my Savior until I reach my inheritance with you. Amen.

WE ARE GOD'S FAMILY

1 John 3:1 *See what great love the Father has lavished on us, that we should be called children of God! And that is what we are! The reason the world does not know us is that it did not know him.*

Moving far away from home to attend a college can be a challenge—you move away from family, friends, and familiarity. By the time you leave for your first Christmas break, you realize that this new home created new families, new friends, and new familiarity. For me, family was my dorm "floormates," my roommates, study groups, and even a friend's family who took me to her home for Thanksgiving every year. How special it is to be part of a family!

God tells us in 1 John 3:1 that we are part of his family. At baptism, he calls each of us his child. We are undeserving sinners and our relationship with the Father is completely one-sided—God graciously loves us and adopts us as his own. This happens not because we are worthy, but because at baptism our sins are washed away and we are covered in Christ's holiness.

Perhaps you get to go home for Thanksgiving, or maybe a friend has invited you to his or her home. As children of God, we can be assured that our Father invites us into his home. He has graciously sent his Son, Jesus Christ, to die for our sins so that we may enjoy a right relationship with him and live eternally in his heavenly home. How special it is to be a part of God's family!

PRAYER Heavenly Father, by your gracious sacrifice, you call me your child. I'm sorry for disobeying your Word. Thank you for forgiving me and showing me your perfect and unconditional fatherly love. Please help me share your love and grace with others so that they also may be called your child. Amen.

A FRAGRANT AROMA

2 Corinthians 2:14 *Thanks be to God, who always leads us as captives in Christ's triumphal procession and uses us to spread the aroma of the knowledge of him everywhere.*

The aroma wafts through the house: tender turkey, savory stuffing, potatoes, beans, succulent squash, and pumpkin pie. It's going to be a Thanksgiving meal to remember.

The aroma wafts through the dorm. The fragrance seeps over the football field, the volleyball court, and the music hall. People are captivated by it. What *is* that smell?

YOU, O Christian! That's right! It's YOU!

The apostle Paul pictures a parade. A king comes back with all the spoils of war. People shout praises, light incense, and strew flowers for their victorious king. It is a time of celebration and thanksgiving!

We are in a triumphal procession. Our King Jesus went into enemy territory. He walked into the dungeon of hell. He took our place. He gave his life over to death only to take it up again in triumph. He marched through hell proclaiming his victory over Satan. He carries you on his shoulders.

You are the aroma of the knowledge of Christ. You taste it every time he renews his covenant of grace with you in the Lord's Supper: "Your sins are forgiven!" You hear his voice comfort you: "Never will I leave you." He's by your side.

Even before you talk, people smell you. They notice that you're different. They perceive the serving attitude that shows itself in action. Let it be seen. Let the smell waft through the air of the world. *You* are in Christ's triumphal procession. Give thanks for that!

PRAYER Dear Lord Jesus, thank you for rescuing me and making me a part of your kingdom. Amen.

GIVE THANKS TO THE LORD

1 Chronicles 16:34 *Give thanks to the Lord, for he is good; his love endures forever.*

Out at their favorite restaurant, a Christian family bows their heads and quietly murmurs a prayer before eating. The youngest child concentrates on the newly learned words while his older brothers and sisters easily repeat the memorized prayer, only half-aware of its meaning.

Before giving this portion of his prayer before the whole nation of Israel, David danced before the ark of the covenant as it entered Jerusalem. The king, God's chosen, a respected and powerful man, was so excited about the presence of the Lord entering the city that he did not care about the expectations and responsibilities of his office—he simply wanted to praise his Lord.

So often when we repeat these words of David, our minds are on the meal before us. While we are thankful for the physical blessings God has provided, we frequently overlook opportunities to dwell on the value of both earthly and spiritual gifts and our naturally sinful, undeserving nature. While far from perfect, David, a musician, poet, and king, chose to dance before the Lord in addition to his other acts of worship. Like David, we can continually reflect on our many blessings, especially Jesus' ultimate gift of our salvation, our treasure in heaven. By focusing our talents in acts of worship, we come closer to God's purpose for us and our prayer lives and relationship with God can be refocused and strengthened.

PRAYER Heavenly Father, thank you for the gifts you shower on me each day. I ask you to strengthen me as my list of responsibilities grows and often distracts me from the promise of your grace. During this time for thanksgiving and family, strengthen my faith, body, and mind, bringing me ever closer to you. In Jesus' name, I pray. Amen.

November 24

ALWAYS THANKFUL

1 Thessalonians 5:16-18 *Rejoice always, pray continually, give thanks in all circumstances; for this is God's will for you in Christ Jesus.*

What do you thank God for and when? Is it after a sports victory, passing a test, or at mealtime? Or is it when being made fun of, after losing a loved one, or after an injury? In most cases, the first few circumstances are situations where we most often give glory to God. But why shouldn't we praise him every moment of every day when he loves us every moment of every day?

To give thanks in all circumstances is not a request but a command. Take time out of your day to think of how God has blessed you recently, remembering that blessings are not rewards but merciful and gracious gifts. Rejoicing always is to be joyful for what our Savior has done for all people, no matter the circumstance. He died so that we may live! Even in grief and pain, we should give thanks and rejoice for the eternal salvation the Lord promises us—knowing that what is earthly is temporary and what is heavenly is eternal. That is our hope.

We have all the reason in the universe to give glory to God even when sin and death are staring us in the face. So next time someone cuts you down or misfortune comes your way, it is your spirit's desire, given by God, to rejoice and give thanks in the name of Christ Jesus in the middle of adversity.

PRAYER Father, thank you for your love and protection and for giving me life every day. Point me to the cross at all times, and remind me of the blessings I've received even when strong emotions cloud my mind. Amen.

November 25

DON'T BURN OUT

Romans 12:12,13 *Be joyful in hope, patient in affliction, faithful in prayer. Share with the Lord's people who are in need. Practice hospitality.*

Sometimes in life, we give up too easily. When things don't go our way or move at our pace, we throw temper tantrums and lose all hope. We forget that our God is greater than anything that is or is to come. We focus so much on what our eyes see as the problem that we become blind to our blessings.

Today's Scripture reminds us of how to be happy in troubled times and where we should focus our thoughts. Let us not be burdened by life trials but rejoice in God's unchanging and unconditional love and grace. I challenge you to not get tired of being thankful. We have a right to be confident in our hope because God's promise will remain with us. Don't burn out on praying, and seek God's Word. It is through prayer and the Word of God you will find your strength to be thankful and the courage to help others even during your times of need!

PRAYER God, thank you for your grace and the many blessings you give me. My prayer is that you continue to open my eyes to those blessings to which I am blind. Give me patience and confident hope throughout my trials and tribulations and a heart to continuously serve your people in their needs. May your love and grace be seen though me, and may I forever be thankful for everything you have done for me. In the name of my Lord and Savior Jesus Christ, I pray. Amen.

I THANK GOD FOR YOU

1 Corinthians 1:4,5 *I always thank my God for you because of his grace given you in Christ Jesus. For in him you have been enriched in every way—with all kinds of speech and with all knowledge.*

We can learn a few lessons from the way Paul praises the Corinthian church. To begin, we are reminded of the importance of thanking God for those people whom he places in our lives. God works in mysterious and subtle ways and often through those around us. It can be difficult or impossible to see just how their actions benefit us. God works to strengthen our faith, helps us through hardship, and brings us earthly blessings through the encouragement and graciousness of others. Too easily we neglect to recognize just how important these people are to us, and we forget to thank God for their role in our lives. Take a moment and consider how God blesses us through the faith of others.

Additionally, we notice something interesting about Paul's phrasing: he is purposefully deferential. Though he is complimenting the Corinthians, he is sure to place all the credit on Christ. He thanks God for God's grace, which was given to the Corinthians. This grace was not earned; rather, it was a gift through Christ. And in Christ, the Corinthians have been blessed in every way. We are reminded just where all blessings come from—they are gifts of God, given in grace through the atoning work of Christ. This is a wonderful reminder that God is the source of all good things.

PRAYER Dear Lord, thank you for all those you have placed in my life. Help me remember that all my blessings, and all good things, come from you as an expression of your grace, through the work of Jesus. In his name, I pray. Amen.

THANK YOU!

Colossians 4:2 *Devote yourselves to prayer, being watchful and thankful.*

Without *the power of prayer, watchfulness, and thankfulness:*

My alarm is blaring. I only got three hours of sleep once I finally finished that paper—after a long day of classes, tiring practice, and work. Time to start again. I need to find breakfast and get ready for the early shift at work before my first class. Another day with obligations and deadlines and limited hours and accumulating assignments. Ugh . . .

With *the power of prayer, watchfulness, and thankfulness:*

My alarm is going off, and the world is dark and silent: a chance for me to pray without distractions. Thank you, Lord! I didn't get much sleep, but I was able to stay alert enough to finish my paper last night and do a good job of it. I developed some of my ideas on my research topic, which will stick with me for life. Thank you, Lord! That cross country practice was challenging, and although I'm sore now, my body will be stronger. Thanks, Lord! Wow. I get to live another day in this special role! Thank you for taking care of my needs— clothes, a bed and shelter, food. I can focus on letting my light shine for you. Help me watch for the opportunities you give me to share the news that all are forgiven by you. Wow! Another day. Thank you, Lord!

PRAYER Help me devote myself to prayer, for by it, I can thank you, praise you, confess my sins to you, and ask things of you. Help me be watchful so that I do not miss opportunities to build you up or waste my time grumbling. Help me be thankful in all things, for I know you bless me in countless ways. Amen.

CHEERFUL GIVING

2 Corinthians 9:7 *Each of you should give what you have decided in your heart to give, not reluctantly or under compulsion, for God loves a cheerful giver.*

It is better to give than to receive. I'm sure you've heard this before. Yet it doesn't always feel that way, does it? It's simply not how our culture works. The world's attitude often has a "What's in it for me?" mind-set instead of an attitude that gives with a joyful heart. One testament to this selfish attitude is seen in our misguided focus on certain holidays. Christmas and Valentine's Day often overemphasize what we get or how much we get.

This cannot be our attitude when it comes to showing our thankfulness to God. It is true that he has already given us so much! Heaven is our home! For this reason, our attitude should be one of sincere thanksgiving—not one of reluctance.

Show thanks to God with cheerful giving. Understand that he has already given you the greatest gift that could be given: eternal life in heaven. Willfully give from the heart. Our encouragement is to refrain from a "What's in it for me?" mind-set and transition to a "How can I serve?" attitude. One way of serving is through giving back to the One who has already given everything. When we give back to God, we aid the advancement of his kingdom and show our thankfulness to him.

PRAYER Dear Lord, you have already given me so much. I am thankful for the gift of salvation you bestowed on me. Please fill me with an attitude that wants to joyfully and willingly support the work of your kingdom. Amen.

HAVE FAITH

Matthew 17:20 *He replied, "Because you have so little faith. Truly I tell you, if you have faith as small as a mustard seed, you can say to this mountain, 'Move from here to there,' and it will move. Nothing will be impossible for you."*

We have plenty to thank God for on a daily basis—family, friends, shelter, food—and the list goes on. But is not one of the greatest gifts we receive from God our faith?

We also face obstacles and hardships on a daily basis. Sometimes it may seem that we can do nothing right and the world is against us. Our work piles up. The cash pile for food shrinks. Relationships get a little rocky. The one thing that remains constant in our lives is God's love for us. Through our faith in God and his love, we can accomplish and get through all other things life throws our way.

In order to continue growing and strengthening our faith, we must be in God's Word to give the Holy Spirit the opportunity to work his miracles within us. Have some personal reflection and devotion time. Attend church regularly and be involved. Participate in Bible studies. Most important, we must be able to share our faith with others. Plant even the tiniest of seeds and the Holy Spirit will do the rest. It would be selfish to keep this amazing blessing to ourselves. Go and make disciples of all nations.

PRAYER Thank you, God the Spirit, for working faith in me. Give me the courage to plant seeds in those who don't know you yet. Bless the family of believers, that we may offer support to one another. Let us not be scared, worried, overwhelmed, or stressed because we know that we can cast all our anxiety on you and you will be with us to overcome all obstacles. Amen.

LOOK TO THE LORD

1 Chronicles 16:11 *Look to the LORD and his strength; seek his face always.*

Celebration was in order. King David and the Israelites had placed the ark of the covenant in its designated place after a powerful defeat of the Philistines. This was one of David's first notable acts as king. God delivered the Philistines into the Israelites' hands and "David's fame spread throughout every land, and the LORD made all the nations fear him" (1 Chronicles 14:17). God's power was evident to David and all of Israel in the brilliant defeat of the Philistines. His power over sin, death, and the devil is even more impressive and, for that, we have good reason to acknowledge his power and always seek him.

David appointed Asaph (who is attributed with writing many psalms) to give praise to the Lord. In this passage, David gives direction to Asaph and his associates that echo psalms that he, David, had written and sung in the past. Through his words we are reminded of the Lord's strength and his power over all creation.

More important, though, we are encouraged to "look to the LORD." This means he wants us to look to his promises in the Bible for help and strength in times of trouble. For in his Word we learn that he is a kind, forgiving, gracious Father in Christ—which makes it safe for us sinners to "seek his face always."

God has truly blessed us, both here on earth and eternally, through Jesus. Let's "look to the LORD and his strength; seek his face always."

PRAYER Dear Lord, please bless me and help me remember to go to you in times of trouble and times of happiness. It is easy to get bogged down in the busy life of college, but I know that if I seek you, you will have my back. Amen.

DECEMBER
JOURNEY TO THE MANGER

PRAY FOR PATIENCE

Luke 1:12,13 *When Zechariah saw him, he was startled and was gripped with fear. But the angel said to him: "Do not be afraid, Zechariah; your prayer has been heard. Your wife Elizabeth will bear you a son, and you are to call him John."*

Some of the greatest moments and surprises in life can emerge during something very routine. This sudden change can feel overwhelming. In these moments, we can find ourselves so immersed in our own interests, timing, and feelings that we lose sight of God's care and plan.

The prophet and church leader Zechariah was in the midst of a similar scenario just months before the birth of our Savior. Zechariah and his wife, Elizabeth, were faithful and "righteous in the sight of God." Despite years of praying for a child, the couple had yet to see their prayers answered. Then, in the middle of faithfully carrying out his traditional duties as a priest, Zechariah was approached by an angel of the Lord. One can only imagine what his first thoughts were after hearing that he and his wife, at such an old age, would soon be expecting a son!

There are times in our lives when we can be just like Zechariah. Years of faithful service, and what seem to be unanswered prayers, can make it seem easy to grow impatient. At these times, we need look no further than Zechariah's story to learn that impatience can lead to doubt and fear. In those moments, just as Zechariah was assured by the message of God's angel, we can be assured by the message of God's Word. Pray for patience to assure you of God's grace, love, and timing.

PRAYER Lord, please give me the patience that you require of me. Amen.

LISTEN TO GOD'S MESSENGERS

Luke 1:18-20 *Zechariah asked the angel, "How can I be sure of this? I am an old man and my wife is well along in years." The angel said to him, "I am Gabriel. I stand in the presence of God, and I have been sent to speak to you and to tell you this good news. And now you will be silent and not able to speak until the day this happens, because you did not believe my words, which will come true at their appointed time."*

Laura worked for the same company for 35 years and in her time there had been promoted through the ranks, eventually landing a position in upper management. She thought she knew what she was doing, and then one day she was called into a meeting. She was told that she wasn't doing her job and was fired.

Zechariah received a similar chastisement when he failed to do his job. Although startled by the presence of an angel, Zechariah was ambivalent about the pronouncement the angel made. His line of questioning shows his disbelief, even words directly from an angel! How could he not believe? How very human of Zechariah!

Just as God sent his messenger to Zechariah, so he sends us messengers. Who has been put in your life to help keep you on the path to heaven? What kinds of consequences did you face? Laura lost her job because she ignored the signs. Zechariah lost his ability to speak. And you? Zechariah was being personally prepared for the coming of the Savior of the world. We are being prepared for Jesus' return. As Christmas draws nearer, we thank God for sending Jesus to die for our sins. As we begin to consider Jesus' birth, let's also consider his return, and ask God to draw us closer to him.

PRAYER Lord Jesus, thank you for remaining with me even when I face doubts and unbelief and am disobedient to you and those you send to serve me. Bless me and come quickly! Amen.

NO MORE SHAME

Luke 1:24,25 *After this his wife Elizabeth became pregnant and for five months remained in seclusion. "The Lord has done this for me," she said. "In these days he has shown his favor and taken away my disgrace among the people."*

"Shame on you!" Did your parents ever say that to you when you were growing up? Mine certainly did!

Elizabeth had no children, which was considered shameful in her day. Perhaps you've experienced your own version of society's ability to shame you for something you lack. Have you been ridiculed for being single, for not having a job, for your body type, or for the clothes you wear or the car you drive? I'm sure you could insert your own personal statement here, and it probably hurts to think about it.

I bet that, at times, Elizabeth felt she was out of God's favor while she waited to become pregnant. I bet she felt isolated and alone. Perhaps she questioned God's presence in her life. Isn't that what we do as well?

In today's reading, Elizabeth is finally released from her shame. How awesome it is that Elizabeth praised God, especially after her long wait!

Though we often join Elizabeth in waiting for a release from the temporary shame of this world, let's spend this Christmas season anxiously awaiting the celebration of Christ's birth, knowing that he came to release us from the *eternal* shame of our sin. Jesus took our shame with him to the cross, and each of us can now erase the phrase "Shame on you!" from our minds. We are free!

PRAYER Dear Father, thank you for releasing me from my shame through your Son, Jesus Christ. Help me so that I don't do anything to bring temporary, earthly shame upon myself, my family, or my school. When my earthly troubles overwhelm me, fix my eyes on the freedom I have in you! Amen.

THE LORD IS WITH YOU

Luke 1:26-28 *In the sixth month of Elizabeth's pregnancy, God sent the angel Gabriel to Nazareth, a town in Galilee, to a virgin pledged to be married to a man named Joseph, a descendant of David. The virgin's name was Mary. The angel went to her and said, "Greetings, you who are highly favored! The Lord is with you."*

It is December. Your finals are coming up, your projects are due tomorrow, and your Christmas presents are yet to be purchased. (And with what money? You have to spend those few dollars on your gas to get home!) You are feeling overwhelmed, out of your comfort zone, and wondering, *Why on earth did I ever think I could do this crazy thing called college?* You are not alone, and God put you here for a reason. I believe there was one person in Bible times who could sympathize with your overwhelmed feelings of wonder, stress, and confusion. She was a young girl, perhaps barely into her teens, and she found out—from an angel, no less—that she had been chosen to carry God's one and only Son.

Though Mary may have wondered if she was the right one for what the Lord called her to do, she trusted in God's promise: "The Lord is with you." You, yes you, in all of your imperfections, failings, worry, and doubt, are here for a reason. The Lord is with you, and he will not let you fall. Trust in his promises. Trust in his Son. Trust in his plan. The Lord is with you.

PRAYER Dear Lord, please forgive me for the times I do not trust you. Help me find a faith like Mary's and follow the plan you have set for me. Amen.

December 5

SURPRISING NEWS

Luke 1:29-33 *Mary was greatly troubled at his words and wondered what kind of greeting this might be. But the angel said to her, "Do not be afraid, Mary; you have found favor with God. You will conceive and give birth to a son, and you are to call him Jesus. He will be great and will be called the Son of the Most High. The Lord God will give him the throne of his father David, and he will reign over Jacob's descendants forever; his kingdom will never end."*

Have you ever received news so surprising that you thought it couldn't possibly be true? You won tickets to your favorite band; you got the job after months of rigorous interviews; you passed the exam that you stayed up all night studying for and got an A.

The account in Luke 1:29-33 describes Mary receiving the news that she would give birth to the Savior of the world. How unbelievable this was, especially because she was a virgin! Mary's response to this news is an example for all believers. Mary was humbled by the angel's words and recognized this as a special way God had chosen to bless her life. She was grateful and sought to live a life of thankfulness. When you hear great news, be humble and recognize how undeserving you are, and glorify God. We also learn from this account that nothing is impossible with God. Never doubt God when he places an opportunity in your life that appears like something you can't handle.

This Christmas season and always, let us recognize the ways God has chosen to bless us. He grants us earthly blessings to fulfill our needs and wants like concerts, a means of income, institutions to gain knowledge, and many other blessings. Remember that God took care of our greatest need through Jesus and for that we can forever be thankful.

PRAYER Heavenly Father, please help me be humbled and thankful for the many blessings you shower upon me daily. I surely do not deserve them. Amen.

GOD CAN DO ANYTHING

Luke 1:34-37 *"How will this be," Mary asked the angel, "since I am a virgin?" The angel answered, "The Holy Spirit will come on you, and the power of the Most High will overshadow you. So the holy one to be born will be called the Son of God. Even Elizabeth your relative is going to have a child in her old age, and she who was said to be unable to conceive is in her sixth month. For no word from God will ever fail."*

Nothing is impossible with God. Easier said than believed, right? Sure, the Bible is filled with stories supporting that claim—Moses leading the Israelites out of Egypt through the parted Red Sea; little David defeating the giant Goliath; Jesus healing the sick, deaf, and blind. The reading for today has the same theme. Mary is told she will have a child even though she is a virgin. Impossible! And not just any child— the Son of God. Unbelievable! Yet the angel reassures Mary that nothing is impossible with God. She believes and trusts what defies understanding, logic, and biology.

What a remarkable faith! How can we have a faith like that? I mean, we don't have angels personally reminding us of that message every time we start to doubt. But we do have something else—Bibles. Bibles do the same thing the angels did—deliver God's message to us. And the words of the Bible are powerful! Want proof? As Christians, we already believe some pretty remarkable things—Jesus died on a cross to forgive all of our sins and he will come again on judgment day to take all believers to be in heaven forever. How much more then should we trust and believe that God can do anything in our lives? When we face challenges and hardships, we know we have a God who can do immeasurably more than we can even imagine. Plus, he always does what is best for us, even if we don't realize it.

PRAYER Lord, as I enter each new day, please help me remember that nothing is impossible with you. Keep me from doubting and help me focus on the strengths I have through you to tackle everything with confidence. Amen.

LOOKING PAST OURSELVES

Luke 1:38 *"I am the Lord's servant," Mary answered. "May your word to me be fulfilled." Then the angel left her.*

The Christmas season is one of the most stressful times of year. Professors want projects and papers completed before you go home for break. You are losing motivation for classes. On top of that, you are expected to buy gifts on a college budget for those close to you.

When you think about a Christmas season such as this, there is much focus on us. How am I going to get this paper written before break? How is my family going to look on my Christmas card? What presents are people getting me?

Mary had the opposite reaction to that first Christmas. She put her own wants and needs to the side and focused on what God asked her to do. She did not worry about what others would think. She simply opened her heart, and God worked through her to create a miracle that blessed all with a Savior who lived and died to defeat sin.

This Christmas season strive to show Christ in the selfless way of Mary. It can be done by making a needed phone call home, even though you are busy. It can be shown by gritting your teeth through the papers and projects instead of complaining. It can be shown through your daily interactions with others that show that Christmas isn't focused on what is here on earth—Christmas is focused on the One who came so that he could be selfless for you.

PRAYER Dear Lord, sometimes I can get caught up in the self-centered attitudes around the Christmas season. Help me look past myself like Mary so that I can focus on you and your amazing coming! Thank you for your selfless act of coming to this corrupt world for me. In your name, I pray. Amen.

December 8

REMAIN DEPENDENT ON GOD

Matthew 1:18,19 *This is how the birth of Jesus the Messiah came about: His mother Mary was pledged to be married to Joseph, but before they came together, she was found to be pregnant through the Holy Spirit. Because Joseph her husband was faithful to the law, and yet did not want to expose her to public disgrace, he had in mind to divorce her quietly.*

It is an American tradition: going it alone. We love frontiersmen and cowboys, inventors and entrepreneurs. From Lucky Lindy to Annie Oakley, we prize the can-do spirit of the self-made man or woman.

What about Joseph? Out of faithfulness he subjected himself to the law and out of love followed the law without shaming Mary. Our primary focus is not Joseph's decision to "do right" by Moses and by Mary. It is rather *God's* decision to promise a Savior and to bring Joseph to faith in that promise.

Joseph knew, as Christians after him have confessed, that to gain salvation one must give up independence. In this realm, we give up and discover that no amount of sacrifice or self-denial can take away the guilt of sin. In a world that celebrates rugged individualism, praises personal accomplishment, and pays homage to the skeptic and the doubter, we trust God's grace alone, faith alone, and Scripture alone.

One aspect of being a college student is developing self-reliance—getting ready to go it alone. It's part of becoming independent and taking your Christian identity into whatever life-role God allows you to occupy, like Joseph. But as a primary focus, you remain dependent: counting on grace alone, trusting through faith alone, confident in Scripture alone.

PRAYER Heavenly Father, give me humble faith like Joseph and lead me to see in Jesus' conception and birth your plan of salvation worked out in human history. Amen.

JOSEPH'S EXAMPLE

Matthew 1:20 *But after he had considered this, an angel of the Lord appeared to him in a dream and said, "Joseph son of David, do not be afraid to take Mary home as your wife, because what is conceived in her is from the Holy Spirit."*

Each December, Christians meditate on Jesus' humility, Mary's trust, and the Father's faithfulness. But this season we should also focus on Joseph. He is a model of godly male leadership—a crucial example at a time when many men are shirking their roles in families and as leaders in the church. Yet he is more than an example to men. Every Christian can learn from Joseph's relationship to the Father.

Joseph was a godly man, described as "faithful to the law." When Joseph was called to be responsible, he stepped up to the plate. At the same time, he was sensitive to Mary's needs. He planned to deal with issues in a way that would "not . . . expose her to public disgrace." Joseph's strength came from his connection to God through the Word and through prayer. When an angel made known to him the will of God—to take Mary as his wife—he gladly embraced it.

God speaks to all of us today in a similar way. But without daily time in the Word, active church participation, and regular prayer, those messages are carried off into the wind, unheard as we go about our self-directed lives. Being faithful to the law like Joseph was, we stay in active communication with the Lord, opening ourselves to his guidance. Through these means, God gives us the strength to be faithful.

PRAYER Father God, let me learn from Joseph's example. Let me be faithful to you. Give me strength to fulfill my responsibilities in serving you. Amen.

GOD IS IN CONTROL

Matthew 1:24,25 *When Joseph woke up, he did what the angel of the Lord had commanded him and took Mary home as his wife. But he did not consummate their marriage until she gave birth to a son. And he gave him the name Jesus.*

How do you think it felt to be Joseph? He was about to marry a woman who suddenly became pregnant. If I were Joseph, I don't know if I'd stay! The good news is that God gave Joseph an understanding heart. He planned to quietly divorce Mary, so she would not be publicly humiliated (Matthew 1:19). He listened to an angel of the Lord when the angel told Joseph that Mary would give birth to the Son of God (Matthew 1:20,21). He trusted that Jesus was there to save everyone from sin. We can learn something from Joseph: be patient and understand that God is in control.

How often are we quick to judge? Not only people, but also any situation that does not go the way we think it should? We don't understand God's plan for our lives or his plan for the world around us. Have you ever doubted God's gift of salvation? Is he truly going to bring us to heaven?

So often, we see the turmoil of this world and immediately think negatively. We think our society is crumbling and there's no hope for humanity. Rather than focusing on the sin in the world, why not focus on God's amazing plan of salvation? God's plan is for all people to receive eternal life!

We see Joseph being patient, and although he may have doubted at first, he listened to God. God brought salvation to the world through Jesus, so we don't need to doubt that God is in control of our lives and will bring us to his heavenly kingdom.

PRAYER Dear God, thank you for granting me eternal life through your Son, Jesus. Help me realize that, even though this world can seem hopeless, you are in control of my life and the world around me. Amen.

TRUSTING FAITH

Luke 1:41-43 *When Elizabeth heard Mary's greeting, the baby leaped in her womb, and Elizabeth was filled with the Holy Spirit. In a loud voice she exclaimed: "Blessed are you among women, and blessed is the child you will bear! But why am I so favored, that the mother of my Lord should come to me?"*

Have you ever played the "getting to know you" game, where you ask someone, "If you could meet anyone who has ever lived, who would you choose?" Mary would be one of my top choices. Can you imagine being a teenage girl who is told that you will soon give birth to a son who will be the hope for all people for all time? Would you simply say, "May your word to me be fulfilled"? What tremendous faith!

Can you imagine what it must have been like for Mary to hold Jesus as a baby, tend to his scraped knees as a child, cook his dinner, wake him up for school, watch him grow from a boy into a man, see him leave home, and then witness him brutally killed on a cross, all while watching him as her son *and* Savior? Oh, the thoughts and questions that must have crossed her mind! But she had faith; she simply trusted the promise.

Elizabeth also believed that promise. It is evident in her words: "But why am I so favored, that the mother of my Lord should come to me?" Two women trusting in a promise. Amazing. By the power of the Holy Spirit, they trusted in a promise given by God. Just like you and me. Amazing.

PRAYER Heavenly Father, things are going to happen today that are out of my control. Some of them may be good and some of them bad. Although I have no control over the situation, you do. When I have doubts and questions, please grant me the same trusting faith you gave these two Jewish women. I believe Jesus' promises, so help me trust. Amen.

MARY'S EXAMPLE

Luke 1:46-48 *And Mary said: "My soul glorifies the Lord and my spirit rejoices in God my Savior, for he has been mindful of the humble state of his servant. From now on all generations will call me blessed."*

Many times when people think of Mary, they think of words such as *blessed, special,* or *chosen.* People may say these things solely based on her role in the Christmas story as the chosen mother of God's Son, Jesus. But I think if we really look at Mary and her personality, we may see an even bigger reason why she has such a positive image.

Put yourself in Mary's shoes. You are a young teenage girl. You are engaged to be married. You have a strong faith in the Lord and have a seemingly decent life. Then catastrophe strikes. You're pregnant! How could this happen? As the story unfolds, you find out your child is God's Son and that you were chosen to be his mother.

As you put yourself in Mary's situation, you realize how crazy and difficult this must have been! I think I would feel a mix of confusion, stress, and maybe even a little bit of anger that my great plan had been torn apart. But Mary responds in great joy and praise for what God has done. She says her "soul glorifies the Lord" and her "spirit rejoices in God," her Savior. She trusted that Jesus would live and die for the salvation of all. Her great faith and trust in God can act as a wonderful example for us as we face many different types of struggles in our lives. We see that God always and only works for good.

PRAYER Dear God, thank you for sending your Son, Jesus, into the world for me. Thank you also for blessing us with an example like his mother, Mary. In Jesus' name, I pray. Amen.

SHARE THE GOOD NEWS!

Luke 1:62-64 *They made signs to his father, to find out what he would like to name the child. He asked for a writing tablet, and to everyone's astonishment he wrote, "His name is John." Immediately his mouth was opened and his tongue set free, and he began to speak, praising God.*

Have you ever had such good news that you just had to share it with the whole world on Twitter, Facebook, and Instagram? Maybe you sent out a text message or Snapchat to your close friends too. Luke tells us that Zechariah reacted in a similar way, except he wrote on a tablet, not via social media, and the news spread throughout Judea by word of mouth, not Facebook newsfeeds.

You'll recall that Zechariah was visited by the angel Gabriel and told the wonderful news that his wife, Elizabeth, would become pregnant. He doubted Gabriel's message because he and Elizabeth were so old, and his ability to speak was taken from him for over nine months!

Can you imagine the shock, awe, and joy of everyone present after an elderly woman had a healthy baby and the baby's father, who couldn't speak for over nine months, suddenly started speaking again and praising God? God the Father certainly made it known that someone special was coming! John paved the way for Jesus, pointing people to the Lamb of God, who takes away the sin of the world. Let us keep our focus on the manger this Christmas season.

PRAYER Dear Lord, thank you for fulfilling all of your promises. Thank you for sending John the Baptist to pave the way for your Son. Fill my heart and move me to share the great news of salvation with everyone I know as I celebrate the birth of Jesus this Christmas season. Amen.

THE WAIT IS OVER!

Luke 1:67,68 *His father Zechariah was filled with the Holy Spirit and prophesied: "Praise be to the Lord, the God of Israel, because he has come to his people and redeemed them."*

Have you ever waited for something to happen? How did you feel while you were waiting? How did you feel when the waiting was over? Way back at the beginning of the world, God promised Adam and Eve that he would send a Savior. This special person would redeem, or buy them back, from their sins and restore their relationship with God. But they had a long wait ahead of them. The people of the Old Testament continued waiting for this promised Savior. The people of Israel endured many hardships in Egypt and in the desert, and at times, they could hardly be considered patient. Eventually, God led them back into the Promised Land, where the Savior would be born. The years continued to pass, more difficulties came, and no doubt people were beginning to wonder about the fulfillment of God's promise.

After his son, John, was born, the priest Zechariah announced something exciting. Reread today's verses. John was born just a few months before Jesus, and this was the big finale of prophecies before Christ's birth. After all the waiting, at last the Savior came! Relief, excitement, and joy filled the hearts of believers. This Christmas season, may our hearts be filled with the same joy that people like Zechariah felt at the birth of their Savior. The wait is over; we are redeemed—spread the Word!

PRAYER Dear heavenly Father, thank you for sending Jesus as my Savior and Redeemer. Help me eagerly proclaim his saving message to others this holiday season. May I ever find joy in you. Amen.

OUTSIDE YOUR COMFORT ZONE

Luke 1:76,77 *And you, my child, will be called a prophet of the Most High; for you will go on before the Lord to prepare the way for him, to give his people the knowledge of salvation through the forgiveness of their sins.*

During biblical times, people would prepare a road for a king to travel on. In the same sense, John the Baptist prepared many hearts for the coming of Jesus. Even though people had been waiting for a promised Messiah, it could not have been easy telling people they were sinful and needed to repent. Jesus fulfilled the message that John proclaimed. He lived and died for our salvation.

Today, we get so caught up in the day-to-day struggles like fast-approaching deadlines, a pile of assignments due before midnight, tough sports losses, and the hurt and drama that come from relationships. We tend to forget the reason we even exist, but our job is not done. No, we do not have to prepare for Jesus' first coming, because it happened over two thousand years ago, but that's not where it ends. If someone does not know God, are we quick to tell that person about him? We have many opportunities to reach out to those we love before it's too late, and yet we often shy away. It's comfortable to blend in; we need to get a little uncomfortable.

Just as John the Baptist led people to the waters of baptism and the star led the wise men to Jesus, so should our lives, guided by the Holy Spirit, lead people to the feet of Jesus.

PRAYER Dear heavenly Father, give me the ability to step outside of my comfort zone to do the work you set aside for me. Work through me and my gifts to bring others closer to you. Amen.

GOD'S TIME LINE

Luke 2:1-3 *In those days Caesar Augustus issued a decree that a census should be taken of the entire Roman world. (This was the first census that took place while Quirinius was governor of Syria.) And everyone went to their own town to register.*

Caesar Augustus held the most power in the world at the time of the birth of Christ. Augustus replaced the Roman Republic with an imperial government, and he expanded the empire to include the Mediterranean world. It was he who desired a census of his Roman Empire for the purpose of taxing the people.

Just imagine the commotion in the Roman Empire while families traveled back to their hometowns, all for the purpose of taxation. Yet, what may have appeared to be the whim of Augustus was actually the plan of God Almighty. God used a pagan ruler to fulfill the prophecy of Micah 5:2 made seven hundred years earlier, which states, "But you, Bethlehem Ephrathah, though you are small among the clans of Judah, out of you will come for me one who will be ruler over Israel, whose origins are from of old, from ancient times."

Perhaps as we close off our semester and get ready for Christmas, there is commotion in your life. Deadlines can be daunting, and we often become caught up in the chaos of preparation for the holidays. In all of this, we should never forget that God works all things out for our good. He is in control of our timeline, and we should never lose sight of him.

PRAYER Heavenly Father, I thank you that you are in control of my life. Help me keep your holy will first in my life, even when commotion comes my way. In Jesus' name, I pray. Amen.

EXPECTATIONS

Luke 2:4,5 *Joseph also went up from the town of Nazareth in Galilee to Judea, to Bethlehem the town of David, because he belonged to the house and line of David. He went there to register with Mary, who was pledged to be married to him and was expecting a child.*

"We're expecting." When you hear a couple announce these words, you fill in the blanks. You wouldn't answer by saying, "Expecting what? What's going to happen?" Instead, you understand that the woman is pregnant. In a way, we have reserved such a special place for childbirth that you don't even have to finish the sentence "We're expecting . . ." We get it! That's awesome! We can't wait to meet the little cutie!

Do you think as Joseph traveled he was excited to see this baby born? Of course! But it wasn't just because babies are cute. After all, this particular baby would live a short life, executed on a cross for things he didn't do. His weak and fragile flesh would eventually bear every sin ever committed and be pierced for them. This would happen because you and I are by nature sinful.

However, what was Joseph and Mary's joy is ours also: this once-baby boy took away our sin and guilt by dying on a cross. He gave us the ultimate gift: perfection in the eyes of God—peace between us and our loving Father. Now we eagerly and joyfully expect the day we are united with him in heaven.

PRAYER Dear Lord, you are a gracious and loving God. You promised to send your only Son to save me from sin and death, and you delivered on every expectation. Thank you for your boundless love and your dependability. Amen.

A TINY, PERFECT BABY

Luke 2:6,7 *While they were there, the time came for the baby to be born, and she gave birth to her firstborn, a son. She wrapped him in cloths and placed him in a manger, because there was no guest room available for them.*

I was sitting at my older sister's dinner table waiting to see what was for dessert. She came in with orange and yellow fortune cookies for us. I immediately cracked mine open, anxious to see what my fortune said. I slowly read, "A baby will be in your next September," and I looked up to see if everyone was reading the same thing.

Nine months later I got the privilege of meeting my nephew. He was asleep in his swaddle, beautiful yet very helpless. He had much to learn—holding his own head up, using his hands and fingers, and learning who was all around him.

Jesus, the Son of God, came into this selfish world as a weak and fragile baby, through the work of the Holy Spirit. This emphasizes how great God's love truly is. Jesus, who is God, gave up the status of being only God to become fully human—a weak baby—simply to save the lost.

During this Christmas season, remember the status we receive from the humiliation of Christ. The beauty of God's love is Jesus and the redemption he won for everyone.

Could you give up everything for Christ? Your status? Your income? Your time? Can you step off your pedestal and help someone lower than you? Think about ways you can exemplify Christ in his humility.

PRAYER Dear Father in heaven, look upon me today as I remember how you gave your perfect Son. Help me reflect the love and grace you have shown to me. Thank you for the tiny, perfect baby who saved us all. Amen.

ORDINARY IS EXTRAORDINARY

Luke 2:8,9 *There were shepherds living out in the fields nearby, keeping watch over their flocks at night. An angel of the Lord appeared to them, and the glory of the Lord shone around them, and they were terrified.*

The verses in today's devotion might be familiar words to you. As you read the passage from Luke, imagine what it would be like to be a shepherd in the fields. Hear the sheep, the wind, and your fellow shepherds talking to each other. Picture going through your routine as you work under the stars and suddenly the angel of the Lord appears.

The shepherds were just doing their jobs when all of a sudden the angel of the Lord appeared with great news of a Savior who would die for the sins of all people. There was nothing special about this group of men, yet the glory of the Lord was revealed to them. You are just like the shepherds. You, along with everyone else in the world, have become accustomed to going through the day-to-day grind without ever looking up. Although the angel of the Lord may not visit you at your next work shift, fasten your eyes on the glory of the Lord.

God chose to reveal his glory to ordinary men. Countless accounts prove that God works through his servants to make his will known. So as you go through your daily routine today, be aware that you are a shepherd. Remember that God has already revealed much about his law, mercy, and love to you. Therefore, look up today and share with others what the Lord has revealed.

PRAYER Dear God, as you revealed your glory to ordinary shepherds, reveal to me your ways. Help me fulfill your will and share your love with others. Amen.

NEVER DOUBT YOUR VALUE

Luke 2:10-12 *The angel said to them, "Do not be afraid. I bring you good news that will cause great joy for all the people. Today in the town of David a Savior has been born to you; he is the Messiah, the Lord. This will be a sign to you: You will find a baby wrapped in cloths and lying in a manger."*

The promise of the Savior is good news to all. During the time of this passage, shepherds were not regarded as important or reputable people of the community. Even though some of the greatest heroes of the faith were shepherds, they did not have a historically good reputation. Particularly, hired shepherds who were unrelated to the owners were often looked at as suspicious, unsavory, and thieving. In some senses, they were some of the lowest and least respected by the community, not even allowed to stand as witnesses in a judicial hearing.

Yet who were some of the first people told the good news of a Savior's arrival? Even for shepherds, perhaps especially for shepherds, it was a message of joy and redemption that the Messiah had arrived. Our Father has a habit of using the lowest and weakest to show his power. He has a habit of showing up in the most humbling ways—like as an infant in a manger. But he also has a habit of treasuring the lowest and weakest as precious prizes to be won.

Next time you doubt your value, remember that the Maker of the universe considers you so valuable and so loved that he sent his dear Son to save you. Even the shepherds, the ones others did not value, were among the first with whom he shared this news.

PRAYER Dear Lord, thank you for giving the great message of your Son to lowly shepherds. Help me remember that all people are valued by you and welcome in your kingdom. In Jesus' name, I pray. Amen.

ETERNAL PEACE

Luke 2:13,14 *Suddenly a great company of the heavenly host appeared with the angel, praising God and saying, "Glory to God in the highest, and on earth peace to those on whom his favor rests."*

Think of the people, places, or things that bring you peace. Sitting next to a fire on a cold winter night while reading a good book? Running? Your favorite musical piece? Whatever brings you peace in this life, it is amazing to think about all God provides for us. How long does that peace last, though?

In our Bible reading, we read about an eternal peace. The angels proclaimed peace for those on whom God's favor rests. However, this deeper, lasting peace does not apply to all. The peace that was being proclaimed the day of Christ's birth was in reality referring to God. After all, one of God's many names used in Scripture is Prince of peace. We have peace through him and what he has done for us. Christ lived and died so that we may enjoy eternal peace with him.

This side of eternity, the peace that we have comes with certain conditions: fighting Satan, the world, and persecution for what we believe. There are times when it feels like there is no peace at all in this corrupt world. It seems to get worse as diseases spread, wars rise, and sin overtakes lives. Just watch the evening news. One encouragement is to keep wondering. Keep wondering what it is like to live with eternal, uninterrupted peace. This wonder will keep each of us hungry to dive into Christ's Word and grow stronger in him. This peace will come when we are in heaven with Jesus someday. There will be absolutely nothing greater.

PRAYER Dear Lord, thank you for sending your Son to bring peace to my life, a peace that lasts. Help me confidently and boldly share that peace with others. Amen.

SHEPHERDLIKE TRUST

Luke 2:15 *When the angels had left them and gone into heaven, the shepherds said to one another, "Let's go to Bethlehem and see this thing that has happened, which the Lord has told us about."*

Trust. The shepherds have just seen an incredible thing—heavenly hosts singing God's praises on earth! They rush off to see the Lord's promise with their own eyes. By having no doubt about what the angels had told them, the shepherds demonstrate an extraordinary trust. They trust that the angels were sent by God, that what the angels are saying is true and happening in their very city, and that this baby Savior is real. With this trust they faithfully set off to see God's promise fulfilled.

Like clockwork I read this story around Christmas every year. And every year I find it amazing that the shepherds had such amazing trust. At the same time, I get a little envious. If I had angels appear to me and bluntly say, "God is real! Come see him!" I think I would have the strongest faith ever! I have not seen God spelling things out for me, while in biblical times it seems God made his power known left and right.

But then I hear God's voice call out to me—urging me to come see that he is real, to draw into him, and to know his power wholeheartedly. He gives me his Word and his fulfilled promises. He gives me his remarkable work in the people around me that help me trust that God is for us and with us and wants us. We can have trust like the shepherds because he is real and he is there as the angels said.

PRAYER Dear Father, please allow me to have trust like the shepherds. Amen.

BE LIKE SHEPHERDS

Luke 2:17,18 *When they had seen him, they spread the word concerning what had been told them about this child, and all who heard it were amazed at what the shepherds said to them.*

I sometimes struggle to imagine what the night of Jesus' birth looked like. The only image my brain can seem to conjure up is that of the common nativity scene. The Bible speaks clearly about the events of that evening. Jesus was in a manger, Mary and Joseph were there, the angels were singing, and finally, so were the shepherds. Now, if I had to rank these characters by importance, the shepherds would come in last. However, the Bible declares that they had an important role.

The shepherds were some of the only people to have seen Jesus that night. These shepherds were actually the only known and recorded witnesses to the birth of Jesus. They not only witnessed the event, but they also testified to their sighting and spread the news of what they had seen. Without this listed witness and them spreading what they had seen, the story may not have spread as far as it did.

These shepherds also act as a great example for believers today. As we grow in our knowledge of the Word and in our faith in Jesus, God calls us to be like the shepherds and tell others about what we have heard! These shepherds may seem to have a pretty small role in the action on that Christmas night, but they served a huge purpose then and continue to serve us today as we hear their account of the story of Jesus' birth every Christmas.

PRAYER Dear God, thank you for blessing me with a Savior. Help me be like the shepherds, who were overjoyed to tell about what they had seen. In Jesus' name, I pray. Amen.

December 24

JESUS IS YOUR SALVATION

Luke 2:30-32 *My eyes have seen your salvation, which you have prepared in the sight of all nations: a light for revelation to the Gentiles, and the glory of your people Israel.*

What are your favorite Christmas "clues"? Weather changes, lights on houses, tree stands in parking lots, holiday displays in stores, Christmas music on the radio?

The Holy Spirit led Simeon to the temple, and despite other clues there might have been (Were the shepherds still talking? Had anyone else noticed angelic singing or a strange new star last week?), it was there, in God's house, that he *saw.*

You're probably home now for Christmas to see your family. Your house might be full of familiar decorations and lots of presents. Or perhaps there isn't much to see at home—not many gifts, not much holiday warmth and cheer, or not even love. Such is the reality of life in this sin-corrupted world.

Whether you are distracted by everything there is to see or disappointed by everything there isn't to see, let this one glorious sight shine over everything: your salvation. There is nothing that matters so much this Christmas, for without it we are lost. Without him, we are lost. The eight-day-old infant in Simeon's arms was already carrying the weight of a perfect life in an imperfect world, was already prepared as the sacrifice for all, both Jew and Gentile.

Do not close your eyes to him this season. Do not let the glitter of your celebrations outshine the glorious light of revelation in that infant's face. He is your salvation, from sin, from death, from hell itself. See it. Marvel at it. Worship him for it.

PRAYER O Christ Child, forgive my blindness to your light. Open my eyes to see you as Simeon did: as my salvation. Amen.

FOLLOW THE STAR

Matthew 2:1,2 *After Jesus was born in Bethlehem in Judea, during the time of King Herod, Magi from the east came to Jerusalem and asked, "Where is the one who has been born king of the Jews? We saw his star when it rose and have come to worship him."*

Imagine following a star across a foreign land—having no clue at all where it was going to take you. This is certainly not Google Maps—no step-by-step instructions and certainly no warnings about the traffic conditions ahead! Simply an extraordinary star in the sky that somehow seems to say to its careful observers, "Follow me—I'll take you to the King." How the Magi knew to follow the star, and knew what it signified, is beyond my understanding. I've heard it said before that the Magi from the east were careful stargazers. While this certainly must be true if they noticed this star, I think it's more interesting *why* they followed it.

They weren't impressed by its size, brightness, or location. All they cared about was the *reason* behind the star. They did not come to gaze at the star closer up, but to gaze at the *One* it celebrated—Jesus Christ, the true Light of the world. When Jesus was on earth, he declared that he was the Light of the world and whoever would follow him would never walk in darkness (John 8:12). When I read that verse, I cannot help but think of the Magi. Jesus spoke this promise to all who follow him, all who by the power of the Spirit are not walking in the darkness of false beliefs.

Take some time to look to the Light of the world by reading and recalling what he says in his Word. And while there may not be a bright star in the sky, we have the promise of an even greater light to follow. May our response to our Savior always be one of worship.

PRAYER Jesus, thank you for being the Light of the world. May I be like the faithful Magi, following you wherever you lead. I love you and praise you. In your name, I pray. Amen.

December 26

HE CHANGED EVERYTHING

Matthew 2:3,4 *When King Herod heard this he was disturbed, and all Jerusalem with him. When he had called together all the people's chief priests and teachers of the law, he asked them where the Messiah was to be born.*

One of my favorite Christmas songs is called "A Baby Changes Everything" by Faith Hill. The first time I heard it, I didn't realize it was a Christmas song. It just sounded like a song about a young girl, unmarried and pregnant. I heard it again several weeks later and decided to listen to the words. It talks about the struggles that Mary and Joseph faced when they found out they were having a baby, about how they worried about what others would think, and how that little baby would change the world.

Matthew 2:3,4 makes me think of that song. That little baby changed everything. He even frightened an extremely powerful king. Herod was afraid of what that baby's birth might mean for his position and power. He was the king and wanted no one to take that away from him. He was so afraid that he had his guards go out to kill any baby that could be Jesus.

If a powerful king is that afraid of a little baby, what does that say about how we should react to this baby? This baby did change everything. We were supposed to end up in hell, but because God sent his Son in the form of a humble baby, we will live forever with him in heaven. Jesus did change everything, which is a constant reminder we need at Christmas with all the holiday hustle and bustle.

PRAYER Dear Lord, you know how I run around all day and forget about what's most important. Your promise to send your Son is something that is so incredible, and I need to remember that all the time. Help me be reminded of that not only during the Christmas season but every day of my life. Amen.

KEEP CHRIST ON HIS THRONE

Matthew 2:7,8 *Then Herod called the Magi secretly and found out from them the exact time the star had appeared. He sent them to Bethlehem and said, "Go and search carefully for the child. As soon as you find him, report to me, so that I too may go and worship him."*

King Herod was a heathen man. He lived a very secular life, filled with the vices of the world. He was full of pride. He was very aware of any threat to his power, and would do anything to remove it. So when the Magi told him about a bright star that led them to Jerusalem—and that they were searching for the King of kings to go and worship—what do you think went through his mind? This section of Scripture is just a snapshot of the encounter, but the rest of the story does not end with Herod bowing down to Jesus in worship.

Herod wanted to know where Jesus was so that he could nip that threat in the bud. What threatens God's throne in your own heart? Be conscious of it, and stay in the Word so that you can keep Christ on his throne. How shortsighted of Herod to think that Jesus would be a ruler on earth! Little did Herod know that Jesus' true kingdom is not of this world, but is of heaven! It is wonderful to know that it was not even possible for Herod's plan to kill Jesus to succeed and that God's plan for our salvation was carried out. No matter what difficulties cross the path of God's divine plan, his ways will always succeed. What comfort there is in that!

PRAYER Dear Lord, thank you for sending your Son, Jesus, to be my Savior from sin. Help me keep Christ on the throne in my heart, no matter what threats may arise, and trust in your promises. In Jesus' name, I pray. Amen.

WHAT IS YOUR STAR?

Matthew 2:11,12 *On coming to the house, they saw the child with his mother Mary, and they bowed down and worshiped him. Then they opened their treasures and presented him with gifts of gold, frankincense and myrrh. And having been warned in a dream not to go back to Herod, they returned to their country by another route.*

What is your "star"? What in your life points you to Jesus? The Magi were led right to Jesus. They understood the significance of the event of his birth, and they had the amazing privilege of worshiping him in person! He would be their Savior—not from worldly danger, but from the eternal danger of hell and separation from God because of sin.

So, what points you to Jesus? Ultimately, it is always God's Word and sacraments that point us to our Savior, but God uses earthly things like people and circumstances as tools to direct us to the means of grace. In the case of the Magi, he used a star. The things God puts into our lives might not seem as miraculous as a bright new star, but they are there.

In the past, your star may have been your parents bringing you to church to be baptized. Now, maybe your star is a friend who is a good example of diligently studying the Bible. In the future, perhaps your star will be something that happens at work that leads you to scour the Scriptures in search of what God says about a certain topic. Be on the lookout for the stars God puts in your life today and every day, and thank him for them!

PRAYER Dear Lord, thank you for the stars in my life that lead me to your Word and sacraments. Amen.

December 29

AM I WHERE I SHOULD BE?

Matthew 2:13-15 *When they had gone, an angel of the Lord appeared to Joseph in a dream. "Get up," he said, "take the child and his mother and escape to Egypt. Stay there until I tell you, for Herod is going to search for the child to kill him." So he got up, took the child and his mother during the night and left for Egypt, where he stayed until the death of Herod. And so was fulfilled what the Lord had said through the prophet: "Out of Egypt I called my son."*

Have you ever wondered if you are where you should be? I think that Joseph probably struggled with this as well. He had entered into a socially unacceptable marriage, his wife had given birth in a stable, and now God was sending him and his family to Egypt because their lives were in danger.

I'm sure Joseph had some of the thoughts that many of us have had, such as, "What am I doing?" or "I don't know what I will be doing in four years, let alone how I'm going to get to Egypt ASAP."

We might not have to worry about going to Egypt, but maybe you have wondered if you are making the right decisions in life right now. Though God does not directly talk to us like he did to Joseph, do not worry. He will use every situation that you encounter for some purpose. Even if you're unsure of what you're doing at this time, pray with confidence that you're where you are supposed to be at this moment and that you will end up being exactly where you should be. Remember, Christ lived and died for us, and that is the only truly important thing.

PRAYER "Christ be my leader by night as by day, safe through the darkness, for he is the way" (CW 367:1). Help me trust you and not doubt your plans. Thank you for bringing me to this point in my life. Please continue to guide me in all that I do. Amen.

December 30

HELP ME BE A GOOD STEWARD

Matthew 2:16 *When Herod realized that he had been outwitted by the Magi, he was furious, and he gave orders to kill all the boys in Bethlehem and its vicinity who were two years old and under, in accordance with the time he had learned from the Magi.*

In this passage we hear the account of the so-called "Massacre of the Innocents." What could drive a man to commit so heinous a crime? Herod had been told by the Magi that a king had been born in Bethlehem. Ignorant of the reality of Christ's kingdom, Herod feared that this baby would displace him from his throne.

This account shows us the sobering reality of the kinds of corruption that come from earthly power, wealth, and status. We wouldn't think ourselves capable of such a terrible act, but which one of us, if we were given the opportunity and the ability, would not abuse our power? The thing Herod feared above all was that, one day, everything he had would be taken from him, and it was this fear that drove him.

Herod lived, as we often do, under the illusion that he was entitled to his power. As followers of Christ, we understand our role as stewards in this life; all we have is not truly ours. They are "on loan" from God, so to speak, given to us to use for his glory and to further the mission of his church. But one day, all earthly things will vanish "in the twinkling of an eye." This should not frighten us but should be a reassurance that all that matters is Jesus' selfless sacrifice, and that, in him, we have the greatest gift—eternal life in paradise.

PRAYER Dear Lord, please help me be a good steward of your kingdom. Guide me to use all I have been given to help others, to praise your name, and to spread your gospel. In Jesus' name, I pray. Amen.

FAITH LIKE A CHILD

Matthew 2:19-21 *After Herod died, an angel of the Lord appeared in a dream to Joseph in Egypt and said, "Get up, take the child and his mother and go to the land of Israel, for those who were trying to take the child's life are dead." So he got up, took the child and his mother and went to the land of Israel.*

Hebrews 11:1 says, "Now faith is confidence in what we hope for and assurance about what we do not see." This passage perfectly exhibits what we see in our reading about Joseph and his faith. God sent an angel to give him direction, and he did not question it. He simply got up, took Mary and Jesus, and went back to Israel from Egypt. He had faith in his God and in the long-awaited Savior that had finally come from his line.

This theme is seen in the Old Testament too. One example is when Abraham is told to leave Ur to go to the Promised Land, the land that would become Israel. Even small children have blind faith in their parents, knowing that their parents would never hurt them. The comparisons are all around us.

In fact, Jesus told his disciples that whoever has faith like children will be the ones who enter the kingdom of God. God asks us to believe in what we cannot see. This can be a struggle, but he gives us his promises that we can hear and believe. We can open our eyes and ears to the message of Jesus Christ and his suffering and death on Calvary in our place.

PRAYER Lord, help me have faith in that which I cannot see. While others may push me from your path, give me hope, strength, and faith through your Spirit to keep my faith in you. Amen.

JANUARY
LIGHT IN THE DARKNESS

A NEW START

1 Peter 2:9 *You are a chosen people, a royal priesthood, a holy nation, God's special possession, that you may declare the praises of him who called you out of darkness into his wonderful light.*

Confetti lies on the floor. Plastic cups of various fill levels riddle the room. Decorations persistently hang around the doorways and down the hallways. How many apartments and houses would you suppose share this scene on January 1—the first day of the new year? New Year's Eve is a big night for some people—a night of celebrating what has passed and anticipating what is to come.

However, sometimes thinking about the past year is not so fun. Many people experienced terrible things this last year; others will not be living in the new one. All of us have made mistakes, damaged relationships, or endangered ourselves this past year. Yet the confetti flies, the champagne is poured, and midnight kisses are shared.

Each year leaves us with something to regret, but each new year also brings a reminder of God's grace. The apostle Peter teaches us about our new identity in Christ in the passage for today.

Thank God for this passage. Peter throws two things at us: who we are and what we're here for. Christ died for you and clothed you with his "new year" righteousness, wiping away every sin of your previous years. You are free to live the rest of your days in God's grace. He did this so that you could revel in your newfound identity and point others to theirs. This year, let us all make the resolution to glorify God in everything we do, because he has made us new.

PRAYER O gracious God, loving Father, thank you for purchasing me into your family through Christ's blood and for making me new in Christ's righteousness. Amen.

THE LIGHT OF THE WORLD

Genesis 1:3-5 *God said, "Let there be light," and there was light. God saw that the light was good, and he separated the light from the darkness. God called the light "day," and the darkness he called "night." And there was evening, and there was morning—the first day.*

Did you ever notice that God created light before he created any sources of light? Before sun, moon, and stars, somehow light existed. Today we know that light is a wave and can hypothetically exist independent of its source, but it does not change how strange this is from a scientific/common sense perspective. How can you have light without a source? Psalm 19 tells us that "the heavens declare the glory of God" and that this created world shouts, "There is a God." His signature is everywhere, yet the way God reveals the creation of this world remains veiled in mystery.

If you are anything like me, you struggle with this. We want our God to be comprehensible, to explain everything with logical certainty and mathematical clarity. We get angry with God for hiding, for making us take him at his word and simply trust him. We feel the doubt creep in. That is when we need to remember that our Savior has died for us for these exact moments: moments when we get angry at him for hiding, moments when we doubt what his Word says, or moments when we feel ashamed at sharing his Word with our friends. Jesus died for all sins, including these. The Light of the world brought not only physical light but also spiritual light into our lives, letting us know that our sins are forgiven and that we're now children of God.

PRAYER Heavenly Father, thank you for creating light, and thank you for sending Jesus, the Light of the world, into this world that has become darkened by sin. Strengthen my faith so that I trust what your Word says. Amen.

GOD'S MAJESTY

Psalm 104:1-3 *Praise the L*ORD*, my soul. L*ORD *my God, you are very great; you are clothed with splendor and majesty. The L*ORD *wraps himself in light as with a garment; he stretches out the heavens like a tent and lays the beams of his upper chambers on their waters. He makes the clouds his chariot and rides on the wings of the wind.*

How often do you sit and wonder? Wonder about what things around the world look like, sound like, feel like? Rather than sit and ponder, do you take out your smartphone to get the quick answer? When I was in college, I took an astronomy class that used some very unique mobile apps to help our stargazing efforts. Now, we could have just completed our work using these highly accurate virtual skies, but this would have diminished the appreciation for God's creation.

When we observe creation, we are free to make our own interpretation. The psalmist shares our response to God's creation. What a wonderful display of God's majesty! Although even nonbelievers can see creation, it is by faith and the Spirit that we stand in awe of God's work.

We also stand in awe of God's work of salvation. Christ died so that we as hopeless sinners could live. So, the next time you find yourself walking under God's tapestry of light, say a prayer of thanksgiving for the ever-present reminder of God's presence and glory.

PRAYER Heavenly Creator, how awesome are your works! When I gaze on the works of your hands, instill in me a spirit of humble awe. Thank you for your constant presence and loving care that are on display in your creation. In my Savior's name, I pray. Amen.

THE PERFECT FRIEND

Psalm 84:11,12 *For the Lᴏʀᴅ God is a sun and shield; the Lᴏʀᴅ bestows favor and honor; no good thing does he withhold from those whose walk is blameless. Lᴏʀᴅ Almighty, blessed is the one who trusts in you.*

Have you ever known a person who was hard to trust? There are always people who do not come through for us on a regular basis or continue to lie and make up excuses. Relationships with these people are often difficult and filled with disappointment, anger, and hurt feelings.

Even when we look at people whom we see as "good" friends, who help us and seem to always have our backs, we see they have flaws. There may have been that one time your mom broke her promise to take you somewhere. Or maybe there was that one year your friend forgot your birthday. No matter how good of friends you think you may have, they are sinful and at one time or another will disappoint.

Thanks be to God! We always have one person who will never let us down or disappoint us. God always comes through for us. In our verse today, it says, "No good thing does he withhold." Not only does he do everything that we need, but he does *everything.* There is not one good thing in this life that is not from him and through him. God will always be there to uplift and strengthen us. The Lord always protects and provides for us as our "sun and shield." Through faith in him and the saving grace of our Savior Jesus, we have salvation. We have every reason to put our trust in him.

PRAYER Dear God, thank you for putting people in my life who are loyal friends to me. Thank you even more, though, for blessing me in every way and always being present. Please continue to strengthen the trust I have in you. Amen.

January 5

LOOKING FOR EXTRA MOTIVATION?

Psalm 36:9 *For with you is the fountain of life; in your light we see light.*

Christmas is over and January is upon us. Gone are the festive lights strewn across town; coming are the days of trudging to class in the muddied snow and watching the sun disappear while still sitting at your desk. During this dark and often dreary period, it can be difficult to have the energy to keep up with schoolwork and even keep going in general. So it may be strange to read today's verse in the midst of these feelings.

Psalm 36 begins with depictions of the attitudes and actions of the wicked. The Israelites knew what it was like to feel burdened and weary by the wickedness of other nations and by their own sin—enough to make them wonder if things would ever look up. But then the psalmist praises the Lord for the refuge and happiness he brings to his children, even in the midst of evil. Furthermore, we are told that God does not just GIVE Christians this life and light, he IS life and light.

Looking for that extra motivation to keep going in a cup (or four) of coffee? Look instead to God's Word. Just as he did for the Israelites, God sent his Son to save you from the darkness of sin, and he will guide you through the dark periods of life until he brings you home to eternal life. Let's be motivated by thanks for that awesome promise and continue to bask in the Son that is close to us in every season.

PRAYER Dear Lord, thank you for granting me salvation through Jesus, the Light of the world. Help me spread this great news to others and hold to this truth even in the darkness. Amen.

January 6

SAFE IN THE LIGHT OF JESUS

Isaiah 9:2 *The people walking in darkness have seen a great light; on those living in the land of deep darkness a light has dawned.*

Basements can be scary. My family lived in my grandparents' basement for a winter when I was young. With the water softener, the deer mount that hung above my bed, and absence of light, sleeping in the basement was difficult for my four-year-old self. So difficult that if it hadn't been for the wood burner on the other side of the basement, each night would have been hours of sheer horror. The light that emitted from the fire was just enough for me to see my parents' bedroom door and my sister on the pull-out couch. This helped me realize that if they were safe, then so was I.

Fear of darkness is not limited to the inability to sleep. How many times have you wished you had turned on the flashlight on your phone after you sustained a stubbed toe or a dented shin while walking through a dark room? A little light is always a great thing. The world is full of sin and darkness. At times, our world is so materialistic and sinful that it's overwhelming. It is great to have a light in the saving grace that Jesus provides for us through his death and resurrection. What a comfort it is to know we are safe.

PRAYER Dear Lord, thank you for sending your Son to redeem me from my sins. Thank you for providing a light to me when I feel as though I am in complete darkness. I pray that I can share your light with others. Amen.

COMMITTED

Psalm 37:5,6 *Commit your way to the LORD; trust in him and he will do this: He will make your righteous reward shine like the dawn, your vindication like the noonday sun.*

Are you committed? Are you committed to your major? Are you committed to continue in the time-zapping sport, theater, or music program? Are you committed to your current relationship? Are you committed to your Savior?

A lot of things can change in college. Perhaps you always wanted to be a vet, but it looks like your skills are in business. Maybe your education has to take precedence over an extracurricular that you have loved for a long time, which can no longer be a priority. In addition, if you are not as compatible with your boyfriend/girlfriend as you thought, it is fine to explore other options.

What about the commitment to your Savior? We are told to be open-minded and tolerant of people in all walks of life. However, the true God of the Bible tells us that he does not share his affection with anyone or anything else. If we change our alliance from God's truth to the ways of the world or our own selfishness, we will walk into the danger of spiritual darkness . . . and worse yet, lose our way to eternal life!

We can be thankful that even when our commitment wavers, our loving God is always committed to us! Even though our interests and attitudes can change, he is always there speaking to us in his Word. We are righteous through Jesus, our Savior. He is the Light that we need to guide us through this life and lead us to heaven. When we are committed to Christ, we can be confident that he will make all things work out for our spiritual good . . . for today and for eternity!

PRAYER Dear Lord, help me show my appreciation for your commitment to me by living a life of commitment to you. In Jesus' name, I pray. Amen.

GOD IS WITH US

Psalm 23:4 *Even though I walk through the darkest valley, I will fear no evil, for you are with me; your rod and your staff, they comfort me.*

Yes, it's that time of year again—when cabin fever seems to reach a peak as the days of bleak light fade into the dark, cold, snowy winter nights. It's the time of year when hopeful resolution-makers have already broken promises to themselves, and a time when people return to a busy work schedule and students return to the grind of academic endeavors.

Perhaps one of the most difficult transitions to manage in January is that of coming down off of the euphoric emotional high that is Christmas. The days preceding Christmas are filled with such hope and joy as we prepare ourselves to celebrate Christ's birth. Now, however, we are thrust back into a "reality" where the message of Christmas is sometimes overshadowed by the sorrows and stress of the world.

Our reading gives us comfort and strength in the face of life's difficulties. We are assured that no matter what disappointments and trials lie ahead in the new year, God is with us. Whether it is the loss of a loved one, a financial or health burden that troubles us, or the many battles that we face with temptation, we are given an everlasting hope. God is with us. The next time we are tempted to fall into the mind-set of hopelessness, let us be reminded of God's promise to us and how Jesus was born so that he could be our Savior to live and die for us.

PRAYER Dear Lord, thank you for leading me into a new year, a time filled with hope and expectation. In this year, guard and guide me through all the snares and disappointments. Though life may not always go according to plan, give me peace and comfort in the knowledge that you are with me always and there is nothing to fear. Amen.

REMINDERS OF GOD'S PRESENCE

Psalm 112:4 *Even in darkness light dawns for the upright, for those who are gracious and compassionate and righteous.*

Ever since I was in high school, I think of angels waving at me when a streetlight goes on or off for no apparent reason. I know it's probably a bulb going out or a short in the wiring, but I prefer to let it simply be a reminder that I am not alone or unprotected. God is watching over me. What reminds you of God's care for you?

Whatever it is, whenever it is, it's because God has made you his. If you did not know your God, there would be times when the darkness would overwhelm you. But since you know that Jesus suffered, died, and rose to life for you, you also know that nothing can overcome you because you are his. There is always light for those who trust in him.

This is the reminder the psalmist wants to give you today. No matter how dark your life may be, you know that Jesus' light will dawn just as surely as the sun comes up in the morning. No matter how bad a relationship is or how your grades are not where you want them to be or that you have not found that special someone yet, you know that there is hope and peace when God is with you.

I think of angels when a streetlight goes out. Another may think of God's care when the stars shine. No matter what reminds you of his presence, you know there is always light because of your Savior.

PRAYER Dear Jesus, remind me in my darkest hours that because of you, I always have light to see me safely home to you. Amen.

THE LIGHT OF SALVATION

Psalm 62:1,2 *Truly my soul finds rest in God; my salvation comes from him. Truly he is my rock and my salvation; he is my fortress, I will never be shaken.*

As a psychology major, studying disorders or abnormal behavior has always interested me. One disorder that interests me is seasonal affective disorder. According to Mayo Clinic's website, seasonal affective disorder, or SAD, is a form of depression that is related to the seasons, and it is often related to the winter months. It causes its victims to feel moody or low on energy, and it may be hard for individuals affected by SAD to function in their daily tasks.

Why may SAD occur in individuals? There are many possible explanations, but one stands out from the rest: light deficiency. The months after Christmas are deficient of light. After the Christmas lights and hype are gone, it may be difficult to face the harsh winter ahead. Winter months are also deficient of physical light. In many places, winter is riddled with gray and cloudy skies. The sun is absent and it's hard for people to find comfort in a world without light.

In a similar way, it is impossible to find hope in a world absent of the light of God's promises.

Jesus fills our dark and dreary world with the light of his salvation. Though the Christmas season is over, God radiates through the gloom with his mighty Word. Jesus has conquered all sin, death, and sadness. Eternal salvation is ours; we have every reason to be glad! May the Son's light shine through the darkness in our lives, and may we gather together with fellow believers to find strength in his Holy Word.

PRAYER Dear God of light, shine through the gloom of this world and keep me grounded in your Word. When I feel sad, remind me that you have conquered all sadness on this earth and fill me with the joy of salvation. Amen.

January 11

FOLLOW JESUS

John 8:12 *When Jesus spoke again to the people, he said, "I am the light of the world. Whoever follows me will never walk in darkness, but will have the light of life."*

Leaving a childhood home and the safety it offers is a daunting experience, especially because a college campus lacks so many of the requirements that make a place home. Since there is no going back, all anyone can do is try to make the most of life on campus. But without the support of home and family, everything is dark and uncertain. How do you decide what to do with your life? How do you cope with tragedy or hardships? These and so many other questions arise in college, and sometimes they are made even worse by an uncertainty of whom to trust in a new environment. Sometimes college feels like walking through a beautiful forest at night on an untraveled path.

For everyone at a loss to find their bearings, Jesus has wonderful words of promise in today's passage. Read it again. What a special promise for anyone living away from home—Jesus is the Light of the *entire world*. No matter how unfamiliar our surroundings, or how far we are from home, Jesus will always be there to light our way. When any struggle arises, Jesus is always there to light our path and guide us directly where we need to go.

PRAYER Dear Lord Jesus, Light of the world, guide me and lead me through the unfamiliar paths ahead. As I am in this transitory home, remind me to turn to you for understanding, and remind me that no matter where I am, I am never outside of your light. Amen.

FOCUS HEAVENWARD

Psalm 89:15,16 *Blessed are those who have learned to acclaim you, who walk in the light of your presence, LORD. They rejoice in your name all day long; they celebrate your righteousness.*

If you're anything like me, you are probably not the most pleasant person to be around seconds after your alarm clock rouses you from your sleep, which always seems far too short. You may groan as you rub your eyes and remember all of the obstacles that you have to face that day. After you down a cup of coffee, you'll be lucky if you are in the mood to mutter a "good morning" to anyone. Can't night just last a few more hours? Do we really have to do this whole "school" thing again?

So often we forget that it is a blessing to wake up to a brand-new day, to once again bathe in the sunlight that is a gift from God. He has not only granted us another opportunity to see the sunrise, but he has sent his Son to win eternal salvation for us! Yet, due to our sinful nature, it's as if the night erases our memory of God's love and faithfulness to us. Instead of mumbling and complaining about how tired we are and about the drama that exists in our individual bubbles, we should be rejoicing in the Lord's righteousness and grace.

Walk around as a child of the light who has been redeemed and promised salvation. There is no reason to dwell on the insignificant problems of today, but there is every reason to dwell on God's gifts to us! Don't trudge around focusing on negativity and gloom, but turn your eyes heavenward to focus on the Son. Challenge yourself to spend every day focusing on these gifts!

PRAYER "Renew me, O eternal Light, and let my heart and soul be bright, illumined with the light of grace that issues from your holy face." Amen. (CW 471:1)

WE CANNOT HIDE

Psalm 139:11,12 *If I say, "Surely the darkness will hide me and the light become night around me," even the darkness will not be dark to you; the night will shine like the day, for darkness is as light to you.*

In this psalm, David is explaining how much the Lord knows us. God knows when we get up and when we lie down, he knows us in our inmost being, and he knew us from the moment we were formed. I don't know about you, but sometimes this scares me. God sees me all the time? Even when I'm copying and pasting content straight from a website into my paper? Even when I'm thinking horrible thoughts about people I cannot stand? I can't even hide my faults because God exposes them to his light. I don't want God seeing me at these times, and I am sure David felt the same way.

However, God does not want these passages to scare us. Yes, they serve as a warning, but more important, they show how much God loves us. Would you believe that God is loving, all-caring, and willing to die for our sins if he did not actually know us? Although he knows all our shortcomings, he still loves us unconditionally. The beauty of this psalm comes from that unconditional love, and we can take comfort in it.

PRAYER Dear Lord, thank you so much for this new day. I am so thankful for your deep love for me, despite all the times you see me mess up. Please strengthen me as I continue through the darkness of sin; only you can bring me to the light of your promise of salvation. In your name, I pray. Amen.

YOU HAVE DELIVERED ME

Psalm 56:13 *You have delivered me from death and my feet from stumbling, that I may walk before God in the light of life.*

Though the month of January can sometimes be a time for relaxation from school and meditation on the celebration of Christ's birth, there are often roadblocks that Satan sets up to distract from God's Word. Perhaps you already realize that next semester is going to be stressful because of schoolwork, and you are already stressing out about how you are going to finish everything in one semester and earn the grades you want. Maybe there are financial or relationship strains that are causing you to lose focus on the hope God has set up for you through Jesus' birth and death.

Whatever your situation may be, you can always take comfort in the fact that God has already brought you through your troubles and hardships. Psalm 56:13 is a good, comforting reminder of this. Not only has God provided us comfort and safety in times of need while we live on earth, but he has saved us from eternal death. There is no better thought than the one that assures us that God has already brought us through hardship, even if we have yet to face it!

PRAYER Dear Lord, hardships are inevitable in this life. Give me the strength and faith to trust that you will bring me through hardship and ultimately bring me to heaven. When I waver in my confidence, remind me that you are always there to guide me through this life until I reach my eternal home of heaven. Amen.

ARE YOU AMAZED?

James 1:17,18 Every good and perfect gift is from above, coming down from the Father of the heavenly lights, who does not change like shifting shadows. He chose to give us birth through the word of truth, that we might be a kind of firstfruits of all he created.

As a child, I loved bundling up in the middle of January, sneaking out of the house at midnight, and finding a patch of unbroken snow to go stargazing. On nights when the moon came out, it bathed the forest in brilliant white light and cast ghostly shadows through the trees. Though the shadows moved as the moon crossed the sky, the brightness from the moon and stars never decreased. To this day, these January sights never cease to amaze me.

How often are you amazed? It's easy to only see the big things in life when we're wrapped up in our hectic schedules. Yet when amazement strikes, do you think about the Creator of those good things? What's God really like? How much does he care about us?

We may not be able to completely comprehend the awesome power and majesty of our God, but we do know of his goodness toward us by how he reveals himself. The epistle writer James points to this fact in James 1:17,18.

Our Creator-God is always good, like the brightest moon in a midnight sky. Although life's shadows may try to loom over you, remember that God made you his child through Jesus Christ. He cares especially for you, and by his Word you can know this love will never change.

PRAYER Thank you, Father, for your unchanging grace as the light of my life. Keep me mindful of all the perfect blessings you give me each day. Amen.

WHAT IS TRUTH?

Psalm 119:129,130 *Your statutes are wonderful; therefore I obey them. The unfolding of your words gives light; it gives understanding to the simple.*

What is truth? Have you ever questioned what truth is after watching the news? Have you ever questioned the truth of God's promises in tough times? At the end of the line, you feel overwhelmed and lost in disillusioned thoughts.

In one of my courses, I was required to study briefly the "Allegory of the Cave" by Plato. Plato details that humans are consistently fulfilled through disillusionment—we come to believe part of the picture and not the whole picture of reality. We thrive on shadows instead of the enlightenment outside the cave. Through reason, humans find their way out of the cave and into the light. Many of our brothers and sisters in the world follow the same roadmap. They embrace reason and see it as the only way for survival but neglect to see the whole picture. Christ, through his servant David, revealed the answer to where we find light in the face of utter darkness—his Word.

What is truth? It is the unveiling of truth and promise that is given to us in the Word of God. It is the fact that Christ has died for our sins. His words were meant for us. How can we respond to the unfolding of his Word? David says by obeying it. In the face of such utter darkness in this world, heeding the call of God as he whispers his truth to our souls and breathes life into our lives is truth. Let us heed his call and seek him in his Word to find the light.

PRAYER Dear Lord, I often struggle over the question of what is truth. Help me remember that the only truth that matters is that Christ has died for my sins. Keep me rooted in your Word. Amen.

BE BOLD

Psalm 91:5,6 *You will not fear the terror of night, nor the arrow that flies by day, nor the pestilence that stalks in the darkness, nor the plague that destroys at midday.*

Consider this story about a courageous Christian who stood before a Roman emperor who was persecuting the church: the emperor demanded that all Christians abandon their faith and deny Christ as Lord. One Christian refused to do so, and in response the emperor threatened him, saying, "Give up Christ, or I will banish you." The Christian, strong in faith, replied, "My home is in heaven, and you cannot banish me from Christ, for he says, 'Never will I leave you; never will I forsake you.'"

The emperor tried again, saying, "I will confiscate all your property unless you denounce your faith." The Christian answered him, "My treasure is stored up in heaven. You cannot take it from me." Finally the emperor threatened, "I will kill you." But the Christian replied, "I am already dead to the world in Christ. My life is in Christ and you cannot separate me from him." The emperor then turned to the others in the room and asked, "What can we do with such faith?"

The Christian in the story understood God's protection. In the frightening times we live in, where so many things scare us—from terrorists to life-threatening diseases—God's Word calms our fears. God promises to be with us through any trouble, and we can face anything that comes our way boldly, knowing that he is in control.

PRAYER Dear heavenly Father, calm me when I become afraid of the darkness in this world. Remind me of your promises to protect me, and keep me ever in the light of your Word. In Jesus' name, I pray. Amen.

LIGHT VS. DARK

John 1:4,5 *In him was life, and that life was the light of all mankind. The light shines in the darkness, and the darkness has not overcome it.*

Were you ever lost in the dark when you were young? It's a little harder to make it back to that safe place we call home when we can't find our way there.

Of the many dual elements in this world, there is none other like light and darkness. They can illuminate or impede transportation and communication. They signify the beginning and ending of a day. They can also signify good and evil or life and death.

In the gospel of John, the contrast between light and darkness is a theme present throughout the book, with Jesus referring to himself as the Light of the world.

We live in spiritual darkness. We are that lost child, trying to make our way back home, but we are incapable of making light on our own. Jesus is our light. He found us in the world, and he is leading us back home, step by step.

The true, spiritual light is something we should never lose sight of. While it may seem to merely be one side to a metaphysical coin, it means so much more. It is the answer to our spiritual darkness. It is also our path back to our true "home" as well.

PRAYER Dear Father, please continue to be the light that guides my path and keeps me from stumbling into the darkness. Help my own light, my faith, point to you. You are the source of all light in a world full of spiritual darkness. In the name of my Savior, I pray. Amen.

FACING THE DARKNESS

Matthew 5:14 *You are the light of the world. A town built on a hill cannot be hidden.*

I was quickly spiraling down the tunnel of depression. I felt anger and sadness every second of every day. I was losing my friends. My grades were dropping significantly, and I felt as if no one understood me. I was overwhelmed with darkness. Have you ever felt this way? Well, as I remained blind to the light that was always before me, someone lit my flame of faith. Jesus pulled me out of the darkness by being my light.

I'm sure most of us know of pain and its darkness, no matter the severity, no matter your story. Maybe some of you have lost a loved one or are struggling with family or friends. My darkness took over after my third ACL tear in basketball. Sports were a passion of mine. When I no longer could play them, I lost a vital part of what I thought was my identity.

It turned out God had bigger plans for me, and he does for you too! Jesus used my darkness to pull me into his Word: the light. Though I felt I had lost a part of who I was, God was actually molding me into who he wanted me to become. He is doing the same for you. The Holy Spirit brought me comfort and peace through his Word. Jesus was my light—is my light—is *your* light. Turn to God for strength. Share with others the peace you've found in Christ, that they may come to the light, for in him there is no more darkness.

PRAYER Dear Lord, please help me turn to you in times of trouble. Send your Holy Spirit to fill me with a faith that trusts in your comforting promises. Help me use your Word to be a light to others. Be with me as I face the darkness in each day. In your name, I pray. Amen.

GOD'S WORD WARMS YOU UP

Psalm 119:105 *Your word is a lamp for my feet, a light on my path.*

Right around this time of year, I tend to get down. It's after the excitement of the holidays and before the beautiful spring weather. The snow starts getting heavy and thick, not like the fluffy flurries that float about in December. It is dreary outside with the clouds and the cold, and you get cabin fever from just sitting inside with little to do. It just feels like there's nothing to look forward to or to celebrate.

It's during times like these that Psalm 119:105 lifts me up. We always have something to look forward to, something that can never and will never be taken away from us: Jesus' love. His Word points us to where we need to go. It lights the way to heaven for us and gives us hope when all seems hopeless. Without his Word there is nothing to look forward to.

So when the winter storms are violent and bone-chilling, we can turn to God's Word to warm us up and be the beacon of hope that we need to brave the ongoing storms of this world. We can use God's Word as a tool to light up others' lives and to inspire us to be the light that he wants us to be for him. God has given us what we need to do his work, and he will bring us safely to his home, where we can celebrate with him.

PRAYER Dear Lord, thank you for giving me your own Word to lift me up when I am down and to instruct me on how to be your faithful servant. Lead me with that Word down a path that is pleasing in your sight. Amen.

LET YOUR LIGHT SHINE

Matthew 5:16 *In the same way, let your light shine before others, that they may see your good deeds and glorify your Father in heaven.*

Balance. This is the key to basic living. In life you're constantly balancing time, money, socializing, tasks, and many other things. To be effective, you cannot focus on just one thing. You need to find a healthy balance. The same is true with balancing your good works and sharing your faith.

As Christians, we have the privilege to shine our lights to others to help lead them out of their darkness and point them to their Savior. As we help our neighbors, are they aware that we are helping them because of Jesus' love for us on the cross? The same is true when we spread the Word: are our neighbors seeing our sacrificial giving because all belongs to God and nothing is ours?

We are called to shine our light in the darkness. By helping our neighbors, we can show them our love because Jesus first loved us. However, we must remember that our salvation comes not from good works, but from Christ's sacrifice. We must also remember to have a healthy balance between our good deeds and sharing God's Word with others. Therefore, let us help our neighbors while sharing the Word with them so that they may be brought from their darkness and into God's light through the work of the Holy Spirit.

PRAYER Lord, you are the Light of the world and only through you can I reflect your radiance. Help me be selfless with your mercy and grace so that I may tell others of your love, because you are love. Thank you for giving me your light so that I need not wallow in darkness anymore. Please be merciful and bring light to the world. Amen.

I AM GOD'S CREATION

Psalm 138:8 *The Lord will vindicate me; your love, Lord, endures forever—do not abandon the works of your hands.*

I am the work of God's hands. I am his creation and he cares for me richly. David writes beautifully and highlights all of God's grace through Psalm 138 as he describes how God cares for me: "When I called, you answered me; you greatly emboldened me . . . though I walk in the midst of trouble, you preserve my life . . . with your right hand you save me . . . the Lord will vindicate me."

Vindicate. Wow. I do not deserve that. I do not deserve to have the Son of God look into my heart, see my sinfulness, and vindicate me—to set me free from my chains and prove before his Father in heaven that I am a redeemed child, welcome to join him in heaven one day. Christ lived and died to restore my relationship with God (Romans 8).

Yet he has done this for me. He has done this for you. Be emboldened, as David writes, and live for the Lord as one who has been vindicated by him. Let the blessing of living a life preserved by God's mighty hand embolden you to do the work God has called you to do. Wrap the enduring love of God around you as the robe of righteousness you can wear into eternity.

We are the work of God's hands, and there is nothing that shines more brightly than his creation. That's you!

PRAYER Dear heavenly Father, light in this darkened world, thank you for creating me and saving me from my own sinful nature. Thank you for erasing the awful blemishes in my heart and preserving my life. Guide my footsteps and remind me through your Word that I am your child, clothed in your love and righteousness, awaiting my home in heaven. In Jesus' name, I pray. Amen.

JESUS IS OUR SUPERHERO

Psalm 18:28,29 *You, Lord, keep my lamp burning; my God turns my darkness into light. With your help I can advance against a troop; with my God I can scale a wall.*

A five-year-old wearing superhero pajamas races around the house, pretending to save his sister's doll. His mom urges him to change into the clothes set out on his bed. She doesn't notice as her son puts on his clothes over his superhero pajamas. The little boy gets to school, and during play time, takes off his outer layer of clothing. With a cape made out of his red jacket, he runs around the classroom, telling his classmates that he will save them. He is a superhero.

As children we fantasize about superheroes. I remember having arguments with friends over who was the best superhero. The idea of superhuman strength, speed, and size are certainly incredible to imagine. The majestic image of superheroes with their capes, bravery, and charm is heart-capturing. The mystery of their disguise and their true identity is intriguing.

We are in great need of a superhero. We often deceive ourselves when we try to fight our own battles, telling ourselves that we can handle them on our own. But the truth is that we need a superhero. We cannot get through one day without one. The world, our individual problems, guilt, shame, sadness, and sin are things we cannot face on our own.

Thank God that we have a Superhero in our lives. He doesn't not wear a cape or put on a disguise. He gives us his identity and shows us his immeasurable power. God's Word shows us the great deeds that our Savior has done. It is through him that we receive our strength. It is with God's love and mercy that we have no fear. The devil and all the evil in the world cannot touch us with God at our side.

PRAYER Thank you, God, for being my superhero. Amen.

January 24

OUR GUIDING LIGHT

Luke 1:78,79 *. . . because of the tender mercy of our God, by which the rising sun will come to us from heaven to shine on those living in darkness and in the shadow of death, to guide our feet into the path of peace.*

Imagine sitting outside, perhaps in a park, in the early afternoon on a sunny summer day. Then think about what that same place would be like only 12 hours later, in the middle of the night. In the midst of darkness, a once-pleasant setting becomes ominous and foreboding. When we cannot see our surroundings, a sense of uncertainty takes over our minds. Light is a comfort.

The sunrise is a beautiful natural phenomenon that is often taken for granted. Although almost 93 million miles away, the sun is big and bright enough to provide enough light to guide us through the day. Imagine if the sun did not rise one day. What would we do? We would feel lost.

Living without the light from the sun is like living without the light of God's Word. The Bible sheds light on our sins and wrongdoings and helps us see how helpless we are. It also shows us our Savior, Jesus Christ, who lived the perfect life that we could not. Through faith, our darkened world becomes filled with light to "guide our feet into the path of peace."

The next time you find yourself in the dark, remember that the sun will eventually rise and bring its light along. When you find yourself spiritually in the dark, find comfort in God's Word and the reassurance that God is our guiding light and will bring us out of the darkness.

PRAYER Dear Lord, thank you for the comfort that is found in your Word. When I feel lost and unable to find my way, help me remember to look to you for light. Please guide my feet into the path of peace. Amen.

NO FINE PRINT

Psalm 117:1,2 *Praise the LORD, all you nations; extol him, all you peoples. For great is his love toward us, and the faithfulness of the LORD endures forever. Praise the LORD.*

We've all been advised to read the fine print before signing a contract or making a large purchase. We wonder what trick might be hidden in a lengthy legal document before we sign it. We understand that not every salesperson has good intentions, and we are taught to be cautious of the dark that may hide in a disguise of light.

During the season of wish lists and gift giving, we were reminded of the great, enduring gift our heavenly Father has given us—himself. Now this psalm tells us that his love and faithfulness endure forever. They endure beyond the Christmas season, beyond the start of a new year, and into the beauty and trials of our everyday walk.

There is no fine print to the psalm we read here. There is no need to wonder at the intention of the writer of this document. Our Creator always has our best interests at heart, and when the Creator of all tells us "forever," he truly means forever.

His love and faithfulness have no end, not because of who we are, but because that is who he is. The shame, the guilt, and the doubt that we feel do not inhibit God's character. Rather, the joy, the peace, and the praise that we give can rise out of this truth. Regardless of who we are, our Father is characterized by a faithfulness and love beyond limit.

PRAYER Dear Lord, thank you for always having my best interests at heart and for never giving up on me. Amen.

WALK IN THE LIGHT

1 John 1:7 *If we walk in the light, as he is in the light, we have fellowship with one another, and the blood of Jesus, his Son, purifies us from all sin.*

It is so easy in life to simply go through the motions of being a Christian. It is even easier to say that you are a Christian and not even bother going through the motions. College is often a time that encourages such behavior because there is so much that is competing to get your attention. Clubs, jobs, projects, relationships, homework, sports, video games, Netflix, band, etc., are all there in your face all the time. It is important to remember that good works without faith are pointless but also that faith without good works is dead.

Christian faith produces good works. This is why Christians can be comforted by every good deed they do. Our good deeds comfort us because they show that our faith is alive and that the Holy Spirit is within us. Our good deeds are not the cause of our salvation. That was won for us through Christ's sacrifice on the cross. They are evidence of a living faith.

Live your faith during your college years. After all, what is more important—your project grade or your eternal salvation? Obviously, it's your salvation. We need to keep this in perspective during the busyness and chaos of college. Spend time in God's Word to nurture your faith and take comfort in your good deeds as a sign that your faith is alive.

PRAYER Dear Lord, thank you for sending your Son to die for all of my sins on the cross. Help me walk in the light with good deeds, which are a fruit of faith. Amen.

STOP WORRYING!

Psalm 46:10,11 *Be still, and know that I am God; I will be exalted among the nations, I will be exalted in the earth. The LORD Almighty is with us; the God of Jacob is our fortress.*

My mom is a worrier. If I had a dollar for every time I told her not to worry, I could probably afford another four years of college. Any time we have this discussion, I think about catechism class. My instructor told me, no matter what happens, God never gives us more trouble than we can handle. He always provides a way for us to get through trials.

When we worry, we make the mistake of trivializing God's power and promises. We do not trust him. God encourages us to quiet our doubts and remember that he is always working for our benefit regardless of what our sinful nature whispers to us. He has already taken care of our biggest problem when he sent Jesus to die for our sins. God does not place roadblocks in our way to complicate our lives, but to strengthen our relationship with him by reminding us that we need to rely on him.

Worrying is an easy trap to fall into and is all too common in our ever-busy lives. Remember that when the due dates are getting closer and projects are piling up, he has got us covered. My catechism instructor took that lesson further. He told us that, since God knows we can handle every trial he allows us to encounter, we should take this as a sort of compliment when we experience particularly difficult tests. Sometimes it may result in a low grade because we did not prepare enough. Sometimes we may be bloodied or broken. At the end of the day, we always get up . . . and every time God provides just the solution we need.

PRAYER Lord, help me remember to rely on you in all things. Forgive me when my trust falters, and strengthen my faith during times of struggle. Amen.

YOLO!

John 12:35,36 *Jesus told them, "You are going to have the light just a little while longer. Walk while you have the light, before darkness overtakes you. Whoever walks in the dark does not know where they are going. Believe in the light while you have the light, so that you may become children of light." When he had finished speaking, Jesus left and hid himself from them.*

You only live once (YOLO). *Carpe diem.* Live in the moment. The idea of taking advantage of every opportunity pervades our society, for good or bad. I'll very willingly admit that there have been times in my life where this mentality has served me well (i.e., forcing my non-morning-person self to watch the sun rise over the Andes mountain range on my last day in Chile). However, there have also been times when it's caused me to do some pretty stupid things (i.e., riding on the roof of an operating car).

I'd like to think that Jesus' words in John 12:35,36 are the New Testament equivalent of YOLO. In this passage, he's talking to his disciples about his impending death and the fact that he (the Light) will not always be physically with them in order to guide them through the sinful, dark confusion of life.

Our time of grace is short, people. As young adults, we've heard it millions of times, but somehow we still seem to operate under the impression that getting old or dying won't happen to us. We weren't called to take the easy route, though. Christ has given us a definite purpose to our lives— to witness for the sake of furthering his kingdom. Brothers and sisters in Christ, let's seize the day before it's too late!

PRAYER Dear Lord, help me live as a child of the light and take advantage of my time of grace to share your message of hope with the people in my life who need it most. In your name, I pray. Amen.

SHADE ME FROM HARM

Psalm 121:5,6 *The Lord watches over you—the Lord is your shade at your right hand; the sun will not harm you by day, nor the moon by night.*

While we see light as being powerful and revealing, it can also harm us and be unreliable. The sun burns us and sets. The moon is also not always reliable. This is why, in this verse, God's protection is described as "shade." His shelter protects us completely and is always reliable, whether we are in the sun or the shadows.

God does not need a flashlight or night vision goggles. He takes us under his wing and guides us through any darkness. Nothing that comes our way will harm us. Even when we are walking through sunlight and it seems that we can see in front of us, God is always by our side, ensuring we do not become too confident in our walk and step away from him.

It takes trust on our part. We are stepping where we cannot see the ground in front of us. We have to simply walk with God, knowing that every step we take will be well-guarded and directed by our Creator. His shade can be hard to see in our lives. We still fall down; we get sick; we sometimes even make the wrong decisions. It can seem as though God is far away and that we are alone. This is why trust is so important and so difficult. However, we can ask God for stronger faith and be confident in knowing that when our faith wavers, God is still watching over and guiding us.

PRAYER Heavenly Father, thank you for watching over me and shading me from harm with your mighty power. Help me trust that I do not need to see the path that you are leading me on but I only need to see your Holy Spirit working in my life. In Jesus' name, I pray. Amen.

LIGHT ATTRACTS

Revelation 21:23,24 *The city does not need the sun or the moon to shine on it, for the glory of God gives it light, and the Lamb is its lamp. The nations will walk by its light, and the kings of the earth will bring their splendor into it.*

Have you ever arrived at a new city in the middle of the night? Nothing looks familiar. Neighborhoods appear forbidding. You may feel scared as you travel toward your destination.

But the next morning, everything looks different in the light.

This reading does not picture an imperfect city on earth, but Jerusalem that is above. There is no night in heaven, because Jesus, the city's lamp, and God's glory give the city light.

Light directs. As long as we are in the darkness of sin, we cannot see God's grace. But in the light we can see all Jesus has done for us. "The god of this age has blinded the minds of unbelievers, so that they cannot see the light of the gospel that displays the glory of Christ. . . . For God, who said, 'Let light shine out of darkness,' made his light shine in our hearts to give us the light of the knowledge of God's glory displayed in the face of Christ" (2 Corinthians 4:4,6).

Light attracts. The nations—meaning the "Gentiles"—will walk by its light, and the kings of the earth will bring their splendor into it. What Revelation pictures has happened throughout history as people from all parts of the world have been attracted to the light of Jesus.

So now we live in the light, and Jesus calls us to shine into the darkness around us. This is something you can do right now. Lighthouses don't need to make a lot of noise; they just shine.

PRAYER Dear Lord, thank you for shining your light on me. Amen.

THE LORD IS MY SHEPHERD

Psalm 23:1,2 *The LORD is my shepherd, I lack nothing. He makes me lie down in green pastures, he leads me beside quiet waters.*

Next to John 3:16, Psalm 23 is probably one of the most quoted passages in the Bible. It's easy to read these familiar words and brush over them. Why are these words so beloved?

The LORD is my shepherd—this declaration means acknowledging that God has chosen to lead us and take care of us.

I lack nothing—a promise to cling to because we know our Shepherd. Because we follow the best Shepherd, we can rest in the fact that we will lack nothing.

He makes me lie down in green pastures—our Shepherd leads us to places that are perfect and for our good.

He leads me beside quiet waters—in our busy, hectic lives, the picture of "still waters" seems almost foreign to us. The meaning of this phrase is clarified further in the beginning part of verse 3: "He refreshes my soul."

Psalm 23 is an honest yet humbling prayer, as it means submitting ourselves to the Shepherd. However, the blessings that come with following this Shepherd—total provision, rest, and restoration—are exactly what we need.

PRAYER Dear Jesus, thank you for being my Good Shepherd. Help me remember to come to you for the rest and provision I so desperately need. In your name, I pray. Amen.

FEBRUARY
WHAT'S LOVE GOT TO DO WITH IT?

FORGIVE IN LOVE

Ephesians 4:32 *Be kind and compassionate to one another, forgiving each other, just as in Christ God forgave you.*

The idea of forgiveness is so amazing. What's love got to do with it? Everything.

Have you ever said the words *I forgive you* without sounding like you really forgive the person? Maybe your roommate hurt your feelings or your significant other lied to you.

Forgiveness seemed like something that would come later—after you were done being upset. God tells us, "Be kind and compassionate to one another, forgiving each other, just as in Christ God forgave you." Wait a second. We are supposed to forgive others just as God forgave us?! God forgave us with the most sincere kindness and compassion possible: he sent Christ to pay for the sins we commit against him. Wow! That is quite the high standard to meet. As sinners who often think of ourselves as number one, we are not so good at suddenly stopping anger in our hearts to forgive another person. The good news is that when Jesus died on the cross, the forgiveness he gave for our sins was complete. It cancels the debt we owe.

Why did he forgive us? This question can be answered in one word: *love*. "God so loved the world . . ." (John 3:16). We definitely do not deserve his forgiveness. In fact, we deserve the opposite: his wrath and punishment. Love for us led God to forgive us. Love for God leads us to forgive others.

PRAYER Dear Lord, when people say, "I am sorry," fill my heart with love so that I can forgive them just as in Christ you forgave me. Because I so often fail at that, thank you for your forgiveness that covers my sins and makes me white as snow. Amen.

TEAMWORK

Ecclesiastes 4:9 *Two are better than one, because they have a good return for their labor.*

When I was 17, my brother and I were driving to see a movie. All of a sudden our car sputtered and eventually came to a halt. We got out and tried to find out what was wrong with the car. Nothing appeared to be wrong, yet it wouldn't run. Then it hit me. I had forgotten to put gas in the car before we left, and we were out. So I pushed while he steered, but the car would not budge. By myself I was not strong enough to handle such a large task. Eventually he came out and helped. The two of us were stronger together and the car began to roll. I was so thankful for my brother's help that day. Without him I would have been stuck.

This story illustrates the power that two people have together. Whether the two people are friends, family, coworkers, or loved ones, two are always better than one. Our passage for the day, Ecclesiastes 4:9, demonstrates this idea perfectly. God has blessed us with people all around us. Working with them as a team yields good results. Relationships are a blessing from God, and we should cherish the ones that we have. Alone we have struggles. Together we have struggles too, but they are far easier to bear with someone working with you. We are always better with a teammate.

PRAYER Dear Lord, thank you so much for the blessing of relationships. Please let me cherish what you have given me and help my relationships grow in your grace. I love you, Jesus. Please help me show it. Amen.

BROTHERS AND SISTERS

Hebrews 2:11 *Both the one who makes people holy and those who are made holy are of the same family. So Jesus is not ashamed to call them brothers and sisters.*

Are you the senior or super-senior on campus? Or a freshman or someone in between? When I was a freshman, I decided that I would do my best to avoid the "upperclassmen." Well, that worked until I got to know my resident assistant. My fear of the old folk lasted about three days. She was amazing. She introduced me to her friends and even invited me to hang out. Who was I that she would ask me to hang out with her cool upperclassmen friends?

Maybe I'm exaggerating a little bit, but that is the type of feeling we have when we think of what Jesus did for us. His humility saved us from eternal death. He stooped way down. He made himself lesser than we could ever imagine and did it for us. The only way that we could be saved was if someone with our human nature could be perfect. Jesus did this. He became fully man, but he was still fully God, which was also necessary because God is the only way to perfection.

Just as my RA was not ashamed to introduce me to her friends, Christ tells us in his Word that he is not ashamed of us. We are the most undeserving creatures—we deserted God. But instead, he redeemed us and now calls us his brothers and sisters.

It's for this reason that we praise him and thank God for loving and caring for us so much that he would give his Son to be our brother through death on a cross.

PRAYER Christ, my brother, your humility and willingness to die on the cross has redeemed me. Please give me the courage to mirror your humility and to share God's Word with everyone so they may also become your brothers or sisters. Amen.

JESUS' FAMILY

Mark 3:33-35 *"Who are my mother and my brothers?" he asked. Then he looked at those seated in a circle around him and said, "Here are my mother and my brothers! Whoever does God's will is my brother and sister and mother."*

Recently I was asked to write out a family tree for a class. We identified parents, grandparents, aunts, uncles, etc. Then we were asked to share it in small groups. We learned that everyone's definition of family is different, and some of us have pretty complicated family trees. The individual experiences we have with our family impact our outlook on life and our other relationships.

Reread today's passage. There are a few points from these verses that stick out:

- Jesus said that whoever follows God's will is his family.

- If we follow God's will, we are members of that circle that surrounds him.

We need to be a family with other believers who are in the circle surrounding Jesus. That means spending time with other believers, getting to know them, and helping them grow as Christians. It also means witnessing to others so they can join Jesus' circle. If some of us have negative experiences with our earthly families, we might not understand how joining Jesus' family is different. Jesus died for us to bring us into his family. Believers must demonstrate his will and his love.

PRAYER Dear heavenly Father, thank you for the strength and support that come from being surrounded by people who are children of God—those who are redeemed, restored, and forgiven. Please help us witness to others so they will want to join your family of believers. Amen.

OWNED, BUT NOT ENSLAVED

1 Corinthians 6:19,20 *Do you not know that your bodies are temples of the Holy Spirit, who is in you, whom you have received from God? You are not your own; you were bought at a price. Therefore honor God with your bodies.*

In history classes, when slavery is covered, one cannot help thinking about how awful it must have been to be a slave—to be bought and sold as property. To be owned by another is not something that one hopes and dreams for. Or is it?

As Christians, we are owned by another. When Jesus died for all humankind, he paid the price for everyone. We are indeed owned by God, but we are not enslaved by him. He gave us our freedom, and we live our lives in thankfulness for this gift.

Even though Jesus gave us freedom, we still may use this freedom poorly. Some take this freedom to be sexually immoral by dishonoring our bodies as "temples of the Holy Spirit." Even though Jesus gave us our freedom, we can still be enslaved by sin. Having sex with anyone other than your husband or wife is throwing away the gift of freedom that Jesus bought for us.

History classes continue to remind people of the awful conditions of slavery. Although we may never desire to be owned by another human, we know how wonderful it is to be owned by God. God owns his children, but never enslaves them. One only becomes a slave to sin. Thankfully Jesus' gift of freedom from sin is constantly renewed through his ever-forgiving love that was displayed in the price he paid for you and me.

PRAYER Dear Lord, please help me honor you by honoring my temple. Thank you for paying the price to make me your own. Amen.

February 6

AN ATTITUDE ADJUSTMENT

Ephesians 4:3,4 *Make every effort to keep the unity of the Spirit through the bond of peace. There is one body and one Spirit, just as you were called to one hope when you were called.*

How do you get along with your roommate, your professors, your lab partner? Sometimes we are put into situations in which we have to deal with people whom we don't know or with whom we do not see eye to eye. Do we shut down? Do we wait for an opening so we can verbally attack when we believe we are wronged? Do we look for reasons to blame others for our failures?

These reactions are common, because we all are innately selfish. We want things done our way, and we will try to manipulate others. When things go wrong, we are eager to play the blame game.

We are eager to look all around us for excuses, but more often than not, we need to look at ourselves to keep the peace! We need encouragement to "make every effort to keep the unity" of our campus community. Things may not always go our way, but our first reaction needs to be one of understanding, patience, and reconciliation.

This attitude doesn't come from within; it comes from what has been done for us. Jesus is the "attitude adjusting agent" we all need and have been given. Through his love, he died for people who wronged, hated, and eventually killed him. However, we are called to love and serve others unconditionally, just as Jesus treated his enemies . . . and I would have to believe you have not met any hostility that severe! Peace isn't just a two-finger mantra; it is a way of life. Live it every day, showing kindness to all, because Jesus is our peace provider!

PRAYER Gracious God, thank you for being an example of how to love unconditionally. Amen.

LIVE IN UNITY

Psalm 133:1 *How good and pleasant it is when God's people live together in unity!*

The passage above sounds so pleasing, yet it can be one of the most difficult pieces of wisdom to live out. As human beings, we've found many ways to disagree with each other, from simple situations to the most complex circumstances. One of the reasons living in unity seems so difficult is because our decisions are biased and based on our personal perception of things.

Instead of life being wonderful and pleasant, we experience a lot of the terrible and ugly areas of life. Some might say we can't help what we disagree on. However, I firmly believe that if we stop looking at situations from our personal perspective and look at life through the lens of our Savior's eyes, things would be different. This does not mean that life would have no disagreements, but it does mean that unconditional love would overpower thoughts we may not have in common.

Christ understood that we all have flaws, but he did not treat us as our sins deserved. Instead, he loved us beyond our sin. He loved us beyond our disagreements. If we can begin to practice and live that out, it truly would be wonderful and pleasant if God's people could live together in unity.

PRAYER Dear Lord, please help me live out the good and pleasant life that will bring unity. You know the paths I walk and the gifts I need. Amen.

THE PRIVILEGE OF FORGIVENESS

Matthew 18:15-17 *If your brother or sister sins, go and point out their fault, just between the two of you. If they listen to you, you have won them over. But if they will not listen, take one or two others along, so that "every matter may be established by the testimony of two or three witnesses." If they still refuse to listen, tell it to the church; and if they refuse to listen even to the church, treat them as you would a pagan or a tax collector.*

It's time for some straight talk. Your friends are just like you: sinful, shameful, wretched beings.

That's a tough pill to swallow at times, especially when they are the source of some of your most important encouragements. However, if you spend more than a minute with any human being on this earth, you will find the same condition as you find yourself in. This gives the opportunity to practice the purest form of Christian love: forgiveness. You received it freely and completely. Your God-given privilege is to assure your friends of that same forgiveness. Easy, right? If that was all that we had to do, this devotion would end here, and you could be on your way—but there is one difficult and essential step before assuring forgiveness can take place.

The Greek word for *brother* here is *adelphos*. It doesn't mean a younger or less important person, but a peer. The order of these steps is also crucial to true repentance. Forgiveness is a personal bond between you and Christ. Shouldn't repentance begin in the same way?

The desired result is a clear conscience and, God willing, a repentant fellow disciple. What a blessing!

PRAYER Heavenly Father, you have blessed me with the fellowship and encouragement of friends for this life. Give me strength to approach my friends with a humble heart, with their eternal souls in mind. In forgiven peace, I pray in Jesus' name. Amen.

SACRIFICIAL LOVE

John 15:12-15 *My command is this: Love each other as I have loved you. Greater love has no one than this: to lay down one's life for one's friends. You are my friends if you do what I command. I no longer call you servants, because a servant does not know his master's business. Instead, I have called you friends, for everything that I learned from my Father I have made known to you.*

We are all familiar with the love passage in 1 Corinthians chapter 13: "Love is patient, love is kind. It does not envy, it does not boast, it is not proud." This is a great explanation of what love is and what it is not, but I think Jesus' talk of love is a little more jarring. "Greater love has no one than this: to lay down one's life for one's friends" (John 15:13). Jesus says the greatest kind of love is sacrificial love: a person willing to give his or life for the lives of friends.

Remember that scene at the end of the action movie, where the hero is willing to jump in front of a bullet/bus/train/ explosion to push someone else out of death's way? That's the love Jesus is talking about. We do not often think about doing that for our friends or family, but we really should. We are reminded of that kind of love every time we read or hear the gospel. We have our forgiveness of sins and our salvation because of that same sacrificial love. Jesus jumped in front of our punishment and willingly took it upon himself.

Jesus did not resent us for it. He actually calls us his friends. His sacrifice has released us from our slavery to sin and death.

PRAYER Jesus, you call me to do what you did for all of us: love one another. The only way I can possibly do this is with your help. I pray for that help today and always. Amen.

CARRY EACH OTHER'S BURDENS

Galatians 6:2 *Carry each other's burdens, and in this way you will fulfill the law of Christ.*

As a not-so-athletic person, I was often wary of going to the weight room on campus. Worried of being judged for my physical weakness, I rarely set foot in that intimidating space. I found that it was much easier to enter if accompanied by a friend. After all, even the strongest football players had to have a spotter when bench-pressing. It would be foolish for them to try to lift all of the weight by themselves. Even the most athletic people get muscle fatigue and their muscles fail.

The safety principles of the weight room can be carried over to the body of Christ. We should never trust solely in our own strength. Our best friend, Jesus, instructs us to put all of our worries and sins on his shoulders: "Cast all your anxiety on him because he cares for you" (1 Peter 5:7). We are not alone in our struggles and temptations. Not only do we have the almighty God behind us, but he has given us a network of believers on which we can rely for support. Find those fellow Christians who are willing to rebuke you and encourage you in combating your personal battles. In the same way, assist other believers in dealing with their spiritual weaknesses without judging. We are to "carry each other's burdens" because we are all children of God, seeking to honor him in our lives. Know that you are not Atlas, bearing the brunt of the entire world on your shoulders. God will give you a hand.

PRAYER "Bind us all as one together in your Church's sacred fold, weak and healthy, poor and wealthy, sad and joyful, young and old. Is there want or pain or sorrow? Make us all the burden share. Are there spirits crushed and broken? Teach us, Lord, to soothe their care." Amen. (CW 492:3)

February 11

NO MORE TEARS

Revelation 21:4 *He will wipe every tear from their eyes. There will be no more death or mourning or crying or pain, for the old order of things has passed away.*

How are you doing? I mean, *really* doing?

It's hard, keeping up with the relationships and responsibilities you already carry. There seems to be no end to it. And sometimes even then, life gets more complicated.

My classmate is in the hospital with leukemia. My best friend's parents are filing for divorce. My brother was in a motorcycle accident. My cousin had a miscarriage. My grandfather just passed away.

Have you been confronted by any of these? Part of you feels like giving up and not doing anything anymore. Part of you feels like you should be the one to suffer directly instead of your loved ones. Either you feel numb and devoid of feeling, or you hurt so intensely that you wonder if it will ever stop.

Someday, it will. Jesus promised that in today's passage.

Jesus empathizes with the pain you are feeling; he has experienced all of it and more. Yet our God is the activator of our relief. He is the one wiping our tears, not leaving our sufferings for someone else to handle. He does it himself.

Sin and regret have been taken away. Strained or severed relationships on this earth will be made new. Our pain is alleviated through him, and it will be gone forever on the Last Day. What a glorious day that will be! We have Christ's care and compassion right now, with the promise of the permanent peace to come.

PRAYER Jesus, thank you for taking on all my pain and that of this world. When I'm in my greatest suffering, remind me of your promises for my present and future. Amen.

February 12

YOU'VE GOT A FRIEND IN ME

1 Corinthians 13:1-3 *If I speak in the tongues of men or of angels, but do not have love, I am only a resounding gong or a clanging cymbal. If I have the gift of prophecy and can fathom all mysteries and all knowledge, and if I have a faith that can move mountains, but do not have love, I am nothing. If I give all I possess to the poor and give over my body to hardship that I may boast, but do not have love, I gain nothing.*

"You got troubles and I got 'em too. There isn't anything I wouldn't do for you. We stick together, we can see it through, 'cause you've got a friend in me." This song from *Toy Story* brings us back to our childhoods. The lyrics are simple, with the phrase "you've got a friend in me" repeating throughout. This song sets a perfect example of what a friendship should be like, but that is easier said than done. Betrayal, gossip, jealousy, and holding grudges hurt friendships. If we really think about it, how often are we good friends?

Our Scripture lesson points out a key ingredient to being a good friend. Without love we lack the proper motive for being a good friend. Our sinful hearts are motivated by "What's in it for me?" Christian love motivates us to ask, "what's in my friend's best interests?" After all, that's how our best friend Jesus always treats us. The ultimate proof is that he died on a cross in our place, to set us free from sin and to save us eternally—that was certainly in our best interests!

When we are hurt by others, we are commanded to still show love, just like Christ always does, even when he's not getting much in return from us. Whether it is your lifelong friend, family member, spouse, or a new acquaintance, leading with love will ensure that you can say with confidence, "You've got a friend in me."

PRAYER Dear Savior, please help me lead by love. Always keep me aware that you are being my best friend every day, and keep me looking to you as the ultimate example of a good friend. In your name, I pray. Amen.

GOD'S WISDOM

1 Corinthians 7:8,9 *To the unmarried and the widows I say: It is good for them to stay unmarried, as I do. But if they cannot control themselves, they should marry, for it is better to marry than to burn with passion.*

Do you think that Jesus wanted to marry "the girl next door"? He was fully human in every way, though without sin.

The Bible says that Jesus' focus was on *his bride,* the Church—he had come to save us! He could not be distracted from God's plan to save the world from sin. He had not come to marry; he had come to die.

Jesus' life choice is "heard" in Paul's words about the single man or woman and the desire to use God's gift of sexuality. As every male or female matures, we are curious and excited—passionate even—about how and when to use this gift. As God's children we ask, "Father, how do I honor you with this gift?"

Jesus' life gives us a hint. Paul's words are straightforward. "God first. God's plan. God's wisdom."

Paul's readers were being persecuted for their faith with a very real sense of Christ's second coming. They seemed to question if marriage should be in their plans. Paul's response? "A life devoted to God and gospel sharing is a good thing. Stay unmarried if you can (God first), but if you cannot control yourselves, then marry (God's plan)."

Is marriage, then, God's solution to one's desire to be sexually active? Yes. "It is better to marry than to burn with passion." God's wisdom.

Sex without marriage is sin, and the desire can be a burden. Marriage is designed to bless . . . if one is burning with passion!

PRAYER Jesus, help me embrace God's wisdom. Amen.

HONOR YOUR PARENTS

Ephesians 6:1-3 *Children, obey your parents in the Lord, for this is right. "Honor your father and mother"—which is the first commandment with a promise—"so that it may go well with you and that you may enjoy long life on the earth."*

At this point in your life, it might sound beneath you to hear someone tell you to obey your parents. I mean, you are legally an adult now, right? You can vote. You can get married. You can serve your country in the military. You can do all sorts of adult stuff. It's the time in your life when you transition from being told what to do to making your own decisions. But do not forget that no matter how old you are, no matter how independent you may be, you will always be the child of your father and mother.

Of course, things are different now. You no longer have your parents tucking you into bed. You no longer have your mom packing your lunch before school. You no longer have your dad teaching you how to properly grip a football. Instead, you now go to bed later than your parents do, you make your own lunches, and you have either mastered throwing a spiral or have given up hope.

Nevertheless, you are still your parents' child, and you are still called to obey them. Paul reminds you to honor your father and mother. Honoring your parents means to show them love and respect. Even though your responsibilities have increased and your independence has grown, God's command to honor your parents has not stopped. It will never stop. Take this command to heart and enjoy the blessings that flow from obeying your parents. It is never beneath anyone to obey what God commands.

PRAYER Dear Lord, I come before you as a child thankful for my parents. Renew in me an attitude that loves your commands. Teach me to always obey the words of wisdom and guidance from my parents. Amen.

February 15

LOVE YOUR NEIGHBOR

Galatians 5:14 *The entire law is fulfilled in keeping this one command: "Love your neighbor as yourself."*

Perhaps one of the most commonly quoted thoughts from the Bible by both Christians and non-Christians alike is from the last part of Galatians 5:14: "Love your neighbor as yourself." Perhaps this is a principle that your parents instilled in you from a young age, encouraging you to treat others as you would have them treat you. This passage instructs us to go beyond just treating people how we want to be treated, but commands us to love them. God doesn't just limit this to loving others when they are kind to us, or loving people when we like them, but to always loving them as we love ourselves.

Keeping this command is not always easy since many times we may not like someone because of something that person has done to us, but we can always look to Jesus as the ultimate example of how to fulfill this command. Even when the people of Jerusalem did not show love to Jesus, and even when the soldiers nailed him to a cross, Jesus did not hate them. He prayed for them while he was dying. Let us always remember Jesus and what he has done when we feel challenged to not love our neighbor as ourselves.

PRAYER Dear Lord, thank you for sending Jesus to be the ultimate example for loving my neighbor. Even when Jesus was not shown love by the people around him, he still loved them and prayed for them. When I am facing the challenge of not loving my neighbor, remind me of the example that Jesus set. Amen.

BE A PEACEMAKER

James 3:18 *Peacemakers who sow in peace raise a harvest of righteousness.*

Ever notice how the majority of what comedians talk about is making fun of other people? I know that's not the style of all comedians, and I know a good deal of it is reflections on the irony in the world around us. But I think it is safe to say that, just as in comedy, we teach it in most other areas: you get ahead in life at the expense of others.

James tells us the opposite. A harvest of righteousness, that is, a load of the good stuff, is the reward not to the violent or stingy or harsh, but rather to those who make peace. How can James say this and fly in the face of how the world actually works? Because the good stuff for James is not the good stuff of the world. The good stuff for James, and the good stuff every Christian wants, is a mind open to hearing about Jesus, Christians living in peace, and neighbors whose first reaction is gentleness with one another—not the sharp, violent tongue of someone trying to get ahead.

If that's the type of environment you want to live in, your goal is to reflect the godly rather than the worldly. Your goal is to reflect to others the perfect love Jesus showed on the cross when he made eternal peace possible for us through his sacrifice. You will "raise a harvest of righteousness"!

PRAYER Jesus, thank you for making peace between me and God through your death on the cross. Reflecting your love, inspire me to be a source of peace in this world. Amen.

PROTECT YOUR FAITH

2 Corinthians 6:14-16 *Do not be yoked together with unbelievers. For what do righteousness and wickedness have in common? Or what fellowship can light have with darkness? What harmony is there between Christ and Belial? Or what does a believer have in common with an unbeliever? What agreement is there between the temple of God and idols? For we are the temple of the living God. As God has said: "I will live with them and walk among them, and I will be their God, and they will be my people."*

When I went off to college, my mom said, "Well, if nothing else, I hope you'll meet a nice boy to marry." I rolled my eyes . . . I was going to college for a degree, not to get married! But if you're like me, you've discovered long ago that your mom is usually right—I'm now married to a nice boy I met in college.

College is often a time when you start dating more seriously, when you might start looking for a life partner. The passage for today talks about the importance of "yoking" yourself to people who share your faith, and this applies to a future spouse as well. It doesn't mean we shouldn't have unbelieving friends. How can you share your Christian witness with people if you never befriend them? But this passage is a warning not to be "yoked" to them, not to let their influence take you away from your God and your faith.

When it comes to getting married, this is especially important. The decisions you make as a couple, the way you raise your children, the choices you make throughout life will be much stronger if your spouse shares your faith and trust in God.

As you make friends on campus, as you meet a possible date . . . keep your faith at the forefront. It's the most important thing you have. Protect it.

PRAYER Dear Jesus, help me protect my faith as I share it with others. Amen.

February 18

ETERNAL SUCCESS

John 15:5 *I am the vine; you are the branches. If you remain in me and I in you, you will bear much fruit; apart from me you can do nothing.*

This Scripture verse will often be debated because it is saying that in order to be successful, one must have a strong relationship with God and a firm belief in Christ's work. An argument to that statement is that there are many successful people in this world who are not believers in God. It seems a strong relationship with him is not necessary.

However, in order to accurately understand this verse, we must define success as Scripture does. Success in this lifetime is temporary. To have a relationship with Jesus is to have success in the time spent on earth and in heaven. When times are getting rough and "earthly" successes are not coming, turn to and trust in Jesus. Know that you have success—a success that was prepared for you when Christ died on the cross. And if you are blessed in the form of several "earthly" successes, know that all blessings come from God and that without him you would never know the blessings of eternal life in heaven with him.

PRAYER Dear heavenly Father, let me not take your work for granted. Please help me maintain a strong relationship with you and to know you more. Thank you for giving me future success when I get to meet you in heaven. Amen.

BE BOLD IN DEATH

1 Thessalonians 4:13,14 *Brothers and sisters, we do not want you to be uninformed about those who sleep in death, so that you do not grieve like the rest of mankind, who have no hope. For we believe that Jesus died and rose again, and so we believe that God will bring with Jesus those who have fallen asleep in him.*

Let's be honest. At our age, it might be the furthest thing from our minds. Why think about it, when it is years down the road? Now let's be really honest. It's impossible not to think about. When we see it in the news, or even experience it firsthand with a good friend or family member, death is always in our rearview mirror, chasing us.

Whether he was being flogged in the courts or stoned in the city streets, Paul knew what it was like to face death. Shying away from it was not his style. Paul wanted his audience to be bold in death, because he knew the glory that was waiting for them in heaven.

Hope in Christ trumps fear in death. You see the correlation Paul makes with Jesus' death and a Christian's death? Because we believe in Jesus' death and resurrection, it is only natural to believe that in our death, we will rise with Jesus, because of the forgiveness he has won for us!

I don't want to be morbid here, but picture your non-Christian roommate or friend dying. It has to be one of the most heartbreaking thoughts in the world. Now picture that person dying with faith in the God who died and rose for us. Better, right? Now picture yourself sharing this good news and the Holy Spirit planting that seed of faith in your friend's heart. God gave us the job to proclaim his Word so that no one might grieve in death. Do it gladly.

PRAYER Dear Lord, help me be bold in death because I know the salvation that awaits me in Christ Jesus. Amen.

GOD IS LOVE

1 Corinthians 13:4-7 *Love is patient, love is kind. It does not envy, it does not boast, it is not proud. It does not dishonor others, it is not self-seeking, it is not easily angered, it keeps no record of wrongs. Love does not delight in evil but rejoices with the truth. It always protects, always trusts, always hopes, always perseveres.*

It's hard to write a devotion on love when you have not experienced it yet, at least in the *romantic* sense.

There seems to be an underlying expectation that you will find a significant other in college who will be the "one." This person will become your spouse, preferably engaged during your senior year, then married the summer following graduation. This will happen just in time for you both to start new jobs and a new life together in your new apartment with your combined mismatching dishes and new bed comforter.

I hate to disappoint you, but this is not how it ends up for most students.

The passage above is from 1 Corinthians 13, the "love chapter." These verses list the definition of love. As important and popular as these verses are, they are easy to overlook. But these verses made much greater impact on me when they were explained to me this way: God is love (1 John 4:8).

So, instead of using the word *love* as you read the passage, substitute *God* for *love*. God is patient, God is kind, etc.

When it comes to love, there may be pressure to be or do all the things listed above, but if we have God, then we have love. If we have faith, then we have those fruits of faith such as patience, kindness, and goodness. With faith in God, we are capable of loving the way God wants us to.

PRAYER God, help me know you better so that I can love better—love my significant other, classmates, roommates, family, and you. Amen.

A FATHER'S LOVE

Proverbs 1:8,9 *Listen, my son, to your father's instruction and do not forsake your mother's teaching. They will be garland to grace your head and a chain to adorn your neck.*

Mark Twain, a great American author, reportedly said, "When I was a boy of 14, my father was so ignorant I could hardly stand to have the old man around. But when I got to be 21, I was astonished at how much the old man had learned in seven years." I know that I personally can relate to this and today's passage. My parents are great examples to me, and everything they've taught me makes me a part of who I am.

God is also our Father. He gives us instruction just as our earthly fathers and mothers do. He may not sit us down at the dining room table or on the living room sofa, but he gave us a great book to turn to whenever we need advice or comfort. In the month of February, the word *love* is thrown around quite a bit. The world has its own ideas and versions of love. I'm sure your parents have told you their love story, and you remember bits and pieces of it.

God's book, the Bible—his words of wisdom and advice for us—shows us the greatest love story ever told. He sent his innocent and blameless Son to die on a cross for us. Due to his great love, we are never alone and will be with him forever in paradise. If you are single, dating, or in a committed relationship, he is always there. Just as your parents always love you, so does God.

PRAYER Heavenly Father, thank you for loving me enough to send me parents that instruct, and thank you for sending your Son to the cross. Help me show that same love to those around me. Amen.

THE MESSAGE OF CHRIST

Colossians 3:16,17 *Let the message of Christ dwell among you richly as you teach and admonish one another with all wisdom through psalms, hymns, and songs from the Spirit, singing to God with gratitude in your hearts. And whatever you do, whether in word or deed, do it all in the name of the Lord Jesus, giving thanks to God the Father through him.*

Even with the busy college lifestyle, there are many wonderful opportunities to start the lifelong habit of putting today's passage into practice. Around most college campuses, there are campus ministries that offer worship, perhaps chapel, prayer groups, vespers, fellowship, and many Bible study groups. What a great time in your life to cement the daily habit of reading your Bible, praying daily, and joining fellow college students in worship and spiritual growth. You have the chance to grow in faith every day by letting Christ's message dwell in you richly. Habits—both good and bad—are hard to break. That's why college is a great time to establish godly habits that will bless your life.

Establishing the habit of a rich spiritual life will fortify you for the spiritual battles you will face in your walk as a Christian. When you are eating lunch with friends and a reputation is being destroyed by gossip, you will be fortified to give a God-pleasing response. When you feel like skipping a class that you know you should attend, you will find the strength to choose wisely. When Christ's message dwells richly in you, you are better equipped to choose a career prayerfully. You will look for the right qualities in dating relationships. You will spend money differently. You will be ready to make God-pleasing decisions in all areas of your life. College is a great time to let Christ's message dwell in you. Take advantage of the many opportunities available, or create some new ones. Then you will receive a truly well-rounded education.

PRAYER Dear Lord, help me always put you first in my life. Guide my decisions and ambitions. Amen.

BE AWARE OF BAD INFLUENCES

1 Corinthians 15:33 *Do not be misled: "Bad company corrupts good character."*

A friend invites you to a pro football game with some former classmates. Football fan or not, you're ready for a good time.

Things go well until halftime. Your companions get a little rowdy. Some of the guys and girls can't keep their hands off each other. One person tries to push a beer into your hand. Then two avid fans start yelling and swearing at the refs.

What do you do? Is there harm in ignoring the person who starts acting suggestively toward you? Is there harm in taking the beer, whether you drink it or not? Is there harm in criticizing the referee if you aren't swearing?

You aren't alone in these challenges. The Corinthian Christians struggled with the pagan lifestyles surrounding them. In love and concern, Paul admonished them in today's verse. Notice that he doesn't tell them to stop associating with unbelievers altogether. He is reminding them to be aware of bad influences.

We all crave acceptance. But there's a difference between *needing* acceptance and *wanting* acceptance. The acceptance we *need* is given to us by faith in Christ. The acceptance we *want* is the acceptance of our peers. Sometimes we get what we want; sometimes we don't. But we always have what we need, in Christ.

At times we risk mimicking bad behaviors and compromising our integrity. Stay rooted in God's Word, secure in God's acceptance of you, and continue being a Christian witness. When you find your endurance slipping as you face temptation, have an exit strategy. Remember, there's no shame in leaving the football game early.

PRAYER Help me be discerning of the company I keep. Amen.

THE BLESSING OF FRIENDSHIP

1 Samuel 18:1-3 *After David had finished talking with Saul, Jonathan became one in spirit with David, and he loved him as himself. From that day Saul kept David with him and did not let him return home to his family. And Jonathan made a covenant with David because he loved him as himself.*

Believe it or not, sometimes college can seem lonely. Homework can keep you from spending time with others, and you might be far away from your family. It's easy to forget about the wonderful blessing of friendship that God gives us to ensure that we are never lonely. Read today's words again.

Jonathan's brotherly love toward David was so strong that he warned David about Saul's plans to kill him so that David would have time to escape. You may not think you will ever have to save a friend's life, but your actions can easily impact your friend's future. Being a trustworthy friend helps those who are suffering silently. You might be the first person a friend with an addiction turns to for help, even before that friend tells family members. You could also end up being the only one in a room of people willing to speak out against the drinking and driving that could potentially happen that evening.

But more often, there will be less extreme situations to show your love toward a friend. Some of the happiest people you know may not even have a stable family to visit during spring break. God surrounds us with friends to make rough days much more manageable, and we have several opportunities to serve him by being a friend to others.

PRAYER Thank you for my lifelong friends who are helping me survive the challenges of college life. Amen.

February 25

CHOOSE WISELY

Proverbs 13:20 *Walk with the wise and become wise, for a companion of fools suffers harm.*

You have probably heard the saying that goes something like this: "You are the sum total of the five people you spend the most time with." It is almost a modern version of Proverbs 13:20. You will become like the people you hang out with, for better or worse.

I have seen this so clearly in my own life. My friend group in the years since college has changed a lot from the friends I spent time with in college. When I realized I was not being true to myself and my God, I intentionally sought friends who would build me up in my faith and allowed some of the unhealthy relationships to fade into the past. What a difference it has made!

Now that you are an adult, you get to choose your friends on your own—no parental opinions involved. Remember that there are consequences to those choices. Do you want friends who will cause you to compromise your values or friends who will strengthen your values? Do you want friends who will make you timid about bringing faith into a conversation or friends who challenge your faith and its presence in your life? Do you want friends who will make it easy for you to stray from God or friends who would not allow you to stray?

God will gift you with great blessings through good friends. Choose wisely and enjoy those blessings.

PRAYER Lord, you've placed potential friends all around me during these college years. Please guide me in choosing friends who will strengthen me in my faith and encourage me to make choices that reflect my values. Help me take advantage of the opportunity to surround myself with friends who will make me wise in your ways. Amen.

FORGIVE ONE ANOTHER

Colossians 3:12-14 *As God's chosen people, holy and dearly loved, clothe yourselves with compassion, kindness, humility, gentleness and patience. Bear with each other and forgive one another if any of you has a grievance against someone. Forgive as the Lord forgave you. And over all these virtues put on love, which binds them all together in perfect unity.*

Forgiveness is something that I've always had trouble with. When people have wronged me in the past, I found myself constantly angry or irritated with them. It could be over something as silly as them being conceited or arrogant toward me, and I found that I was unable to be kind to them or to carry on a decent conversation with them. I know it's a fault of mine, and it's something that I'm always praying about as I ask for forgiveness and strength to put my selfish ways aside.

Sometimes as I ask for forgiveness, I find myself thinking, "If I can't forgive someone for something so little that they did to me, then why would Jesus ever want to forgive me?" But Jesus not only forgives us, he died to save us. If he can forgive us for every single sin that we have ever committed, then why can't I forgive those who have done so little to me? Who am I to take forgiveness from Jesus when I myself cannot forgive?

We are all sinful. Jesus wants us to forgive the way that he forgave us. This means we do not just have to forgive once, but over and over again no matter what. God has showered his grace upon all people.

PRAYER Dear Lord, you always forgive me for my sins even though I do not and never will deserve it. Please give me the strength to forgive those around me. I know that I am no better than anyone else, but you still forgive me when I do wrong. Thank you. Amen.

THE IMPORTANCE OF GOOD FRIENDS

Proverbs 12:26 *The righteous choose their friends carefully, but the way of the wicked leads them astray.*

I walked down the line, peering carefully into each sweet face, wondering who had a chewy secret to hide.

Tears started to well up in Aniyah's eyes. *Nope,* I thought, *it's not her. True remorse.* However, Grace's eyes had not met mine since I asked all the Bubble Gum Babes out into the hall for the interrogation.

The kindergarten room is a friendly place, but take a piece of gum from a friend, chew it with a guilt-ridden conscience, and get caught by a teacher? It's every gal for herself.

After a speech about honest kids being the bravest kids, I asked each student if she was chewing gum and who gave it to her. These righteous little lambs, the greatest in God's kingdom, lived up to their title that afternoon. They turned their dear friend in and apologized: tearstained faces, white-knuckled hands, sniffly hiccups, and all.

Being assured that they were forgiven and that God no longer sees our sins due to Christ, each little girl walked back knowing that she had chosen the right path.

We can all chew on a stick of these five-year-olds' wisdom. I can recall more than one time when I have been led astray by poor choices in regard to friendship . . . most of the time due to my own sinful selfishness.

They seem so simple, yet the lessons we learn in kindergarten and in Proverbs seem only to be harder to follow as we get older. Choose good friends, lest your big, sticky bubble pops, and you're left with a mess to clean up.

PRAYER Lord, forgive me when I have gone astray, and thank you for bringing me back each time. Amen.

OUR HERO

1 John 3:16 *This is how we know what love is: Jesus Christ laid down his life for us. And we ought to lay down our lives for our brothers.*

Heroes. Their stories fill our lives. Batman. Frodo Baggins. Veterans. They all fight for something greater than they are, and we honor them for it.

I often daydream about what I would do in crisis situations (I probably do this way too often). How would I handle myself? Would I jump in front of a bullet for the woman sitting near me at the movie theater? I daydream that I heroically save the day, but the reality is that none of us knows how we will react until we are in that situation.

Jesus, our mightiest hero, laid down his life for us. We did not deserve his love, and yet he gave the ultimate sacrifice. We are saved from unending sorrow and pain—an awesome example of how to love those around us. His sacrifice is the motivating fire that inspires us in all we do.

And so I encourage you, brothers and sisters, to share the love and help those in need. The ways one can contribute to this endeavor are many and vary greatly. However, if a Christian is unwilling to aid others, it might be time to get a checkup on his or her spiritual health.

Don't just daydream about being a hero. Be a hero.

PRAYER Dear Lord, thank you for my hero, Jesus, who died on a cross so that I could live. I ask you to be with me and give me the strength to be a hero and love those around me. Amen.

MARCH
CROSS TALK
FOR THE WALK

OUR GOOD SHEPHERD

Isaiah 53:6 *We all, like sheep, have gone astray, each of us has turned to our own way; and the LORD has laid on him the iniquity of us all.*

The image of Jesus as the Good Shepherd is perhaps the most well-known depiction of Christ, and for good reason. Descriptions of Christ as a shepherd abound in the gospels, and this illustration is an extension of the image painted by Isaiah. In this image, we are sheep who think that we know what's best. We seek our own path, not aware that leaving our shepherd exposes us to great danger. When Jesus compared himself to a shepherd, he observed that the shepherd, who truly cares for his sheep, is willing to lay down his life to protect them. This is precisely the kind of description presented in Isaiah. We, like sheep, foolishly choose to chase after the desires of our heart. We seek sinful pleasure and selfish goals, to put others down and to forsake God's grace. It is for these sins that Christ died in our place. As our Shepherd, he paid the ultimate price to protect his sheep from eternal death.

Let's stay close to our Good Shepherd by regular worship. He is our true protection from Satan and the evils of the world. He is the one who leads us, as the psalmist writes, beside quiet waters, along the right paths, and even through the darkest valley of death. Our Good Shepherd's guidance is a comfort for us even amid our greatest fears. In this knowledge we may have peace as we follow our Shepherd.

PRAYER Dear Lord, you are the Good Shepherd. You alone lead me on the path to heaven, and you alone laid down your life to bring me safely there. Forgive me for times when I stray, and help me follow your guidance. In your name, I pray. Amen.

KING JESUS

Zechariah 9:9 *Rejoice greatly, Daughter Zion! Shout, Daughter Jerusalem! See, your king comes to you, righteous and victorious, lowly and riding on a donkey, on a colt, the foal of a donkey.*

If there is one event in biblical history that I wish I could have seen, it would be Palm Sunday. As a child, I always loved holding my palm branch high in church while we sang about laying our cloaks in front of the foal that Jesus was riding. It wasn't until much later in my life that I realized how amazing this event truly was. This event was foretold for years, and here it was coming to fruition. Today's verse—as well as many other prophecies—was used to validate that Jesus was in fact the "king" about whom they had been told. It was a way to "cross-check" and be sure that it was indeed the Son of God who was on his way into Jerusalem.

Sometimes we have doubts about things in this life and even our faith. What if God doubted us? We certainly have all done more wrong in our lifetime than Jesus did in his perfect life. If Jesus turned the tables and yelled, "Crucify them!" to us, there would certainly be justifiable reason to do so.

But God does not doubt us. There is never a second where he feels anything but love for us. It is important for us to remember this when we may doubt the genuineness of Jesus being our Savior-King. Put yourself in the place of those people on Palm Sunday and "rejoice greatly, Daughter Zion!"

PRAYER Lord, help me look past my doubt and hail you as King. Amen.

VICTORIOUS KING

Matthew 21:8,9 *A very large crowd spread their cloaks on the road, while others cut branches from the trees and spread them on the road. The crowds that went ahead of him and those that followed shouted, "Hosanna to the Son of David!" "Blessed is he who comes in the name of the Lord!" "Hosanna in the highest heaven!"*

A child doesn't like being separated from his parents. When they go out, he may lose sight of them and panic seizes his heart. The relief of safety and comfort seems far off until he is reunited with his parents again. The emotion can be like that of the infantry in battle, giving up all hope, but then the artillery arrives unexpectedly and saves the dwindling corps.

Life can hit us hard. We don't achieve the goals we set for ourselves. We feel enslaved to temptation and guilt. We are unexpectedly disappointed time and again by our closest friends and family. What relief is there in sight? Will we break free from this exhausting cycle? Will we be saved from misery and death?

In Christ, the answer is yes. God searched through the crowd for you, his lost child. On Palm Sunday, our Jesus strode into the heart of the battle. Christ's eyewitnesses praised God for sending in the cavalry. God came in the flesh to destroy the enemy: our sin, death, and the power of the devil. The misery that advances on every side cannot outdo the might of Christ our King, who has given us comfort and relief in victory.

PRAYER Lord God, I praise you on Palm Sunday as my King, my Savior, and my protector. Keep me in your care always, that I may serve you as your kingdom comes. Amen.

THROUGH THE LITTLE THINGS

Luke 19:39,40 *Some of the Pharisees in the crowd said to Jesus, "Teacher, rebuke your disciples!" "I tell you," he replied, "if they keep quiet, the stones will cry out."*

We've all been there—you sit down at a restaurant and receive your food. Should you pray out loud? Not everyone around you is Christian. Many opt to pray silently. There's no right or wrong, but the motive behind why you would not want to pray could be wrong. Are you praying *so that* others see you, to show how "good" you are? Or are you ashamed of your faith? afraid to show people what you believe in?

When Jesus arrived in Jerusalem riding on a donkey, his believers did not feel ashamed of him. They praised his name, because they knew who he was. But there were others in Jerusalem who had rejected him already. Where do we stand?

Through the little things, we can witness our faith. Through these little things, we can make an impact on other peoples' lives. Do not be ashamed to proclaim Jesus' name. "If they keep quiet, the stones will cry out." The name of the Lord still will be proclaimed throughout the earth.

As the rain and the snow come down from heaven, and do not return to it without watering the earth and making it bud and flourish, so that it yields seed for the sower and bread for the eater, so is my word that goes out from my mouth: It will not return to me empty, but will accomplish what I desire and achieve the purpose for which I sent it. (Isaiah 55:10,11)

PRAYER Dear Lord, please help me not to be ashamed of you. Thank you for dying on the cross for my sins, including my sins of omission. Help me proclaim your name until my time of grace is done. Amen.

THE ANOINTED ONE

Matthew 26:7 *A woman came to him with an alabaster jar of very expensive perfume, which she poured on his head as he was reclining at the table.*

A relaxing footbath can be the perfect stress reliever for many people. Even if you have never experienced one, nearly all will agree that the clean and fresh feeling after a shower is a great way to start the morning. It gets you looking and smelling good for the day ahead. In this devotion's passage, a woman prepares Jesus for his "day" on his journey to the cross.

Other accounts of this occurrence are mentioned in the gospels of Matthew and Mark, but John also notes that the woman poured it on Jesus' feet as well. The oil chosen for this moment in Christ's ministry on earth was rare and difficult to obtain. Anointing someone's head with oil was a custom during the time of Jesus, but pouring oil on his feet signifies deep humility and attachment to the Savior. The woman simultaneously honored her Lord as well as prepared his body for the upcoming events of Holy Week. Her act also demonstrated how Jesus is the Lord's Anointed One, chosen specially to save all people from their sins. The next time you take a shower or enjoy a footbath, remember this important point in Christ's journey to the cross for you and mirror the great faith this woman had in her Savior.

PRAYER Dear Jesus, grant that I am always refreshed by your Word. Anoint me with the Holy Spirit, as the woman anointed you for your walk to the cross. Keep me strong in my faith in you, my Savior, because you sacrificed yourself for me. In your holy name, I pray. Amen.

WHAT DO YOU VALUE?

Matthew 26:10-12 *Jesus said to them, "Why are you bothering this woman? She has done a beautiful thing to me. The poor you will always have with you, but you will not always have me. When she poured this perfume on my body, she did it to prepare me for burial."*

Think of something valuable that you own. Not necessarily for sentimental reasons, but because it has high monetary value: perhaps your car, an autographed jersey, a jewelry collection, or even the money in your bank account. How hard would it be to part with it? Not many people would be able to freely give away something of high value.

The woman poured an expensive jar of perfume on Jesus' feet. The disciples were astonished and upset that she "wasted" something so pricey, when it could have been sold and the money given to the poor. While their idea had good intentions, Jesus reminded them of the earthly concepts of rich and poor. Jesus was not always going to be with them, so the woman was taking advantage of the time she had with him. By her actions, she showed him more love and respect than if she had simply sold the perfume.

We enjoy things that we consider valuable. There is a sense of comfort in being financially stable. However, Jesus reminds us that money is only earthly. It is around during our time on earth, but once we die and enter eternity, it will have no relevance. Rather than focusing on and worrying about monetary things, a well-lived life focuses on the truth of God's Word, which prepares us for eternal life.

PRAYER Lord, thank you for all the earthly blessings you have given me. Help me remember what truly matters in life and focus on spiritual matters above earthly ones. Remind me to look to you in times of good and bad and to look forward to the day when you will return. Amen.

BLAMELESS

Mark 14:18,19 *While they were reclining at the table eating, he said, "Truly I tell you, one of you will betray me—one who is eating with me." They were saddened, and one by one they said to him, "Surely you don't mean me?"*

Judas betrayed Jesus for 30 pieces of silver. It seems unfathomable that someone could do this to their friend, much less the Son of God. Jesus even warned his disciples about it. Jesus was giving him another chance to repent, and yet Judas still led Jesus to his death.

It can be easy to blame people. It's so easy to forget our own sins and bad choices. We say, "Surely I have not done anything as bad as Judas, Lord." We're able to forget that God demands *perfection*. He doesn't ask us to be pretty good. We forget that it was every single one of our sins that led Jesus to be whipped, beaten, mocked, and nailed to a cross.

Jesus warns us about our sins too. He tells us to surround ourselves with friends who will guide us on his path and tell us when we are straying. Sometimes we need those reminders. If we start to think that we can do no wrong, it's a short hop away from wondering why we need a Savior in the first place.

It's certainly easy to blame others. It would be just as easy for Jesus to blame us for his suffering and death. Instead, he loves us, protects us from harm, and sees us as holy and blameless. Jesus lived and died for the forgiveness of our sins. We are blameless only through his sacrifice.

PRAYER Lord, as I view your walk to the cross, let me be repentant for my sins but also open my heart and mind to realize that I put you on that cross. Remind me of your grace and compassion, and thank you for overcoming the death that I could not overcome. Amen.

March 8

A LOVING WARNING

Mark 14:21 *The Son of Man will go just as it is written about him. But woe to that man who betrays the Son of Man! It would be better for him if he had not been born.*

When I was a kid, I was mesmerized by the warning labels on the side of electric control boxes. I couldn't help but stare at the picture of the stick man with his stick hand in the wrong place. I would wonder, *What would I look like if I stuck my hand in there? Would I also have a jagged red aura around me?*

One thing I never thought was this: *How dare you, box! That is a horrible thing for you to picture! Do you want me to be electrocuted to death!?*

This passage from the Last Supper is kind of like that. I can't look away. Really, Jesus? How can you talk that way? Don't you know Judas is going to end his own life out of despair?

But these words of Jesus are not a wish; they are a warning. Jesus told his disciples that God's plan of salvation was through Jesus' suffering, no matter what, "just as it is written about him." He was going to die to save everyone—his disciples, Judas, you, and me.

That was inevitable—Jesus would allow himself to be betrayed to save us all.

Do you hear his loving warning? "Judas, it does not have to be you. Please, don't go down the path you are going. It leads only to death. Let me save you too."

Jesus gives us loving warnings in his Word. Listen to him, and rejoice that he saves you, just as it is written.

PRAYER Dear Jesus, thank you for your love and your warnings. Amen.

A MEAL TO REMEMBER

Mark 14:22 *While they were eating, Jesus took bread, and when he had given thanks, he broke it and gave it to his disciples, saying, "Take it; this is my body."*

As we continue our Lenten journey to Calvary, Christ and his disciples are in the upper room for the Last Supper. Here, Jesus institutes the Lord's Supper, something that is still celebrated today in churches across the world.

The time is coming for Jesus to bear his cross, our cross. But before he goes, he gives his disciples a final meal to remember. Certainly they never knew that two thousand years later, Christians would still come to the table and receive the body and blood of Christ—the same blood he was about to shed for you, for me, for all people. The same body nailed to the cross for the forgiveness of all our sins.

As we continue through the season of Lent, remember the true meaning of the bread and wine in Lord's Supper. It is the real body and blood of Christ, under the bread and wine, given for you on the cross, to forgive you and draw you closer to God, so that you may join in the heavenly banquet on the Last Day.

PRAYER Dear Lord, thank you for sending Jesus to this earth to suffer and die for my sins. Help me bear my cross daily with joy and come to your table willingly in repentance to be forgiven. Amen.

JESUS' BLOOD FREES US

Mark 14:23-25 *Then he took a cup, and when he had given thanks, he gave it to them, and they all drank from it. "This is my blood of the covenant, which is poured out for many," he said to them. "Truly I tell you, I will not drink again from the fruit of the vine until that day when I drink it new in the kingdom of God."*

In January of 2015, an old couple was struck by an SUV and killed while walking home from attending the church where they were lifelong members in Caledonia, MN. This sad story portrays how bad things can happen in even the most innocent situations. You don't have to look too far to see distress in this world in the form of wars, hunger, poverty, abuse, or natural disasters. No matter how hard we try to build a stable society, these problems will always occur. Human nature makes people question why bad things happen to good people, but Jesus' work on earth gives us peace that we can never achieve on our own.

In Mark 14 Jesus refers to the blood he would shed in the near future to save all of humankind from eternal damnation. The words "blood" and "poured out for many" affirm the promise of salvation made to all believers. Whenever trials occur in life, remember that "the kingdom of God" is ours, and it lasts forever. Earthly suffering is only temporary and is our reminder to spread the good news to every nation.

PRAYER O Lord, help me remember that you are in control in every situation. Your blood frees me from eternal punishment, defying my legal destiny as a sinner. Use every hardship as a reminder to prioritize my life according to your will. Amen.

TURN TO GOD IN PRAYER

Luke 22:41-43 *He withdrew about a stone's throw beyond them, knelt down and prayed, "Father, if you are willing, take this cup from me; yet not my will, but yours be done." An angel from heaven appeared to him and strengthened him.*

Finals week. It's not here yet, but it's coming—the week when it seems there is just too much to handle. Not only will you have six cumulative exams and two papers due in a matter of four days, but for the entire semester you know you will have to go through it. Someone else can relate to something similar.

Jesus lived his whole life knowing that he would have to take on the whole world's sin while being tortured and crucified. It's possible he felt like it was too much to handle. Jesus gives us a solution to what we should do when our plates are full and overflowing. At the Mount of Olives, Jesus prayed, "Father, if you are willing, take this cup from me; yet not my will, but yours be done." Jesus was not afraid to turn to God in prayer when he felt weak. We see our Savior in a position we have been in ourselves, wishing there were a way to not suffer. Unlike the times where we have just turned to despair, though, Jesus turns to God. God answers in his own way. We know how the rest of that night and the next day went; God's will was done. But Jesus was not ignored. "An angel from heaven appeared to him and strengthened him." Jesus' prayer was answered.

Whether it's finals week or a different form of suffering that we face, Jesus shows us what we need to do. We are to pray. We pray to the God who will listen and give us what we need.

PRAYER Dear Lord, help me remember to always pray to you when I feel weak. Your will be done. Amen.

COME TO THE CROSS

Luke 22:47,48 *While he was still speaking a crowd came up, and the man who was called Judas, one of the Twelve, was leading them. He approached Jesus to kiss him, but Jesus asked him, "Judas, are you betraying the Son of Man with a kiss?"*

It's hard to believe that the instigator of Jesus' arrest was from among his most trusted inner circle. Judas, one of the 12 disciples, had long been secretly planning this moment. I wonder what inner torture Judas must have experienced while trying to hide such a conspiracy from the Son of God. Little did he know that Jesus knew the plan all along. After all, he is God! When Judas kisses Jesus, Jesus does not ask why he is betraying him, but rather, why he is doing it with a kiss. A kiss would be a familiar, friendly greeting—certainly not something one would expect from someone who is going to betray you!

Judas' betrayal reminds me of what I try to do when I come to the cross. I often try to hide my sins behind nice words of praise or thankfulness. What really needs to be brought to the cross is my sin. Let us not be like Judas and try to hide our sins behind false fronts. Jesus knows our hearts and went to the cross so that we are fully forgiven. A repentant heart comes to Jesus in humility and honesty.

PRAYER Jesus, please help me come to you with complete honesty and humility. Thank you for the forgiveness and freedom that is found in coming to the cross. Amen.

BOLDLY PRAY FOR STRENGTH

John 18:4,5 *Jesus, knowing all that was going to happen to him, went out and asked them, "Who is it you want?" "Jesus of Nazareth," they replied. "I am he," Jesus said. (And Judas the traitor was standing there with them.)*

Imagine waking up knowing exactly how your day was going to go—and it was bad. First, one of your best friends posts on Facebook some of your opinions of others you told her in private. Taken out of context, they sound pretty horrible and spiteful. Second, while driving, you are pulled over. You were not doing anything wrong, but the police officer finds drugs, which are not yours, and arrests you. Finally, you contact your boyfriend to bail you out, but he claims he does not know you. Talk about getting up on the wrong side of the bed!

If you knew all this was going to happen, I doubt you *would* get out of bed. Betrayed by a friend, wrongfully accused, and disowned by someone you love—sounds like what happened to Jesus. He knew the terrible chain of events of his passion, yet he willingly gave himself up. Jesus carried out God's will and trusted this was for the best. Which it was—as believers, we now have forgiveness and the gift of salvation! Even though we do not know the exact difficulties in our lives, we do know we will have them. Therefore, it is important to keep in mind Jesus' courage as we face struggles. Many people pray to be kept from troubles and hardships. And this is alright! Even Jesus asked God if he could be spared from his horrific suffering and death. But how much more could we demonstrate our trust in God if instead we prayed for strength to face our problems and overcome them?

PRAYER Dear God, as I face troubles, please give me the boldness not to avoid hardships but to overcome them with your help. Talk to you soon! Amen.

March 14

THE BIGGER PICTURE

Luke 22:50,51 *One of them struck the servant of the high priest, cutting off his right ear. But Jesus answered, "No more of this!" And he touched the man's ear and healed him.*

Have you ever jumped the gun or gotten ahead of yourself? It's easy to worry and get frustrated when we don't know exactly what is coming next. This can cause us to lose sight of the bigger picture and respond poorly. In this passage we can easily relate to the disciple of Jesus. We often act before we should and without considering what our actions really mean. Just as Jesus' disciple had no real grasp of what his actions meant, we can find ourselves in similar situations, whether at work, in class, or with our family and friends.

Thankfully, God knows what happens next. God has a plan, and he never jumps the gun or gets ahead of himself. His plan for our lives is complete, and he always keeps the bigger picture in mind. Jesus had that bigger picture in mind when he scolded his disciple and healed the man's ear. Jesus was not there to lead a rebellion; he was there to make his way to the cross to die for our sins. God's plan is the most perfect plan. Jesus' walk to the cross means that we don't have to walk to our own cross. We don't have to suffer for our sins because Jesus has already paid that price for us.

PRAYER Dear God, thank you for sending Jesus to pay the ultimate price for me. Thank you also for reminding me that your plan is more important than my own. Keep me patient and steadfast as I face the uncertainties in life. In Jesus' name, I pray. Amen.

March 15

OVERCOMING AWKWARDNESS

Luke 22:61,62 *The Lord turned and looked straight at Peter. Then Peter remembered the word the Lord had spoken to him: "Before the rooster crows today, you will disown me three times." And he went outside and wept bitterly.*

When was the last time you felt awkward? Perhaps it was after giving a speech or after spilling food on yourself. Or maybe you said something weird or embarrassing on a date. No matter who you are, you are always going to run into some awkward situations in life. Here is a question to ponder: is being a Christian awkward?

During Holy Week, Jesus was wanted dead by several powerful figures in Jerusalem. Peter was afraid of even being associated with Jesus. This put Peter in more than just an awkward situation; Peter feared for his life. Peter let his fear take over and denied that he knew Jesus three times.

How many times have we been in situations where denying Jesus is the easy or safe thing to do? It likely was not a life-threatening situation, but a situation in which being a Christian was uncool or not the popular way of thinking. How do we resist giving in to what is easy and pursue doing what is right?

Jesus tells us that it will not always be easy being a Christian in this world. We may even face hate or scorn for our convictions. However, we know that everything we do serves a higher, heavenly purpose. We are not on this earth to serve people but to serve and glorify God for his great gift of salvation to us. Our God is greater than any awkward situation this world throws our way.

PRAYER Lord, thank you for sending your Son to wipe away the sins of all. Help me overcome feelings of awkwardness and instead testify my faith to the world in all that I do. Amen.

GROWTH IN THE KINGDOM

John 18:36 *Jesus said, "My kingdom is not of this world. If it were, my servants would fight to prevent my arrest by the Jewish leaders. But now my kingdom is from another place."*

What are the most meaningful experiences you have had? What memorable vacation can you recall?

When I reflect on my 28 years of life, I realize God has allowed me to take some wonderful vacations with family and friends. He has allowed me to have jobs throughout high school and college, and then directly after college he started crafting my professional life that has led me to some amazing experiences.

There are some experiences that take the cake, and they all seem to have a common factor. That common factor is sharing God's Word. In college I was able to take two mission trips—one to Tennessee and one to South Carolina. Both were to mission congregations in which the group was given the opportunity to canvass a neighborhood.

I currently have the privilege to teach Sunday school to first and second graders. It is quite amazing seeing childlike faith and what they grasp at such a young age and in such short lessons—it is truly the Holy Spirit at work.

Looking into my future I am excited to continue with my involvement at church. I also look forward to partaking in an international mission trip. Because as the Lord says, "My kingdom is from another place." The sole reason we exist is to one day reach our eternal heavenly home. Let's make that known and continue to grow his kingdom!

PRAYER Dear Lord, there are so many ways to serve you. Please help me use my personal gifts to help his kingdom to continue to grow. Amen.

NOT ALWAYS AS THEY SEEM

John 18:37,38 *"You are a king, then!" said Pilate. Jesus answered, "You say that I am a king. In fact, the reason I was born and came into the world is to testify to the truth. Everyone on the side of truth listens to me." "What is truth?" retorted Pilate. With this he went out again to the Jews gathered there and said, "I find no basis for a charge against him."*

Things aren't always as they seem. I might see my fellow student, seemingly uninterested in pulling his weight on a project, not knowing his time is spent caring for a dying parent. I might struggle with a coworker who's continually harsh and cruel, and later overhear her crying in the restroom.

My friends might look at me and think I'm a model student, the one who always does the right thing, the one who always seems to be in control. But they don't know my secret sins. They don't see the things I struggle with every single day. Things just aren't always as they seem.

I wonder what Pilate really thought about Jesus. Pilate was told by the Jewish leaders that Jesus was a troublemaker and a nuisance. And yet things are not as they seem. God used this King, Jesus Christ, to accomplish our salvation. Jesus tells Pilate that the reason he was born was to testify to the truth. Born to be our King. Born for sinners like me, and like you, and for those around us: friends, coworkers, and complete strangers.

How grateful I am that things aren't always as they seem. I am thankful for this clear reminder. I have a Savior who took my sins so seriously that he gave his own life so that I could live with him eternally in heaven. I am a redeemed child of God. May I remember this in my dealings with others. In every face I see, may I see a soul redeemed by Christ.

PRAYER Dear Lord, thank you for your grace. Because of what Christ has done, I am your child. Remind me to see others through these eyes of grace. Amen.

GOD WORKS FOR OUR GOOD

Luke 23:23-25 *But with loud shouts they insistently demanded that he be crucified, and their shouts prevailed. So Pilate decided to grant their demand. He released the man who had been thrown into prison for insurrection and murder, the one they asked for, and surrendered Jesus to their will.*

February 2, 2005, started as a normal Wednesday for my family. It was not until I was pulled out of music class that afternoon to take a phone call that the world seemed to fall apart. My older brother was on the line. He was with my mother as they stood outside our home while the fire department desperately tried to put out the flames that destroyed everything.

Most people say that would be a devastating experience. Looking back, I consider that experience to be one of the best and most important things to happen to my family. The outpouring of love that we received from family, friends, and complete strangers showed us how God works even the most tragic of earthly events for the benefit of his children.

On the day we know as Good Friday, Pontius Pilate sentenced Christ to an undeserved death. It was a tragic event in the eyes of any human: the excruciating pain from the flogging, the crushable weight of a cross on his shoulders, hanging from that tree until his lungs gave way and could no longer offer breath to his body. What an awful image to think about. But think of the good that came from it! Without Christ's death we could not possibly hope to be welcomed into heaven with open arms, free of sin and any impurity. It is because of the terrible death of Jesus that we know God's unending love and that we shall know eternal life.

PRAYER Dear Lord, I thank you for the sacrifice of your only Son that I might live forever with you in heaven. Help me continuously see the ways you look after me both in times of despair as well as in times of joy. In your name, I pray. Amen.

WE NEED TO GROW?

Isaiah 44:3-5 *I will pour water on the thirsty land, and streams on the dry ground; I will pour out my Spirit on your offspring, and my blessing on your descendants. They will spring up like grass in a meadow, like poplar trees by flowing streams. Some will say, "I belong to the LORD"; others will call themselves by the name of Jacob; still others will write on their hand, "The LORD's," and will take the name Israel.*

One of my favorite parts of spring is the regrowth and rebirth I see everywhere. Many of these springtime wonders are either experiencing life for the first time or in a way they could not before because they are no longer threatened by the twin threats of cold and snow.

Similarly, we are spiritually refreshed or reborn when the life-threatening influences of sin and sorrow are removed from our hearts. God is a source of light to guide us even when we, by ourselves, cannot overcome sin. He is a loving Father who warms us with his love, a love that is so strong he was willing to give up his life to forgive our sins. The Holy Spirit calls us to faith, and yet this path is often more like hiking on a rough, muddy trail than a walk in the park. In the end, it's worth it. We are the plants who need to grow, and God is the light and warmth that sustains us.

PRAYER Dear God, help me keep my life centered on you the way a sunflower constantly keeps its face turned toward the sun. I need you in order to live and grow. No matter what circumstances surround me, your love never changes, the way the sun still warms a plant no matter what soil it takes root in. Help me grow in your love. Amen.

THE JOY OF THE CROSS

Matthew 27:28-30 *They stripped him and put a scarlet robe on him, and then twisted together a crown of thorns and set it on his head. They put a staff in his right hand. Then they knelt in front of him and mocked him. "Hail, king of the Jews!" they said. They spit on him, and took the staff and struck him on the head again and again.*

It hurt, but I couldn't stop looking at it. *Why are they doing this to him? Stop it! He doesn't deserve this!* I cried to myself.

The mockery, cruelty, and pain. It crushes me every time. It hurts so badly, but I can't look away. I want to stop it, but I can't. The worst part is even though I'd like to blame the soldiers for doing this, I can't. I'm right there with them. This happened to Jesus because of my sins. Everyone can say the same. It is our fault. We made Jesus go through this agony. It hurts to know this.

But before despair drags you down, know this: although it hurts at first, we keep looking because the more we look, the less and less it hurts until there is no more pain. The hurt goes away because this is where our Savior won salvation. This is where Jesus gave us the crown of life. This is where Jesus loved us so much that he died for us to live. This is the heart of the gospel.

Instead of looking at Jesus' passion and feeling the hurt, look at it and feel the joy. Our sins have been forgiven! Our pains have been healed! Our lives have been taken back from the evil clutches of Satan and brought under the protective wing of God!

PRAYER Almighty and merciful God, it hurts that I am responsible for your death on the cross. Help me see the cross as the means by which my hurt is taken away and replaced with joy. Thank you for your Son, Jesus, who brought me salvation. Amen.

JESUS BEARS OUR BURDENS

Matthew 27:32,33 *As they were going out, they met a man from Cyrene, named Simon, and they forced him to carry the cross. They came to a place called Golgotha (which means "the place of the skull").*

Ever been in the wrong place at the wrong time? Like during a dumb prank by your freshman roommates, a battle between coworker and boss, a protest that got a little crazy?

We know very little of Simon of Cyrene. Mark simply says he was "passing by" (15:21). Maybe he didn't know what was happening that day; maybe he didn't know who Jesus was.

Put yourself in his place. A crowd is exiting the city as you're entering, jeering at or weeping for the beaten, bleeding man in their midst. He's a criminal. They're headed for the execution grounds. Hopefully they'll pass quickly, and you can continue on your way . . .

But, no. The man falls under the beam he carries, and a soldier grabs your arm. "You! Pick that up." You try to protest, but he puts his hand on his sword and insists. "I'm just an innocent bystander," you mutter, but you help him up, shoulder the beam, and follow in his faltering footsteps.

Truthfully, there were no innocent bystanders that day, nor any day before or since. Regardless of their sympathies for or against this Jesus, the crowd was guilty of his death. We are, every last one, guilty of his death.

Though he couldn't carry the cross all the way to Golgotha, he could carry our sin. Even though Simon may have participated reluctantly, Jesus walked on willingly.

As you walk with Jesus, walk with an unburdened conscience. What weighed you down has been removed forever.

PRAYER I praise you, O God my Savior, for you daily bear my burdens (Psalm 68:19). Amen.

A CALL TO REPENTANCE

Luke 23:28-31 *Jesus turned and said to them, "Daughters of Jerusalem, do not weep for me; weep for yourselves and for your children. For the time will come when you will say, 'Blessed are the childless women, the wombs that never bore and the breasts that never nursed!' Then " 'they will say to the mountains, "Fall on us!" and to the hills, "Cover us!" ' For if people do these things when the tree is green, what will happen when it is dry?"*

Even as Jesus walked to the cross, a crowd followed. From that crowd came the sounds of women crying and mourning for Jesus. The words that Jesus spoke to them were a call to repentance. He was warning them that a time was soon coming when they would wish they were dead. A time they would wish that they never had children. Jesus was warning them that destruction was coming.

Is that a call to repentance for you too? As Jesus walks to the cross for you, is there something going on in your life that is leading you to destruction? Is it the material that you view on your computer screen? Is it the liquid that you drink or the green leaves that you inhale? Is it the anger you have for another? Is it the violence that you display? Yes, these things, when left unchecked, will bring destruction. These sins, when committed with an unrepentant heart, could cause you to feel like the inhabitants of Jerusalem—wishing that the mountains would fall on you to crush you rather than having to experience the pain of God's judgment and destruction.

If this is you, heed Jeus' warning. Follow him on his walk to the cross. Fall at the foot of the cross and beg for his mercy and forgiveness. And, with each drop of blood that falls from the cross onto your body, Jesus reminds you that he has forgiven you. That's why he went to the cross in the first place. Faith and trust in him will make all the difference on the day of judgment. That will now be a day of rejoicing.

PRAYER Jesus, make me whiter than snow and give me the strength to live for you. Amen.

THE ULTIMATE ACT OF HUMILITY

Philippians 2:8 *Being found in appearance as a man, he humbled himself and became obedient to death—even death on a cross!*

It's hard to be humble. Especially in a self-centered society that strongly encourages entitlement, it's a challenge to make sacrifices for the benefit of others. Deadlines and priorities keep our minds full and take our time away from simple acts of kindness, much less truly forfeiting ourselves for another.

Jesus' sacrifice is incomprehensible. Instead of the honor and privilege that he deserved, Jesus chose submission and humble service. Paul explains it to us in Philippians 2:8. God's justice required sacrifice; his great love led Jesus to the cross to take the burden of our sin on himself. Mark 10:45 says, "For even the Son of Man did not come to be served, but to serve, and to give his life as a ransom for many." He died for our benefit, that we may be released from the guilt of sin and turn our thoughts toward the hope of heaven.

This ultimate act of humility fills us with gratitude. We'll never fully understand why God became man and died for every undeserving sinner, but his example and generous love inspires us with a desire to serve others.

When we're surrounded by temptations to be proud and selfish, remember Jesus. Share his love through acts of service that place others first.

PRAYER Heavenly Father, thank you for sending Jesus to give his life as a sacrifice for my sins. Jesus, thank you for leaving the glory and comforts of the heavenly throne to willingly sacrifice yourself for me. May this perfect example of humility embolden me to serve others with love. Amen.

WE AREN'T ALWAYS RIGHT

Luke 23:34 *Jesus said, "Father, forgive them, for they do not know what they are doing." And they divided up his clothes by casting lots.*

"You don't know what you're doing!" Has someone ever said this to you? Is your first reaction a defensive comment or anger? Or do you ask God to forgive that person?

We like to think we know what we are doing. We have a knack for thinking we are always right. However, God's Word tells us that we are sinful and not always right.

The very people that welcomed Jesus into Jerusalem were convinced that he was their king and the Son of God. Yet, just a few days later, those very people were convinced that Jesus should be crucified. They thought they knew what they were doing. The people thought they were watching a criminal, not their Savior, being sentenced before Pilate. Jesus at any moment could have proven he was the Son of God. Instead he turned to his Father and prayed on behalf of the very people who sentenced him to an excruciating death.

We often don't know what we are doing. We don't know the plan God has for us, but we do know we have a loving mediator who asks God to forgive us when we stray. How great is it that even in the midst of persecution our Savior pleaded for those who were sentencing him to death! We like to think we know what we are doing. Let us remember that we aren't always right. Instead, let us be like Christ and ask for forgiveness.

PRAYER Dear Lord, thank you for Jesus, who willingly went to the cross for me. Lead me to be more like him and ask for forgiveness for both my enemies and myself. Amen.

A LESSON FROM A CRIMINAL

Luke 23:42,43 *Then he said, "Jesus, remember me when you come into your kingdom." Jesus answered him, "Truly I tell you, today you will be with me in paradise."*

As one examines the events leading up to Jesus' death on Good Friday, it is easy to get caught up in the helplessness and forsaken state that Jesus was in. He was mocked, ridiculed, and beaten to the point of exhaustion by the time he arrived at Golgotha. Even in this state of complete humiliation, he still modeled true love to those around him. In today's passage, we see his grace and mercy to the criminal hanging on the cross next to him.

We as Christians can not only draw strength and comfort from Jesus in this situation, but also from the criminal on the cross with Jesus. Although he was guilty and could have easily mocked Jesus when everyone else did, like the other criminal on the cross, he rebuked the other criminal and put his faith in Jesus. Because of his faith, Jesus promised him salvation and eternal life.

This criminal is a great example to us for looking to Christ in our times of need and helplessness. We may never end up on a cross to die, but we each will carry our own unique burden or cross in life. Faith alone in Jesus is what grants us eternal salvation in Christ.

PRAYER Dear Lord, at times I may be tempted to forsake you because of the cross I carry in your name. Remind me of Jesus' love for me that led him to the cross to die. Give me strength and courage to stand up for my Savior as the criminal on the cross did. Amen.

WHAT WONDROUS LOVE IS THIS

John 19:26,27 *When Jesus saw his mother there, and the disciple whom he loved standing nearby, he said to her, "Woman, here is your son," and to the disciple, "Here is your mother." From that time on, this disciple took her into his home.*

The word *love* has often been abused in our modern culture. What do you understand about love? Many regard the greatest act of love to be dying in the place of someone else. In this Lenten time, we are reminded that Christ died a brutal death on a cross—a death not meant for him, but for us. Christ demonstrated love to those who scoffed at him and to the criminals who were being executed with him.

Even dying, Christ did not forget to care for his mother. He provided security for her, and he empowered John to take care of her. Would you be able to show such love in death? Sadly, the answer is no. We think first and foremost of ourselves, but Christ lived a perfect life in our stead and loved perfectly to fulfill for us the love we were incapable of. Christ loved for us and satisfied God's demand.

The love of Christ continued through John's actions of caring for Jesus' mother. Look how the love of Christ motivates! By faith, John carried out the request of Christ, knowing and believing that Jesus was the Son of God.

How does it feel knowing that Christ died for you and promises to take care of you? What love! Let us continually thank God for living a perfect life for us, dying in our stead, and finally rising from the dead to proclaim his victory. Rejoice in the love that he has lavished on us. Rejoice in faith that Christ takes care of us—he was thinking of you on the cross. What wondrous love is this!

PRAYER Dear Lord, thank you so much for sending your Son to save us. Your love is incomprehensible. Help us mirror that love as we interact with those around us. Amen.

WE WILL NEVER BE ABANDONED

Mark 15:34 *At three in the afternoon Jesus cried out in a loud voice, "Eloi, Eloi, lema sabachthani?" (which means "My God, my God, why have you forsaken me?").*

As a child, your parents needed to assist you with almost everything. As you grow older, you are expected to take on more and more responsibilities, but your parents are still there to guide you. As a college student living hours away from home for the first time, you may feel abandoned. The people you relied on are now hours away, and the phone is your most personal means of communication. This Easter season let us take a moment to focus on the cross.

Our feelings of desperation will never compare to the desertion Jesus felt on the cross. Arguably some of Jesus' most famous words from the cross found in Mark 15:34 relate how Jesus was forsaken by God. Jesus had to take upon himself all our sins and feel the pain of abandonment by God so that we could be a part of God's family. These words show us what sin does—it separates us from God. While we must learn to provide for ourselves on this earth, we cannot earn heaven or get to heaven apart from God. Jesus' suffering means we have the hope of eternal life.

You may feel neglected as you watch your parents drive away from your dorm or apartment window, but that is a normal part of life. Thank your heavenly Father that you never have to feel abandoned by him because Jesus took that pain upon himself for us on the cross. Our sins can no longer separate us from the love of God.

PRAYER Lord Jesus, the cross you bore for my sins was beyond anything I can imagine. Because of you, I will never be abandoned by my Father. Thank you for bearing the punishment that my sins deserve. Amen.

I AM THIRSTY

John 19:28 *Later, knowing that everything had now been finished, and so that Scripture would be fulfilled, Jesus said, "I am thirsty."*

So seemingly insignificant. Jesus is thirsty. In the grand scheme of this eternally life-altering event, was it really worth the Holy Spirit's time to make sure that we knew that Jesus was thirsty?

It was some three years earlier when Jesus said, "For truly I tell you, until heaven and earth disappear, not the smallest letter, not the least stroke of a pen, will by any means disappear from the Law until everything is accomplished" (Matthew 5:18).

As Jesus mustered up whatever waning strength he had left, he spoke this single word in the Greek, "I am thirsty." Why? Because Psalms 22 and 69 said he would. The least stroke of a pen had to be fulfilled. Even as he gasped that single Greek word, he was not doing it for himself. He was doing it for you . . . that the Scriptures might be fulfilled . . . that your salvation would be completed. That's how much your salvation meant to Jesus. That's how much you mean to Jesus.

College can be a lonely time. You're stuck in between two worlds—the social world and the professional world. And somewhere between those two, you might wonder who your friends really are. That's a lonely feeling. Your Savior promises that he will never leave you or forsake you. And if you ever doubt it, see all the Scriptures fulfilled on the cross, even down to the cry of a single word. "I am thirsty."

PRAYER Lord Jesus, remind me daily through your Word that you love me and care for me more than anything. Amen.

IT IS FINISHED

John 19:30 *When he had received the drink, Jesus said, "It is finished." With that, he bowed his head and gave up his spirit.*

τετέλεσται is the Greek word that means, "It is finished." What was finished? Jesus' task as the only Son of God was completed, and so he died. He could have lasted longer, but he gave up his spirit with purpose.

How many times have you said, "It is finished"? What were the circumstances in which you said it? I can imagine that most of the time it occurs after writing a ten-page paper, completing a semester-long project, or concluding a big presentation. We say, "It is finished" with a sense of relief. We no longer have to spend time on the task and no longer have to worry about it.

When Jesus spoke the words "It is finished," it would make sense to have been with relief or resignation at the end of suffering. But this was Jesus' hour, an hour to which he had willingly gone, and Christ was declaring that he had completed God's plan of salvation.

It was a declaration. A resolute truth. Jesus had lived a perfect life and died a terrible death so that we could know the perfection of heaven. We have confidence in our salvation because we have done nothing to deserve it. We are sinful and cannot earn it. Instead God sent his Son to die in our places. He finished the task for us. What is finished? The only thing that truly matters.

It is finished.

τετέλεσται.

PRAYER Dear Lord, thank you for loving me enough to send Jesus to die on the cross for my sins. I deserve nothing but punishment and yet have salvation through Christ. Give me confidence in this resolute truth. Amen.

HE DIED TO FORGIVE US

Luke 23:46 *Jesus called out with a loud voice, "Father, into your hands I commit my spirit." When he had said this, he breathed his last.*

The small, sterile room was dimly lit. The only sound was the slow, labored breaths straining through Mom's cracked, dry lips. The rest of us watched helplessly. My tears fell silently. Dad sat stone-faced and exhausted on the edge of the bed, holding Mom's unresponsive hand. My sister cried into her purple handmade scarf. Occasionally, the sound of the hospital paging system would pierce the silence, our grieving good-bye disturbed by the outside world—a world that just kept on going while ours felt frozen. And then the breathing stopped. It was over. Mom had left this world.

Have you lost someone dear to you? It's a life-changing moment that causes us to question whether we did enough to show that person our love. Today's passage recounts Jesus' last breath. He was not resting peacefully in a hospital bed surrounded by close friends and family. He was hanging from a cross—brutally beaten and disfigured, nearly naked in front of the angry masses cheering his demise. Those who supported him stood quietly by, fearing for their own safety. And why was he being tortured and humiliated in this way? Because of us. Because of the endless mistakes we have made and continue to make every day. And because of his immense love for us. He died to forgive us for our faults!

If you could go back in time and be there—standing at the foot of the cross, looking up at the beaten, innocent hero who has rescued you from eternal death—what would you say? What would you do? How would you make sure he knows that you love him? Picture that moment—and live out your love for him today and always.

PRAYER Lord, I love you. Amen.

DEATH IS NOT THE END

Job 19:25 *I know that my redeemer lives, and that in the end he will stand on the earth.*

The Russian writer Vladimir Nabokov famously spoke before dying, "A certain butterfly is already on the wing." His final words might give the impression that death can be peaceful, quiet, and almost natural. In fact, we often hear in our university science classes that death is a natural part of biological cycles.

As another writer, David Gerrold, said, "Life is hard. Then you die. Then they throw dirt in your face. Then the worms eat you. Be grateful it happens in that order." Death is ugly. And it's not natural. Try explaining that it's natural to any mother mourning a child, any soldier that has seen comrades die, any adult child visiting their aging parent. Death is certainly an inescapable feature of life, but it's not natural. It's alien, and it's terrible.

Job's words are important because they show us that four thousand years ago people already knew that God was going to defeat death and the sin that caused death. Job knows that his Redeemer will live, and Job knows he will live as well. The rest of Scripture fills in the details: we need not fear sin and death, because Jesus has dealt with our sin and death on the cross. Though we may die one day and contribute to the biological cycle of life, our Redeemer promises us that we will not stay dead. So Christians do not fear death as the end, but see it as a door that we step through to real life.

PRAYER Heavenly Father, death at times seems so far off. Remind me constantly that it is not natural and that it is the very terrible consequence of sin. You have taken care of my sins and death on the cross. Therefore, I know I have nothing to fear. Amen.

APRIL
REST FOR THE WEARY

A WAKE-UP CALL

John 11:25,26 *Jesus said to her, "I am the resurrection and the life. The one who believes in me will live, even though they die; and whoever lives by believing in me will never die. Do you believe this?"*

Here's an undisputed fact: college students like naps. More specifically, they like to sleep deeply and often. There's nothing like crawling into bed, closing your eyes, and ignoring your responsibilities completely, or better yet, pretending you have none whatsoever.

I know I enjoy being able to take a brief respite from life's stresses and give my responsibilities over to an unnamed time in the future. However, even when I wake up, the tasks I have to accomplish are still there, staring me in the face. At times like these it's useful to remember that there's another type of rest I can take. It's "letting go and letting God," as the popular adage puts it.

No matter how frustrated, stressed, lonely, or depressed I am, God is there, guiding me along life's path. In fact, God is so amazing he not only came to earth as a human to eat, sleep, and encounter the frustrations of life like the rest of us, but he also died and *rose from the dead for our sins*. Think about it. God is both our powerful King and loving Father, to name just a couple of his many roles. With him beside us, there is nothing we need fear in this life, for God has taken care of our eternal life. Now, how's that for a wake-up call?

PRAYER Lord Jesus, awaken me to your presence and show me your will for my life. Amen.

WE CANNOT BE SHAKEN

John 10:28-30 *I give them eternal life, and they shall never perish; no one will snatch them out of my hand. My Father, who has given them to me, is greater than all; no one can snatch them out of my Father's hand. I and the Father are one.*

Sometimes I get so overwhelmed by my to-do list I find myself paralyzed, unable to take the next step forward. The amount of things I need to get done completely consume me and become all I can think about. Overtaken by fear and dread and stress, I even lose sleep going over and over it all in my head.

At times like these I need to pull back and go back to God's Word for a reality check. Yes, that test is going to be terrifying, and that paper I haven't started yet feels like it might kill me, but there's a bigger picture here. No matter what happens, my Father's got me in his hands. I really have nothing substantial to fear or stress out about.

I once heard a pastor say that there is no need for fear on this earth. The worst thing that could happen to you, he said, is that you will die, and if so, then you are in heaven. What an obvious yet important truth. One of my favorite authors reminded me of this same truth when referring to our worries about our lives crumbling around us: "We are part of a kingdom that cannot be shaken."

You as a Christian cannot be shaken. You *can* take that next step forward. You *can* live with confidence and peace instead of stress and fear.

PRAYER Dear Shepherd, the next time I feel overwhelmed and my hands feel full, remind me that your hands are also full— they're holding on to me. Amen.

CHRIST IS RISEN!

1 Corinthians 15:20-22 *Christ has indeed been raised from the dead, the firstfruits of those who have fallen asleep. For since death came through a man, the resurrection of the dead comes also through a man. For as in Adam all die, so in Christ all will be made alive.*

The weeks leading to Good Friday are like the preparation of a master baker, carefully assembling all the ingredients to bake the most perfect cake. In contrast, Christ's resurrection from the dead on Easter morning can seem like the frosting on top: a fantastic addition, but maybe not as significant.

False! Yet without understanding, we may not see the importance of Jesus' resurrection. The early Christians in Corinth were also confused over this, and some false teachers worked to convince them that Christ had died for their sins but was not raised to life. Our passage shows that the apostle Paul was not about to let the Corinthians wonder.

Why is the resurrection important? When Jesus died, defeating sin and death, he became "the firstfruits" of that victory, the living result from breaking death's power. His resurrection confirms the restored relationship between God and mankind, fulfilling the promise of salvation God first gave to Adam and Eve.

Christ's victory also means we have the promise of the resurrection for all people in the near future, affirming once again that our faith is well founded and worth sharing.

Jesus' resurrection *is* the frosting, for the cake would not be complete without it. What a glorious sight it will be when we too are resurrected and join him in the victory feast of heaven.

PRAYER Lord, thank you for fulfilling your promises. I look forward with joy to the day I am resurrected and join you in heaven. Amen.

April 4

WE ARE VICTORIOUS

1 Corinthians 15:55-57 *"Where, O death, is your victory? Where, O death, is your sting?" The sting of death is sin, and the power of sin is the law. But thanks be to God! He gives us the victory through our Lord Jesus Christ.*

It's April. That means that the semester is nearing its end, but that end still seems far out of reach. It's a time of much stress with projects and papers on the horizon. And yet it's a time of joy because the celebration of Christ's victory over death, Easter, usually falls in this month.

Read 1 Corinthians 15:55-57 again. What does the passage mean? Sin brought us under death's power, and the law of God gives sin its power. God's law reveals our sin and condemns us to death for that sin.

These are not comforting truths. This is a comforting truth and the only truth that truly matters: our Lord Jesus Christ is victorious over the condemnation of the law and over death through his death and resurrection. Death is a scary thing to think about, but it has been conquered and we have no need to fear it any longer.

If we already have victory over death and have no need to worry about it, then it seems sort of silly to worry about such small things as college projects or papers. Finish the semester strong and give thanks to God, for he has given us the victory through our Lord Jesus Christ. We are forgiven children of God.

PRAYER Dear Lord, college is often a very stressful time. I ask you to reassure me of your victory and provide encouragement to finish strong. I give thanks to your holy name for sending your Son to give the ultimate sacrifice for the ultimate victory. Amen.

WE ARE RECONCILED

Romans 5:10 *For if, while we were God's enemies, we were reconciled to him through the death of his Son, how much more, having been reconciled, shall we be saved through his life!*

Now is the point in the semester that things often get long and drawn out. It's easy to get stressed out when final projects, papers, and tests begin to pile up. It can seem so difficult to keep up with everything. When stress begins to weigh you down, it's important to put things into perspective.

The passage in our devotion can be split up into two parts: a negative and a positive. It uses this logic: if God did something difficult, then he would do something easy. The negative part states that we were *enemies* of God and *death* was required. God's loving power addressed both of these negatives. Christ came to this earth, lived a perfect life, and died on a cross. The results of this are the positives of the verse. We have been *reconciled*, and Christ has *risen* from the dead.

Having been reconciled, we are now friends with God and our living Savior. This gives us full confidence in our faith. When judgment day comes or when we depart from this world, we will enjoy eternity in heaven. Rejoice in Christ's Easter victory, for that is the only thing that truly matters.

PRAYER Dear Lord, it's easy to forget about your victory over death when I am assaulted by the worries and things of this life. Please give me the strength to do a good job with these earthly things but remind me to keep things in perspective. Christ has died. Christ is risen. Christ will come again. To you be the glory. Amen.

April 6

STAND ON THE SOLID FOUNDATION

Matthew 28:2-4 *There was a violent earthquake, for an angel of the Lord came down from heaven and, going to the tomb, rolled back the stone and sat on it. His appearance was like lightning, and his clothes were white as snow. The guards were so afraid of him that they shook and became like dead men.*

I remember exactly when it happened. Our family had just sat down to eat dinner. The television was allowed to be on so we could watch game three between two northern California teams, the San Francisco Giants and the Oakland A's, in the 1989 Bay Area World Series. The television transmission went fuzzy . . . the announcer's voice faded in and out . . . and then there was silence. The screen went black.

Moments later, we figured out what had happened. It was an earthquake. Due to the national sports coverage of the World Series, this "shaker" became the first major earthquake in the United States that was broadcast live.

Matthew recorded for us another famous earthquake that announced the glorious resurrection of Jesus. On resurrection morning, Mary Magdalene and the other Mary came to see the tomb and found an angel sitting on the stone. It seems significant that an earthquake marked both Jesus' death and his resurrection. Both signaled that great and mighty acts of God were taking place. It's as though God our Father was tying the crucifixion and the resurrection of his Son together with a seismic knot.

As we head into the final days of the spring semester, focus on the Easter joy in Jesus' resurrection that is yours no matter what "quakes" attempt to separate you from his love. Stand on the solid foundation of Jesus Christ and his victory won for you!

PRAYER Blessed Savior, help me stand firmly on the victory won on Easter morning! Amen.

AN INCREDIBLE JOY

Luke 24:5-7 *In their fright the women bowed down with their faces to the ground, but the men said to them, "Why do you look for the living among the dead? He is not here; he has risen! Remember how he told you, while he was still with you in Galilee: 'The Son of Man must be delivered over to the hands of sinners, be crucified and on the third day be raised again.'"*

There's a certain feeling on campus at this time of year. Winter is finally over and the weather starts to change, bringing new life. But there's also the overwhelming realization that the end of the school year is coming fast. Are you ever just downright *afraid* that you will not be able to finish everything on your list? And is that fear all-consuming—the only thing you think about?

These worries are about the human, everyday problems we have. Thankfully, we don't need to be afraid when it comes to our spiritual lives. We have the knowledge that Jesus died and rose again. We know for a fact that *he* is the one true Savior, the Son of God. Imagine how much fear the women must have felt walking up to his tomb. Their Lord had died. They lost sight of what was important and were blinded by their fear. Then they were given the words of encouragement that are in our devotion today.

What joy and comfort they must have felt! It can be matched by the same joy we feel every day, knowing that Jesus died for all of our sins. Yes, those projects and presentations are important and you do need to finish them. But if you ever get stressed and worried or lose sight of what is important, just take a moment to remember the seemingly impossible thing that Jesus has done for you—he has saved you from something even worse than an incomplete project.

PRAYER Dear Lord, forgive me for losing sight of what is truly important. Words cannot describe the thanks and comfort I feel from knowing that you sent your only Son to do what seemed impossible. In your name, I pray. Amen.

SPREAD THE JOY

John 20:16,17 *Jesus said to her, "Mary." She turned toward him and cried out in Aramaic, "Rabboni!" (which means "Teacher"). Jesus said, "Do not hold on to me, for I have not yet ascended to the Father. Go instead to my brothers and tell them, 'I am ascending to my Father and your Father, to my God and your God.'"*

For those of you who struggle with poor eyesight, you can relate. Whenever I don't have my glasses on or contacts in, I can only focus on what is directly in front of me. Everything else is a blur! Because of this, I usually don't try to focus on the other details around me. I need help to take away my nearsightedness.

In this section of Scripture, Mary felt the same way. She was so focused on what was right in front of her. She was in the midst of going through an emotional roller coaster; her Lord had been brutally beaten and crucified just a few days ago, and now the body was suddenly gone. Her nearsightedness over the loss of Jesus prevented her from seeing the other details around her. Jesus had to reach out to her by calling her name, and then she could see. He helped turn her nearsightedness into 20/20 vision! She found her joy in the Savior and hope in his redemption. Jesus rejoices with Mary, but then he tells her to spread that joy.

In this Easter season, it is easy to get caught up in everything else. The end of the semester is coming closer, and sometimes it feels so near and yet so far. I encourage you to instead focus on the joy of the Savior and spread it to others as Mary did.

PRAYER Dear Lord, help me turn my nearsightedness on the problems of this world into 20/20 vision this Easter so that I can show this joy to others. In your name, I pray. Amen.

April 9

BE JOYFUL

Luke 24:25,26 *He said to them, "How foolish you are, and how slow of heart to believe all that the prophets have spoken! Did not the Messiah have to suffer these things and then enter his glory?"*

Life is filled with troubles. Cancer, brittle bones, uncertainty, homelessness, poverty, violence, and loneliness are just some that Satan weaves into our lives. We can dwell on them. We can wallow in them.

Or we can get joyful. Luke lets us eavesdrop on a conversation we desperately need to hear. Read today's passage again. The disciples were in a funk. They were wallowing. They were feeling the weight of a world of sorrow, for their Lord had left them. Their faith was blinded by the troubles they had just witnessed.

Jesus reminds the disciples to stop being foolishly sucked into these trappings of sadness and sorrow. Be joyful! Jesus suffered. He took it all on! He overtook the devil and crushed his head. He lives in glory; the same glory that will be ours one day soon. The disciples learned that day to be joyful.

We do not get a face-to-face reminder from Jesus to be joyful. We do, however, have the assurance in his Word that we have the ultimate reason to rejoice! These earthly sufferings are temporary, and one day we will rest from the daily labors and struggles that bog us down. Be joyful, my friends. Our joy now is soon to be magnified in the presence of our Savior.

PRAYER Dear Savior, you know the sadness that I have. You hear it, even when I do not come to you with it. There is a lot of stuff right now that I cannot seem to shoulder on my own. Help me bear it and be joyful in it. Remind me daily through your Word that though I do not deserve it, you have won salvation for me—a joyful eternity with you. In your name, I pray. Amen.

YOU ARE WITNESSES

Luke 24:46-48 *This is what is written: The Messiah will suffer and rise from the dead on the third day, and repentance for the forgiveness of sins will be preached in his name to all nations, beginning at Jerusalem. You are witnesses of these things.*

Most Christians today would probably admit that they wish they could have been alive while Jesus walked on earth; they wish they could have seen how wonderful and awesome he was. While "faith is confidence in what we hope for and assurance about what we do not see" (Hebrews 11:1), to see Jesus' face and hear his voice would have been amazing. When our relationship with God feels weak, when we wonder where his presence in our lives is, the desire for such reassurance often grows stronger.

Jesus' disciples observed his ministry firsthand. They had witnessed God's promised work of salvation and now would preach this message to the world. This was God's plan— what was revealed through Scripture.

We may not have been firsthand witnesses, but we have all the evidence we need in Scripture to prove that Jesus was the Messiah who died and rose for the forgiveness of our sins. This truth continues to bring us joy, reassures our faith, and reminds us of the hope we have in heaven. This is the message that needs to be preached to all nations.

PRAYER Heavenly Father, thank you for sending your Son, Jesus Christ, to be my Savior and for revealing your truth through the words of Scripture. Cast away all doubts, increase my faith, and help me share this truth with others. In Jesus' name, I pray. Amen.

WHAT A RELIEF!

John 20:27-29 *Then he said to Thomas, "Put your finger here; see my hands. Reach out your hand and put it into my side. Stop doubting and believe." Thomas said to him, "My Lord and my God!" Then Jesus told him, "Because you have seen me, you have believed; blessed are those who have not seen and yet have believed."*

Maybe things don't feel very peaceful right now. You feel like the semester's been going on forever, and there's still a month left. The end is in sight, but you know there will be challenges, like finals, before you get there. Or maybe you're at the end of your academic career and the end of the semester will bring a new set of challenges, like finding a job.

Know who could probably empathize? Jesus' disciples. They believed Jesus was the Messiah, and they knew heaven would be waiting for them at the end of their lives, but they knew they would have to face some pretty tough challenges before they got there.

God knows how we are feeling. He knows our every thought and need. Perhaps that's why, when Jesus first appeared to his disciples in John 20:19, the first thing he said was, "Peace be with you!" Then again, when he appeared to Thomas in John 20:26, the first thing he said was, "Peace be with you!" And in John 20:28, after addressing Thomas' fear and doubt, the first thing Thomas said to Jesus is part of today's passage.

You do not have to wait until the end of the semester, until you are at your dream job, or until you are home in heaven to experience that same peace, that same relief. We have 24/7 access to that same peace through prayer and God's Word. Try to take refuge in that when you start to stress.

PRAYER My Lord and my God! Thank you for the eternal peace you've given through the sacrifice of your Son. Help me take refuge in your Word and promises when I start to grow "world weary." Amen.

JOY IN JESUS' ASCENSION

Luke 24:51,52 *While he was blessing them, he left them and was taken up into heaven. Then they worshiped him and returned to Jerusalem with great joy.*

This concluding chapter of Luke is an action-packed one. It recounts Jesus' resurrection, the appearance of angels to the women, Jesus' ministry on the road to Emmaus, his appearance to his disciples, and, in our reading today, his ascension. We may be surprised to see that the disciples returned to Jerusalem with joy after seeing Jesus ascend. Why weren't they confused, stunned, or terrified? If we look back a few verses, we see that Jesus had "opened their minds so they could understand the Scriptures" (verse 45). That is, he had enabled them finally to understand that he was the Messiah. His purpose was to die and to be resurrected, and ultimately, to rejoin his Father in heaven. Even though he had told them repeatedly that he would die and be raised, that he was the Messiah, it was not until now that they fully grasped his mission.

We have the advantage of having the full Scriptures; the foresight that the disciples lacked is the hindsight that we are afforded through their written accounts. Ascension is not a time of sorrow, as if Jesus has left us forever. Rather, we rejoice with the disciples in the knowledge that Jesus' ascension means that God's eternal plan for salvation is complete, and in this joy we remind ourselves that Jesus will return again one day to gather all believers together into heaven.

PRAYER Dear Lord, you provided your disciples with an understanding of your work that led them to great joy. Please bring me joy also, knowing that your ascension reminds me of the culmination of your redeeming work. Help me wait patiently and eagerly for your ultimate return. In your name, I pray. Amen.

April 13

GOD IS OUR STRENGTH

Isaiah 40:28,29 *Do you not know? Have you not heard? The LORD is the everlasting God, the Creator of the ends of the earth. He will not grow tired or weary, and his understanding no one can fathom. He gives strength to the weary and increases the power of the weak.*

There's a time for everything, as the saying goes: a season for this and a season for that, a time to bear stress and a time to share that struggle. Life can be difficult; we undergo many burdens that can pile up quickly. We need the wisdom to discern which responsibility to shoulder, when to delegate, and when to cast all our troubles on Jesus. Often we seek the counsel and comfort of friends, and we forget the One who can help us most: the Wonderful Counselor.

Before we despairingly call or text a friend, confess our emotional pain to a stranger, or even shout out frustration in the frantic hope that help will appear, we need to go to God. He, who is all-powerful, has promised to strengthen us through any situation. Unlike humans, God never feels overwhelmed or worn down. This passage tells us that he has an understanding that absolutely no one will ever comprehend. And he has promised to help us in every need! What a blessing it is to know that God is our strength. Our crushing burdens become carried burdens. When we've been carried by God, we are able to help carry others.

PRAYER Heavenly Father, thank you for always being here for me, even when I forget that you are. I turn all of my burdens and concerns over to you. Please guide my every step and keep me in your Word. Amen.

ETERNAL REST

Matthew 11:28-30 *Come to me, all you who are weary and burdened, and I will give you rest. Take my yoke upon you and learn from me, for I am gentle and humble in heart, and you will find rest for your souls. For my yoke is easy and my burden is light.*

I love to travel, but traveling can be exhausting. There's nothing quite like plopping down in my own bed the first night when I return home. There's just something comforting about sleeping in my own bed that can't be replicated. Coming home for holidays or weekends when I was in college, I always seemed to get a great night's rest in my own bed. There was great comfort in that place for me.

No matter how great that night's sleep in my own bed may have been, that rest was only temporary. The stresses of life, school, work, athletics, relationships, etc., never stop. They just keep coming, and it's exhausting. The good news for us is that our Savior Jesus knows firsthand how exhaustive this earthly life is, and he offers us rest that's not temporary, but eternal. Jesus calls to us in our struggle in today's passage.

An easily overlooked message in this section of Scripture is the practical advice Jesus offers when he encourages us, "Learn from me." We learn from Jesus by seeking him and his wisdom in the inspired words of the Bible. Further, he physically comes to strengthen us through his real presence in the bread and wine at Lord's Supper.

What great encouragement to have a Savior who knows our struggles and reaches out to us with open arms—the same arms that were outstretched on the cross bearing all the sins of the world—so that one day we may rest eternally in peace and joy with him in heaven.

PRAYER Lord Jesus, help me see clearly that your victory on Easter morning is the assurance I have that life's struggles are temporary and your love is eternal. Amen.

GOD KNOWS WHAT WE NEED

Joshua 10:8 *The LORD said to Joshua, "Do not be afraid of them; I have given them into your hand. Not one of them will be able to withstand you."*

When I was a kid, I really wanted my own dome tent for camping. I loved camping, and I actually had a pup tent, but dome tents were cooler, so I thought I needed one. I wanted it so much that I prayed to God for one many times. I eventually received a dome tent, but not when I thought I needed it. I got one a few years later when my feet were literally sticking out of my pup tent, and I bought it with my own money.

Sometimes we feel like our plans and goals have to happen the way we plan them. We are uncomfortable with the idea that we're not in control all the time. Proverbs 16:9 says, "In their hearts humans plan their course, but the LORD establishes their steps."

Joshua must have been really nervous before the battle, but God had this victory in his plan. He assured Joshua, "Not one of them will be able to withstand you." Ultimately, we find out later in Joshua 10 that God confused Israel's enemies and "more of them died from the hail [that God sent] than were killed by the swords of the Israelites" (verse 11).

In Matthew 6:26, Jesus talks about how God takes care of even the birds. Jesus does not want us to spend our time worrying about earthly plans, wants, needs. He wants us to spend that time seeking his kingdom.

We have Jesus' assurance that if God wants something for our lives, whether it is in our plans or not, we can trust that God will make sure it happens for us.

PRAYER Dear Lord, thank you for giving me what I need when I need it. Amen.

WE ARE HIS

Psalm 42:11 *Why, my soul, are you downcast? Why so disturbed within me? Put your hope in God, for I will yet praise him, my Savior and my God.*

I used to resent this verse. I labored under the heaviness of depression for several years, and this verse seemed to mock me.

"Why are you downcast and disturbed?" the cheery voice chirped in disbelief. Subtext: "There's no reason to be! Just put your hope in God and you'll feel so much better."

Having survived my depression, by God's grace and modern medicine, I see this verse more clearly. It does not mock. Rather, it is the heart of God for all who suffer.

"Why my soul, are you downcast?" The question needs to be asked. Examine your circumstances. Your emotions are real. Acknowledging them can open the path to understanding them, and perhaps reaching some mastery of them, rather than being mastered by them. And there are those around you who can help.

But understanding is not enough. The Bible is not a self-help manual; our greatest goal in life is not happiness or even emotional equilibrium. The Bible is the Word of God, which he uses to accomplish his greatest goal for us: to save us, make us his, give us hope.

He reaches out to you in these few sentences, inviting you into his sheltering arms. Regardless of how badly your psyche is cracked, regardless of the toll sin has taken on your life and self, you are *his*, no matter what. He suffers with you, and he suffered *for* you. He suffered in every way possible, died, and triumphed over suffering and death, so your sojourn in this sin-soaked world is temporary and never alone.

PRAYER Even if with tears and pain, help me still praise you, O Lord, for you are my Savior and my God. Amen.

STAND ON THE ROCK

Psalm 40:1,2 *I waited patiently for the LORD; he turned to me and heard my cry. He lifted me out of the slimy pit, out of the mud and mire; he set my feet on a rock and gave me a firm place to stand.*

King David was stuck. He felt as though his feet were sucked into the bottom of a deep pit of clay. Unable to move, he slowly sank. Doubts and fears are a horrible pit that sucks in many children of God. Yet God has enough power to help the weakest and the grace to help the most unworthy sinners if they place their trust in him. The psalmist David waited, praying, hoping, believing that God heard his prayers and would save him. We are told in the Bible that those who wait patiently for God do not wait in vain.

God's grace pulled David up out of the proverbial pit and placed him on a rock. Read today's passages again. The rock that David stood on is the same rock on which our souls can stand firm: Christ. Like David, our souls are filled with joy and peace in believing in Christ as our Savior. We can be confident knowing that God hears us and saves us. We can trust in him and his mercy. If you are ever stuck, look to this passage as an example of how patience, trust, and God's saving grace preserve you.

PRAYER Dear Lord, forgive me for not having patience when I call to you for help. I know you hear me. Please help me believe like David that you will pull me out of whatever pit I am stuck in. Keep my faith firm in you as I stand on Jesus, my rock. In his name, I pray. Amen.

GOSPEL MOTIVATION

2 Corinthians 5:14,15 *Christ's love compels us, because we are convinced that one died for all, and therefore all died. And he died for all, that those who live should no longer live for themselves but for him who died for them and was raised again.*

Why do you do what you do? Why do you do your homework? Why do you get to work on time or take care of your children day after day? Paul tells us in 1 Corinthians 10:31, "So whether you eat or drink or whatever you do, do it all for the glory of God." We are not perfect at that, are we? Sometimes we go through the motions, or we do things for very selfish reasons, and yet we know Jesus did all of these things perfectly for us.

It is an amazing thing for our motivation to be the gospel because of what Christ did for us. It takes something drastic to make that change. It is not something we can just do ourselves—to start living for Christ and living for others. Because of "him who died for them," I can move from the past (and my old self) to the future (with my new self).

Christ's impact on our lives is transforming. Think of when a friend does something nice for you, and you want to do something nice in return. That is a great thing. And yet, think about the motivation that comes from Christ. It is so much more. When we understand and take to heart what Christ did for us, we not only want to live for Christ, but we want to live for others. We understand that Christ did not just do this for us, but for the whole world. Showing love for others is one small yet important way to spread that simple yet important message.

PRAYER Dear Lord, thank you for your gospel. Forgive me for the times I go through the motions in serving you and those around me. Give me joy in service that all things may be done to your glory! Amen.

THINK ABOUT SUCH THINGS

Philippians 4:8 *Finally, brothers and sisters, whatever is true, whatever is noble, whatever is right, whatever is pure, whatever is lovely, whatever is admirable—if anything is excellent or praiseworthy—think about such things.*

No matter how much preparation or planning we do, everything seems to come crashing down at some point. Homework piles up, financial strains grow, our health plummets, work becomes more demanding and time-consuming—and that is just in the current semester. What about the semester following? Or after graduation? It's easy to feel overwhelmed.

It's so easy to start dwelling on negative thoughts when we hit this point in our lives. That's the exact opposite of what we should do! It seems like the natural progression for our thoughts to be consumed with this negativity, but the apostle Paul offers up a different opportunity in Philippians 4:8. Paul realizes that it is smart to be conscientious of our thoughts manifesting into action. It's also important to remember that even though we have problems and troubles that we choose to dwell on, there is something bigger than all of them put together. Something that is true, noble, right, pure, lovely, admirable, excellent, and praiseworthy. That something is our God . . . and our God is also one other crucial thing above all of that—love.

The next time worldly stress, tasks, and troubles encircle you, just remember to dwell on what is important. Put everything in perspective; focus on the positive. But, most important, never forget to take it up in prayer. That is the thought that truly counts.

PRAYER Dear Father, please help me to not lose sight of the blessings you have poured out for me. Remind me of your love and the reassurance I always have in you. And help me to lead others this realization as well. In the name of my Savior, I pray. Amen.

April 20

VICTORY IN CHRIST

Deuteronomy 20:4 *For the LORD your God is the one who goes with you to fight for you against your enemies to give you victory.*

It's really hard to think during difficult times that you've already won the victory over your situation. Some of my most stressful times were in high school and college. Every bad thing that could possibly happen did. No, I'm not talking bad as in I did not get the new Jordans that were out. I'm talking homeless, hungry, poor, feelings of not being good enough, feeling like I would never make it kind of bad. In the midst of chaos, how can I possibly think to myself, *I have won the victory over my situation?*

It took God's Word, prayer, and the realization that I was not fighting the battle. The only possible way that I could have victory is when God fights the battle. I had victory in Christ alone. Deuteronomy 20:4 tells us, "For the LORD your God is the one who goes with you to fight for you against your enemies to give you victory." During difficult times, do not be distressed and do not be worried. Instead, sing your victory in Christ.

My prayer for you is that you know God's strength is made perfect in our weakness. Even though our sorrows may last for a night, joy is surely coming in the morning! Through your current circumstances, both the good and the bad, God gets the glory.

PRAYER Lord, let me know that you are my source of strength and you give me the victory. Amen.

April 21

NOTHING IS TOO HARD FOR GOD

Jeremiah 32:27 *I am the L*ORD*, the God of all mankind. Is anything too hard for me?*

As the stresses of life, school, and work grow, there are times you will feel inadequate and ill-equipped to fulfill the roles you have. Sometimes it's the daily grind that exhausts you or unspeakable tragedy that weighs heavier than you can bear. The good news is that you do not need to carry them alone.

If you are struggling to juggle responsibilities or difficulties, remind yourself to stop for a minute and cry out to God for a renewing of his strength inside of you. The burdens in life are too much to carry when you try to carry them on your own.

In Jeremiah, we are reminded that our Savior is the Lord of all mankind. He is sovereign over all things and died for the sins of all. There is nothing too challenging for him. This is the one whose strength I want to fill my heart during challenging times.

God is never early and never late, even though we often wish he would make himself evident a little sooner. However, he always has a way of showing up right on time. If you are feeling too weak to carry the burdens weighing on you now, cry out to him. Trust that even in the stillness, he is still strong. He will grant you the strength. His greatest desire is that whatever joy or burden you have, it will draw you closer to knowing him. Allow the challenges you face today to remind you to rest in his strength when your own is running low.

PRAYER Lord, remind me to reach out to you when I am in need of relief from the struggles around me. Amen.

WHY BE AFRAID?

Isaiah 44:2 *This is what the L*ORD *says—he who made you, who formed you in the womb, and who will help you: Do not be afraid, Jacob, my servant, Jeshurun, whom I have chosen.*

Who do you turn to when you need help? Whether it's help making an important decision, completing a project for class, or picking out an outfit for a special event, we usually turn to our closest friends or family. They know us best. We rely on them to be there when we need help. But have they ever let you down or been unavailable to help when you really needed them? We have probably all experienced this at least once. Although there can be uncertainty when relying on earthly relationships for help, we can always count on our heavenly Father.

Isaiah 44:2 reminds us that God made us and formed us. How comforting it is to remember that we have a God who made us and knows us better than even our closest friends or family. This means that he knows exactly what we need help with, and he will always be there to follow through with his promise of helping us. Just as the passage says that God chose Jacob to be his servant and that he need not be afraid, the same holds true for us, as he tells us at our baptism.

With all the temptations, struggles, and trials we face during our college years, we can face them without fear. With concern, yes. But with fear? No. The Lord formed us and he knows us. He has chosen us to be his children at our baptism, and he even died to save us—so why be afraid?

PRAYER Lord, you are an awesome God! Your promise of helping me is so comforting, yet I often fail to solely rely on you. Thank you for the special people you've put in my life to help me through my earthly struggles until you take me to be with you forever in heaven. Amen.

PRAY FOR GRACE

Romans 16:20 *The God of peace will soon crush Satan under your feet. The grace of our Lord Jesus be with you.*

It's that time of the semester. Projects are coming due, papers need to be finalized, and exams are approaching faster than it seems possible. I know the feeling. One thing I have learned, though, is that even though school is extremely important, what's most important is to remain conscious of your faith. Temptations may come from all sides to fudge on a paper, lie about an "emergency" to get an extension on a project, or from any number of things during a stressful time in life.

This passage is from Paul's letter to the Christian church in Rome. The last sentence is Paul's prayer that Christ's grace be with the Christians there, among many heathens and people of different faiths. Sound familiar? Whether at a Christian or public university, we can be surrounded by this, and we need to pray for grace all the more.

Stay strong in the comfort that "the God of peace will soon crush Satan under your feet"! With God's help, you can overcome those temptations! With God's help, you can take a step back, breathe, and realize that everything will be okay. You will get everything done. God has already crushed Satan when Christ died on the cross for our sins and rose again in victory.

PRAYER Heavenly Father, in this time of high stress, give me strength and comfort to know that you are here. Bless the efforts of every student, that they do their best work to your glory. Please crush temptations of any kind, and bless me with the grace of your Son, Jesus. In his name, I pray. Amen.

GOD WILL UPHOLD YOU

Isaiah 41:10 *So do not fear, for I am with you; do not be dismayed, for I am your God. I will strengthen you and help you; I will uphold you with my righteous right hand.*

These words were directed to the captive Israelites, but they are also directed toward us, because through faith all believers are descendants of Abraham. It's easy to despair in this world, yet God comforts us by promising to strengthen, help, and uphold his people. You have probably experienced a pep talk where a friend or coach encourages you and the team/band/group to stand tall in the face of difficulty and danger. This is a pep talk from the almighty God who delivers on his promises and offers more than optimistic words.

God promises to uphold us with his righteous right hand. The righteous right hand symbolizes power, strength, and that which is straight, true, and correct. We who are anything but righteous are upheld through God's deliverance. Our almighty God offered up his Son to live a perfect life, die a brutal death on a cross, and rise again in victory.

As the craziness of the end of the semester hits you, know that your God has not deserted you. As you look to a future of unknowns, know that your God has fulfilled and will continue to fulfill his promises. As you have doubts and worries, know that your God made the ultimate sacrifice and you are now forgiven.

PRAYER Dear Lord, you are the Alpha and the Omega. Thank you for sacrificing yourself in order to save me and all people from our sins. You keep your promises. Help me remember that you have promised to strengthen, help, and uphold me as I finish the semester. Amen.

PERSEVERANCE THROUGH TRIALS

James 1:2-4 *Consider it pure joy, my brothers and sisters, whenever you face trials of many kinds, because you know that the testing of your faith produces perseverance. Let perseverance finish its work so that you may be mature and complete, not lacking anything.*

I remember at work one summer I was talking to my coworkers about Jesus. I don't know what specifically we were talking about. All I remember was at one point saying, "Jesus died for your and my sins." Immediately following that statement was laughter. That laughter still rings in my head. The devil uses it to tell me to stop trying, but the Holy Spirit uses it to help me persevere. In everything we do, whether it's telling people about Jesus, or just finishing off the never-ending semester, there will be trials and tribulations that test our faith. The Bible tells us, however, to be joyful. These trials cause perseverance—a quality that builds our character to be more mature in our faith in God.

During this time of year, it's so easy to become lazy in our work. It's so easy to forget our purpose in life. It's so easy to neglect God's Word. Outside forces are at work to make your life seem like it has no meaning. These are all tests of your faith. The devil tries to use these tests to tear you down spiritually, but the Holy Spirit uses these to produce perseverance in your life. Take advice from the Holy Spirit. Finish strong and hold on to God's Word. These tests will make you more mature and complete in Jesus Christ.

PRAYER Dear Lord, help me always be joyful through tests and the trials that come my way. Instill in me perseverance to finish this semester strong. Amen.

GOD IS OUR REFUGE

Deuteronomy 33:27 *The eternal God is your refuge, and underneath are the everlasting arms. He will drive out your enemies before you, saying, "Destroy them!"*

Life can be overwhelming. Have you ever gotten to a point when you just want peace, quiet, and to shut everyone and everything out? You feel like everything is collapsing and you are being attacked on all fronts. There is a war going on, inside and around you! From the time Adam and Eve fell from a perfect relationship with God, sin has thrived, corrupted, and consumed the hearts of humankind. You've felt it and have seen the evil of this world. Sometimes we are led to ask, "Is there no relief?"

God is our eternal refuge. We have a Comforter and protector who never stops fighting for us. We have a God who wishes to embrace us in his love and grace. He will not let go or abandon us.

God does not hesitate to drive out our enemies before us. God has overcome sin, death, and the devil. He faced and defeated our enemies in our stead. Will he who conquered our foes and who promised to be our eternal refuge not take care of us for eternity? The power of our God is huge. He pursues our enemies, drives them away, and destroys them.

There is relief in our Lord and Savior. He promises to be our eternal refuge and to destroy our enemies. Sin is tragic. It continually corrupts and leads us away from God. We will continue to be attacked, but our outlook is no longer bleak. Christ is caring for us. Let us call upon him for refuge!

PRAYER Dear Lord, you are my refuge and my Savior. Remind me of this in times of trouble and when I feel overwhelmed. There will be tough times ahead, but you have the victory that truly matters. Amen.

YOU ARE FORGIVEN

Romans 8:38,39 *I am convinced that neither death nor life, neither angels nor demons, neither the present nor the future, nor any powers, neither height nor depth, nor anything else in all creation, will be able to separate us from the love of God that is in Christ Jesus our Lord.*

Do you remember that one time that you messed up bad . . . like, really bad? I'm not talking about getting grounded for a week for staying out past curfew. I'm talking about that time you did something, you knew it was wrong, and you were scared about what was going to happen when someone found out about it.

I've got the best news you could hope for: your mistake was addressed on the cross. There Jesus was punished for what you did wrong and offers you forgiveness. Our God is amazing. There is no force in the universe that is stronger than his love for us, and there is nothing that can tear us away from him. He loved us enough to send his Son to die for our sins. God no longer sees our sin because of Christ's sacrifice.

It's scary when we mess up. It can be scarier to face the repercussions of our actions. Rest assured we have the blessing to approach our mistakes with the absolute assurance that God will not hold our sins against us.

PRAYER God, thank you for loving me. Thank you for taking away my sin. Thank you for forgiving me when I don't do the right thing. Thank you for your Son. Amen.

GOD IS ALWAYS WITH US

Deuteronomy 31:8 *The LORD himself goes before you and will be with you; he will never leave you nor forsake you. Do not be afraid; do not be discouraged.*

I've always been afraid of growing up. Now I'm out of college with a full-time job. Getting here was one of the scariest things I've ever done. It meant interviewing with strangers for jobs I was not sure I could do or would like. It meant figuring out if I should move back home to my family or stay where I went to college with my friends. It meant leaving a life full of school and little responsibility to move into something new. It was scary and still is sometimes.

Jesus has my life planned. It doesn't have to be scary because he already knows and has made a path for me. All I really have to do is trust him and rely on him to help me get to where I need to go. Consider Deuteronomy 31:8. We don't have anything to be afraid of because God is with us always. We have nothing to be afraid of because Christ died for our sins. We now have eternal victory over sin, death, and the devil.

When life gets scary or we are facing a troublesome situation, all we have to do is turn to the Lord. He will be waiting, ready to take us in his arms. He will never leave us and will be there whenever we need him.

PRAYER Dear heavenly Father, I know that I am weak and doubt the plan that you have for me. Please remind me that you are always there for me and that you are my best friend. Thank you for always holding me in your hands. Amen.

GOD IS OUR EVERLASTING HELPER

Hebrews 13:6 *We say with confidence, "The Lord is my helper; I will not be afraid. What can mere mortals do to me?"*

Life as a college student presents a host of unique challenges. Many people expect that, as a college student, you will graduate and begin full-time work at a job that is specific to what you studied. Economic events of the last decade have made for an increasingly competitive job market, leaving many people to pursue careers in fields that they are not necessarily suited for. Some are left unemployed. Acts of violence and threats of war seem to highlight the news, and there doesn't seem to be hope for resolution.

Our age group is often inundated with messages that attempt to draw us away from our Christian faith or that mock and discourage Christians for the faith that they have. At such a delicate phase in life when financial burdens are piling up, the pressure to succeed has never been more present, and when family members are diagnosed with illnesses or die, it's easy to forget God's promises to us.

The passage today brings comfort in the face of daily pressures and reminds us that God is our everlasting helper. There is nothing on this earth that can change that. The next time we are reminded of the sin-stained state of our earthly lives, let us remember that we may say with confidence that God is our helper and paid the price for our sins. We need not fear tomorrow.

PRAYER Dear Lord, sometimes I lose sight of your promise to always be with me and guide me. When the discouragement from living in a sin-filled world seems too overwhelming, remind me of your promise to always be with me. Amen.

THE BLESSING OF REST

Genesis 2:2,3 *By the seventh day God had finished the work he had been doing; so on the seventh day he rested from all his work. Then God blessed the seventh day and made it holy, because on it he rested from all the work of creating that he had done.*

The semester is nearing an end soon. But first, there's a lot of work to be accomplished. Papers, presentations, and exams. Oh, my! Throw in a job, sports practices, and club meetings on top of that. And before you know it, each day is filled with work. Sometimes it seems as though you can never get any rest. But rest is essential. Even God knew its importance since he rested after he finished all the work of creating the world in six days.

Because our work is never-ending, we continue to need to find time to rest—physically, mentally, and spiritually. Take time for yourself to do activities you enjoy with people you like. And most important, spend time with the God you not only like, but love. It's simple, really! Go to a church service for an hour, do a 15-minute home devotion, or talk to God for a few minutes each morning. When it's difficult to take a break from our work, we can always bring Jesus all our worries or stresses and find comfort in his love for us. Because of his death and resurrection, we can rest assured that our eternal lives will be in heaven. What peace this message brings us!

PRAYER Hello Lord, when I am overwhelmed with all the work I have to do, please give me time to rest. Help me take time for myself as you did and reflect on your love and continuous blessings. Talk to you soon! Amen.

MAY
BLESSINGS FOR THE JOURNEY

IN HIS HANDS

Jeremiah 29:11 *"For I know the plans I have for you," declares the LORD, "plans to prosper you and not to harm you, plans to give you hope and a future."*

Do you remember what you wished for at New Year's? Maybe you hoped for good luck, good health, motivation for new habits, or the resolve to get rid of bad ones. New Year's is when we look to the future with optimism.

In the academic year, May is that same season of hope. Spring semester is ending, and you're on the threshold of new beginnings. It's a moment when the future embraces the present, filled with promise.

Some possibilities are exciting: passing grades and summer vacation, a job waiting for you after graduation, acceptance to a prestigious graduate program, or maybe the final preparations for your soon-to-be-married life. Yet the future can be intimidating: you'll be relocating far from loved ones, or your summer work still won't cover tuition.

It's sometimes hard to believe the future will be positive. Yet that's exactly what God has in store for us. He makes this clear in Jeremiah 29:11.

Whatever your future holds, immediate and far off, God's design is for you to prosper, to have hope in a future he has orchestrated especially for you. When you face trials, God will use them to draw you closer to him, as a father draws his beloved child into his arms.

So even as you shoulder more adult responsibilities, hold to that childlike trust in God, the one who holds your future in his loving hands.

PRAYER Heavenly Father, thank you for your undeserved love in every aspect of my life. Teach me to always trust in your plans for me and to seek your guidance in all I do. Amen.

WE ARE CHOSEN

Ephesians 1:11 *In him we were also chosen, having been predestined according to the plan of him who works out everything in conformity with the purpose of his will.*

We all want to be chosen. In our younger years, we want to be chosen as friends and picked for teams. In high school, we want to be chosen for dates or dances. In college and beyond, we want to be chosen for jobs and lifelong relationships. Life is full of choices. Sometimes they have short-term consequences, and sometimes they mean a great deal more.

But what about eternity? What about that moment when we face God for our own personal judgment? What about heaven and hell? Paul's words in the passage for today are some that mean everything for our eternity.

Reread that passage and let it sink in a minute. For Jesus' sake, God has chosen you for an eternal relationship with him. It wasn't because you were going to excel in any way. It wasn't because you were going to be better than anyone else. It wasn't because you impressed him so much. It was all because of what Jesus would do for you when he came into our world to sacrifice himself for all sinners of all time. God chose you to be cleansed, made alive, and set apart for his special purpose. What a gift! What grace! What love!

As you plan for your future, remember that God chose you for his purpose. He guided your life to this point and will not forsake you. Won't you live today as one chosen by God? Won't you look past the hardships and obstacles of today and focus on your heavenly home? Won't you rest securely, knowing you are his?

PRAYER Loving Father, remind me today and every day that you have chosen me in Christ. Let me always make my plans based on your eternal plans for me. Amen.

BLOOM WHERE YOU'RE PLANTED

2 Corinthians 2:14,15 *But thanks be to God, who always leads us as captives in Christ's triumphal procession and uses us to spread the aroma of the knowledge of him everywhere. For we are to God the pleasing aroma of Christ among those who are being saved and those who are perishing.*

Last spring a little green plant stuck its head out from between the sidewalk slabs going to our front door. In a matter of weeks it blossomed with beautiful little purple flowers. What courage this small viola had, daring to grow between the sidewalk cracks in a heavily trafficked area! Many guests commented how amazing it was that this little flower continued to grow and blossom in this unlikely place.

We are at that point in the semester where many of us will be transplanted—some back home for the summer, some to different academic settings, many to new or different jobs. Some will return to familiar settings. Others of you will venture into the desert and wilderness where you have not gone before, places that weren't part of your plan—hostile environments. God's plans for your upcoming days are noted in the passage.

Just like that wayward viola on our front walk, God has equipped you and will plant you just where he wants you to accomplish the task he has for you: his plan, not your plan. Rooted in the Word, watered with the waters of Holy Baptism and warmed by his love, you can bloom where you are planted—the "aroma of Christ among those who are being saved and those who are perishing." Bloom in full confidence in God, who always leads us in triumphal procession in Christ!

PRAYER Lord, having full confidence in you, enable me to bloom where you plant me so that I might be the aroma of Christ to those you put in my path. Amen.

YOUR PROFESSOR'S SHOES?

John 13:12-15 *When he had finished washing their feet, he put on his clothes and returned to his place. "Do you understand what I have done for you?" he asked them. "You call me 'Teacher' and 'Lord,' and rightly so, for that is what I am. Now that I, your Lord and Teacher, have washed your feet, you also should wash one another's feet. I have set you an example that you should do as I have done for you."*

What color are your professor's shoes? Do you know? Chances are, your professor has multiple pairs of shoes that vary in color depending on the outfit. Are your professor's shoes dressy? Are they comfortable? Are they running shoes? Whatever they are, these are the shoes that your professor will use to teach you valuable skills and knowledge that will help you in your life.

In the time of Jesus, tennis shoes didn't exist. Jesus and his disciples walked around in sandals, collecting dirt under their toenails and building up mighty calluses on their heels. In this passage, Jesus teaches his disciples the valuable skill of servant leadership. He wasn't rude. He didn't comment on how dirty someone's feet were or if one toe was strangely longer than another. No. He washed his disciples' feet and was willing to do so. Just as he was willing to do something much, much more difficult to serve you and me, he was willing to let himself be nailed to a cross to pay for our sin. That is servant leadership at its peak.

The next time you walk into a class, take a moment to notice your professor's shoes. Let these shoes serve as a reminder to seek out ways to serve others every day.

PRAYER Dear Lord, Jesus was the ultimate servant. Please help me seek out ways to serve others for the rest of my life. Amen.

TRUSTED WITH MUCH

Luke 16:10 *Whoever can be trusted with very little can also be trusted with much, and whoever is dishonest with very little will also be dishonest with much.*

When I was a youngster, my parents decided one day that they were going to give me an allowance. However, unlike many of my friends who received allowances of $5 or more, I simply received 50 cents each week. The idea was not that I'd open a 401(k) or buy a used vehicle, but rather that I'd slowly develop an understanding of personal finance. If all went well each year, my parents would endow me with a 25-cent year-end raise.

I never did quite make the Forbes 50 in my grade school days the way my "high income" friends did, but I did learn to be somewhat responsible with what little money I had. As the passage suggests, a similar relationship can be found across other fundamental areas of life as well.

We have all been entrusted with something to varying degrees. But all of us who are in Christ have been entrusted with the greatest gift of all—God's grace, salvation, and Word of Truth. Whatever other gifts God has given you, know that there are many ways in which they can be applied: some for good—others, not so good. Since all of our sins have been taken away through Jesus' perfect life, death, and resurrection, let us not squander our gifts no matter what their amount. Rather, use them wisely by helping others out of love for God.

PRAYER Dear God, please help me be a good steward with all that you have given me. I am not perfect, and I do not always use my gifts wisely. Please grant me the strength and judgment to act in a way that lets others see you in me. In Jesus' name, I pray. Amen.

JESUS HOLDS IT TOGETHER

Colossians 1:16,17 *In him [Jesus] all things were created: things in heaven and on earth, visible and invisible, whether thrones or powers or rulers or authorities; all things have been created through him and for him. He is before all things, and in him all things hold together.*

"You've got it so together." Has anyone ever said that to you? If you're like me, when you hear those words, your first thought is, *If only you could see what's going on inside of me!* Truth be told, living in a world where anything can happen as I look at the future, I have things anything but "together." Same for you?

Read Colossians 1:16,17 again. You see, *you* can't hold anything together. Neither can I. We need only look at our frailties and insecurities and sins to realize that we *can't* hold it together. But Jesus can. He's the one who made all this. In him, it's all held together.

Have you ever heard of laminin? It's a glycoprotein that promotes cell adhesion. It's not an overstatement to say it's the glue that holds us together. Without it, we would literally fall apart. Laminin is shaped like a cross. Isn't it cool that the protein that holds us together *physically* looks just like the cross that holds us together *spiritually*? Feeling unraveled as you look to the future today?

Remember that the One through whom all things were made is also the One who loved you enough to die for your sins. He'll hold it together for you today.

PRAYER Lord Jesus, you made all things and you hold all things together. Your cross proves that you love me enough to hold things together for me today. Amen.

NOT OF THIS WORLD

John 17:16-19 *They are not of the world, even as I am not of it. Sanctify them by the truth; your word is truth. As you sent me into the world, I have sent them into the world. For them I sanctify myself, that they too may be truly sanctified.*

May is a time of commencements. While most think of a commencement ceremony as marking the end of an educational experience, the message of commencement is actually the opposite. "To commence" is to begin. In other words, a commencement marks the beginning of the rest of a graduate's life.

Most commencement speakers encourage graduates to go out in the world using their intellect and skills to find success. Themes often include the following: find your niche; set your course; rule the world.

Followers of Jesus have a different perspective. In fact, their perspective is unknown to the unbelieving world. Christians are aliens here on earth. We are foreigners—people who do not belong. *We are not citizens of this world.*

What makes us different? Jesus tells us. It's him. We are sanctified by the truth of God's Word. Faith, created in our hearts by the Holy Spirit through the gospel in Word and sacraments, sets us apart from everything else in this world.

This does not mean we should avoid the world and hide away until the Lord returns. On the contrary, Jesus sends us out into the world as his disciples. We are to engage the world as salt and light. We are to share the gospel and be a witness to all of the certain hope we have in our hearts. However, as we move through life, Christ's people must realize we do not belong in the same way that Jesus did not belong. We are heirs of glory, and our home is in heaven.

PRAYER Lord, thank you for reminding me that I am not of this world, but of your heavenly home. Amen.

PRODUCE GOOD FRUIT

Matthew 7:17,18 *Every good tree bears good fruit, but a bad tree bears bad fruit. A good tree cannot bear bad fruit, and a bad tree cannot bear good fruit.*

We are entering the end times of the school year. Some of us will be done with college, and some of us will be returning after a summer of working a couple of jobs to help pay for college. In either case, it is important to meditate on what type of fruit you produce.

Fruit is often used to describe good works of faith. This comparison makes a lot of sense. If someone believes that Jesus came to this earth, died, and rose from the dead for all people's sins, then the reaction to such love are good works, or fruit. If someone rejects Jesus, his or her fruit won't be the good fruit that Jesus is looking for. Bad trees bear bad fruit. Good trees bear good fruit. The good trees are those who trust in Jesus.

Good fruit is inviting. By proclaiming the truth of God's Word and performing good deeds, you can be a tool that God uses to bring people to faith in Christ as their Savior. Brothers and sisters, I urge you to produce good fruit as you end the semester and begin your summer.

PRAYER Dear Lord, thank you so much for sending your Son to die on a cross for my sins. Due to your love, I am now able to be a good tree and produce good fruit. Help me produce this good fruit and be wary of those who would like to lead me astray. Amen.

YOUR GREATEST NEED

Isaiah 43:1 *This is what the LORD says—he who created you, Jacob, he who formed you, Israel: "Do not fear, for I have redeemed you; I have summoned you by name; you are mine."*

Whether you are deciding your career path, studying to get your dream job, or nearing the end of your college journey, we have all felt the anxiety that goes along with college life. Sometimes that anxiety can bring fears of choosing the wrong career, failing a test, or not getting a job after graduation.

Fortunately, these are little fears compared to the greatest fear—the fear of eternity in hell. This is a fear that we should have and that we deserve as sinners who have not followed God's will. However, for believers, Christ has overcome the fear of hell. Jesus Christ has redeemed us, or bought us back, from the world in which we live. It was a high price— one that only God could pay. Jesus had to be fully God and fully man. He died on a cross in order to be punished for our sins (sins that he never even committed!). Because of Jesus, we do not fear the furnace of fire, but we rejoice and thank God that we will be with him in heaven one day.

So as you encounter different decisions and outcomes that life brings, be comforted that your greatest need has been fulfilled—the need for a Savior from eternal death. Christ has died, Christ has risen, and Christ will come again.

PRAYER Dear Lord, while I know sometimes life seems a little crazy and stressful, I am comforted in knowing that you love me so much that you would give me my greatest need—a Savior. Whatever direction my life goes, help me shine my light that others may also find that same comfort. Amen.

GOD'S HANDIWORK

Ephesians 2:10 *For we are God's handiwork, created in Christ Jesus to do good works, which God prepared in advance for us to do.*

"So, what do you plan to do?" Since senior year of high school, that question is probably all too familiar for us. As college graduation draws closer, the more realistic the question becomes. "So, what am I going to do?" It often can seem daunting. I mean, how can we really know for certain? We may have ideas, but what if those fail?

When doubts like this creep into our minds, we can turn to God's Word for comfort. God created us all to be different. This is evident just by looking at nature. There is not just one type of flower, tree, or animal. If there were, just think of how dull our world would be. Our Creator enjoys variety. God carefully instilled in us unique gifts and talents and called us his own. We are each a segment in his masterpiece of creation, which glorifies his name.

Instead of doubting whether or not we will achieve our goals or be successful, we should focus more on how we can utilize our talents, no matter the setting. When we give back to God through our gifts, we are carrying out his plan to keep us connected to him. We may not know what job we will have, where we will live, who we will marry, or how much we will make. Yet instead of saying, "I'm not sure" to the familiar question of what we plan to do, we can say with confidence, "To be God's handiwork, in whatever plan he has for me."

PRAYER Heavenly Father, calm my doubts about my future. Keep me connected to you and guide me in using my talents to praise you. Amen.

GOD'S GARDENING TOOLS

1 Corinthians 3:5-7 *What, after all, is Apollos? And what is Paul? Only servants, through whom you came to believe—as the Lord has assigned to each his task. I planted the seed, Apollos watered it, but God has been making it grow. So neither the one who plants nor the one who waters is anything, but only God, who makes things grow.*

Think about planting a flower. Have you ever noticed that you can follow the directions perfectly and yet never see the seed grow? How can something with all the correct resources not grow?

Paul speaks of spiritual growth in these verses. He gives us three simple steps about how we can be utilized by God to help others grow. First, like Apollos and Paul, each of us has been assigned the task of serving others. Second, Paul tells us to plant seeds. We can help individuals take root in God's love by sharing his Word with nonbelievers. Third, we are encouraged to water and nourish the faith of others. Simply by encouraging and supporting others through fellowship, we can be God's gardening tools.

Paul recognizes it is God who makes things grow. While God may utilize his servants as means of providing the correct resources, it is ultimately the Holy Spirit that works faith in each person. Therefore, be prepared to plant and water seeds wherever you may go. Serve others by showing concern for their faith life. Finally, pray that God will help both you and others grow in his love.

PRAYER Dear Lord, please use me as your servant to plant and water the seeds of your love so others may come to know you. Send the Holy Spirit to help me grow and become closer to you. Amen.

May 12

GO AND TELL

Mark 16:15,16 *He said to them, "Go into all the world and preach the gospel to all creation. Whoever believes and is baptized will be saved, but whoever does not believe will be condemned."*

Can you imagine life without your faith? Can you imagine not believing in something bigger than you or not having that comfort that you are a saved child of God? What if your parents, sibling, spouse, significant other, friend, or coworker never shared this good news with you? Where would you be today?

We have that very opportunity and responsibility to share the good news with others! How will you proceed? We are to "go into all the world and preach the gospel to all creation." How cool is that? If you are anything like me, it can be an extremely exciting opportunity yet also scary and intimidating. However, it ends up being the work of the Holy Spirit. One way in which I choose to honor this passage is by signing up for a program called Malawi's Easter for Kids. I have the opportunity to share the good news with hundreds of kids whom I will get to see in heaven someday! I feel incredibly blessed to have this opportunity.

How do you choose to share the good news? Canvassing, service trip, choir, youth group leader, Sunday school or vacation Bible school teacher . . . where does your passion lie? Find it and start spreading the good news!

PRAYER Lord, thank you for choosing me to go out into the world and share your good news with all. Please be with me and help me on this journey. Amen.

DON'T CRACK THE EGG

1 Corinthians 16:13 *Be on your guard; stand firm in the faith; be courageous; be strong.*

As a child, my family had a trampoline. My siblings and I would jump on that trampoline just about every day. To keep things lively and interesting, we would play the game "don't crack the egg." The game basically required you to sit in the fetal position in the middle of the trampoline and attempt to not change position while everyone else jumped around you. This game is kind of terrifying because the whole time you are worried about all of your limbs going everywhere, as you are thinking to yourself, *If only I could find a way to keep my limbs from flailing!* The whole game would be a lot easier if there were someone else just holding your limbs close to your body.

In the same way, life can be kind of terrifying. We are never too sure when we might fall apart because the world is moving so quickly around us. I know my life is always throwing new obstacles in my way. However, there is somewhere we can find comfort as we leave college for the summer or possibly forever, as 1 Corinthians 16:13 reminds us. Sometimes it's difficult to stand firm and be on our guard all of the time, but we aren't doing it alone. God is holding us together. He is the hand that helps us stay together in "don't crack the egg." We can be courageous and firm in our faith with the helping hands of God holding us together.

PRAYER God, as we all move in different directions at the end of the school year, help us remember that through you we can stay strong and be courageous in every obstacle. Keep your guiding hands around us each and every day. Amen.

GROW OR DIE

Hebrews 6:1 *Let us move beyond the elementary teachings about Christ and be taken forward to maturity, not laying again the foundation of repentance from acts that lead to death, and of faith in God.*

Is Continuing Education in the plan for your relationship with Jesus Christ?

Continuing Ed is a buzzword of the professional world seen as a solution to the business mantra "Grow or die!" The thought is that if you are not growing in craft or profession, you are almost certainly failing. And to "lose your competitive edge" is to become obsolete.

Obsolete is *not* good in the world of careers, loan payments, and rent.

Continuing Ed is "growth on top of what one has already achieved." College is a great example of achievement meant for growth. Are you done with your first year of college? What's your game plan for the summer to build on your year? Are you about to graduate? How will you build on what you've achieved?

What about your relationship with Jesus? He gave you faith to love him and his gift of eternal life. Does continuing education—growth—play a role in your future with him?

"Let us move beyond the *elementary* teachings about Christ and be taken forward to *maturity*." All healthy relationships grow through time . . . effort . . . communication. "Grow or die" is true of the Christian's relationship with God.

"I am the vine; you are the branches," Jesus said. "If you remain in me and I in you" (relationship), "you will bear much fruit" (growth). "Apart from me you can do nothing" (John 15:5).

PRAYER Let me plan to grow my relationship with you, Lord Jesus! Amen.

WALK IN LOVE

2 John 1:6 *This is love: that we walk in obedience to his commands. As you have heard from the beginning, his command is that you walk in love.*

Whether it's your first or fourth year of college, the month of May is sure to be filled to the brim with final projects, exams, job searches, and many other stressors. In the midst of this chaos, it's easy to fall into negative patterns and pick up habits that reflect anything but the life of a thriving Christian.

Perhaps relationships that you worked to build up seem to be falling apart at the seams; you begin to worry and your trust in God's plans wavers. Maybe you aren't achieving the grades you wanted; cheating on your work looks like a tempting option to give your grade a quick boost. Sometimes the stress from looming deadlines is too much, and instead of turning to God in your personal devotion, you make "me time" and socializing a higher priority.

God's Word for today gives us a good reminder of how we are always to act. Today we are encouraged to always walk in love, in obedience to God's commands. This means that we are to put all of our trust in God despite what may be happening in our lives. The things we worry about now are actually insignificant in the grand scheme of life, but it is difficult to not stress about them. The next time we are tempted to worry or put God on the sidelines, remember the words of 2 John 1:6 that remind us to walk in love and obey God in his commands.

PRAYER Dear Lord, guide me through these final weeks of the school year that I may put forth my best effort in everything I do. Give me a heart and faith that looks to you for the path that you want me to follow. Amen.

OUR TESTIMONY

1 Thessalonians 1:7,8 *You became a model to all the believers in Macedonia and Achaia. The Lord's message rang out from you not only in Macedonia and Achaia—your faith in God has become known everywhere. Therefore we do not need to say anything about it.*

In order to truly understand these verses, we must look at the verses that come before it. Paul is writing to the Thessalonians and praising their example—"for you welcomed the message in the midst of severe suffering with the joy given by the Holy Spirit." Because of how they walked through suffering with joy, the gospel spread throughout the area. In fact, their testimony was so well known that Paul did not have to say anything further about it.

What kind of example are you setting? I once heard a quote that expressed the idea that we may be the only Bible those around us "read." They see it through our example and ask why—how we handle difficult situations, how we show love to those around us, and even how we do the work put in front of us. As we venture into the next phases of our lives, what reputation goes before us? Hopefully it's one that's characterized by the same qualities the Thessalonians were praised for. We may not experience the intense suffering that they did for their faith, but our testimony can still ring out in the way we live our everyday lives. May our faith in God become known everywhere so that he receives all the glory!

PRAYER Dear Jesus, help me be a bold and willing follower of you so that your name becomes known to others because of my testimony. Thank you for giving me what I need to live this life well. May I not waste the opportunities you give me! Amen.

THE LORD'S PURPOSE

Proverbs 19:21 *Many are the plans in a person's heart, but it is the* L*ORD's purpose that prevails.*

I could not believe it. I had not been a klutz or prone to injury before, but I guess something went wrong. With one slip, I fell down the stairs I had successfully scaled thousands of times before. With that, I found myself in urgent care looking at a significantly disfigured lower leg bone. How could that be? This was not in the plan! I was applying for jobs around the state and working full time. I could not stop now!

It could have been very easy to become discouraged or even angry with God. He had let something stop me in my tracks. It was not in *my* plan! While I was stewing in self-doubt and frustration, God had something else in the works. Reread today's passage. This small but powerful bit of Scripture comes from Solomon, whose father was well acquainted with struggling with God's plan. David wanted to build a temple for the Lord, but he was told that his son Solomon would get that privilege. I am sure David had elaborate plans of what this great temple would look like, but those plans were not in line with the Lord's purpose.

Rather than getting discouraged, focus on the opportunities that are presented at difficult times of redirection. Trust that it is God who is doing the redirection for your ultimate good.

PRAYER Heavenly Father, teach me to pray as your Son taught: "Your will be done on earth as in heaven." I know your purpose for my life will succeed, but help me trust more confidently in the times I lose focus on your plan. May my life be yours for the shaping. Amen.

PLAN WITH CONFIDENCE

Proverbs 16:9 *In their hearts humans plan their course, but the LORD establishes their steps.*

Are you a planner? Or do you have a "winging it" personality? Does one style tend to work better for you than the other?

Either way, your thoughts are probably very focused on what is in your near future: semester project deadlines, final tests, maybe a summer internship or job, and perhaps your graduation date. The pressure is on, and it can be overwhelming. Sometimes you plan and everything seems to fall perfectly into place. Other times, nothing goes according to any intentions you set. Planning can be both a blessing and a source of great frustration.

In finalizing your next set of goals, what will your focus be? Are you living and planning primarily for yourself, or do you have God's mission for you in mind? Look again at what the writer of Proverbs 16:9 shares with us.

This means that when it comes to your future, you get the best of both aspects. God is firmly in control and he has promised to work everything for your good. Yet you have an active and crucial role in this future of yours too.

By his power in forming you and by his power in the gospel that forgives you, God has given you the intelligence and compassion to go out into the world as his representative. You're free to choose your own adventure! Plan with confidence, knowing he is with you every step of the way.

PRAYER Lord God, thank you for being with me in all my life's journey. As I consider my plans for the future, be my great Counselor and lead me in the direction where I can make the biggest impact in the mission to spread your kingdom to the ends of the earth. I do this all for the glory of your name. Amen.

CLEANSE MY HEART

James 4:8 *Come near to God and he will come near to you. Wash your hands, you sinners, and purify your hearts, you double-minded.*

Your mind says salad, but your taste buds say cheesecake. Your professor says, "Papers due tomorrow," but your friends say, "You can't miss the season finale!" Sometimes two impulses beg for your attention, and you have to refuse one or the other.

Remember the prodigal son (Luke 15:11-32)? One impulse told him that his father loved him. But he had two impulses. The other told him to go experience all the world's adventures, pains, lusts, and learning experiences. So he picked one. He refused his father. He chose to follow the world's impulse.

Two impulses. The book of James calls that familiar dilemma being double-minded. You're about to get more familiar with the dilemma. You're stepping into "the real world" full time. Maybe you'll have a place where you hear God's Word every day. Maybe you won't. Either way, your double-minded dilemma is about to show you God's law and his love right alongside the world's adventures, pains, lusts, and learning experiences—two impulses. Sound stressful?

There's good news. "Come near to God and he will come near to you." Prioritize God's will over the world's will. And when you choose sinful pleasure instead of God's will, then go back to him, like the prodigal son. Lift your eyes back to the gospel. You'll find your Dad running to you. He never stopped loving you. As you draw near with regret to repent, he draws near with love to forgive you. Every. Single. Time.

PRAYER Heavenly Father, cleanse my heart from double-mindedness. Fix my eyes on you. Forgive me and draw near to me. I ask it for Jesus' sake. Amen.

STOP LIVING THE "ME FIRST" LIFE

Mark 10:43-45 *Whoever wants to become great among you must be your servant, and whoever wants to be first must be slave of all. For even the Son of Man did not come to be served, but to serve, and to give his life as a ransom for many.*

It's May. To add to the stress, this month signals the end of another, perhaps your final, school year. Sometimes an anxious graduating student will be told by a mentor, "Life's tough out there, so do what you can to get ahead." Even if the phrase is not stated, the sentiment is present.

We could criticize the tenets of our society for promoting selfish greed and cutthroat pursuit of gain, but is not the seed of these attitudes already in our hearts? This month, have you evaded someone who needed you so that you could fill out another application, study a little more, or polish up that paper? Have you been begging God to help you get through May, but not saying a word of thanks for the blessings and people that surround you?

If you're living the "me first" life, then stop. The Christian's life is different. How do we know? Because Christ came to earth to give up everything for our sake. He laid his life down to destroy the accusations Satan raised against us. He set you free from the life of "me first" by putting you first in his life. Now you are called to do the same for others.

PRAYER Precious Jesus, you suffered greatly for my sake to make me holy. Let me live in holiness with you. Amen.

POSITIVE INFLUENCE

John 15:4 *Remain in me, and I also remain in you. No branch can bear fruit by itself; it must remain in the vine. Neither can you bear fruit unless you remain in me.*

Influence can be a powerful thing. I think of Spider-Man and, if we swap the words *power* and *influence*, Uncle Ben would say, "With great influence comes great responsibility."

Some have already tuned out, thinking, "I'm no leader; I don't influence others." You're sorely mistaken. We all have influence! The way you walk and talk, the clothes you wear, and the choices you make influence people around you. The real question is whether or not your influence is positive or negative.

Whether it's your buddies asking you to go to an underage drinking party or your boss yelling at you for some unjustified reason, you have the opportunity to influence those around you for better or for worse. Everything you do or don't do, everything you say or don't say, has the power to influence those around you. That is a huge responsibility, and one you should never take lightly.

If you truly want to positively influence those around you, it is an absolute must that you stay connected to the most influential person who has ever lived—Jesus Christ. He personally took away the sins of the whole world, removing the great divide between our holy God and us. There can be no greater influence than giving someone the gift of eternal life! Because Christ has not just influenced but has changed our hearts and lives in such an amazing and powerful way, our entire lives become an opportunity to powerfully influence those around us and point them to our Savior.

PRAYER Dear Lord, keep me in your Word so that I can stay connected to the One who took away my sins. Help me have a positive influence on others and point them to the most influential person who ever lived. Amen.

FURTHERING GOD'S KINGDOM

John 15:7,8 *If you remain in me and my words remain in you, ask whatever you wish, and it will be done for you. This is to my Father's glory, that you bear much fruit, showing yourselves to be my disciples.*

Have you ever really wanted something? I mean really, really bad? Whether you got what you wanted or not, I would hope that you took time to pray about it. The real question is if you prayed that God's will be done or that he gave you what you wanted in the moment.

Reread today's words. Jesus is not saying that we will automatically get whatever we ask for. He is explaining that we can only pray correctly and approach our Father with a true request when we know Christ's teachings. When we understand that prayer requests should also be aimed at furthering the kingdom of God and not just our own personal gain, our prayer life will change drastically.

As you complete another year of higher education and take another step toward adulthood, now is an excellent time to reevaluate your own prayer life. If you need to make a change, transition from asking only for things that benefit you personally to praying for things that Jesus taught us to pray for. Pray that God's will be done to further his kingdom in us and through us. Pray that we may bear the fruits of faith and glorify his name. Let us start right now.

PRAYER Dear Lord, I thank you for revealing your holy will to me in the Scriptures. Thank you for bringing me safely through another school year. Please guide my life and let my decision making to be pleasing to you. I ask that you would continue to bless me as you see fit and use me as your instrument to further the kingdom. In Jesus' name, I pray. Amen.

SERVE THE LORD

Joshua 24:15 *But if serving the L*ORD *seems undesirable to you, then choose for yourselves this day whom you will serve, whether the gods your ancestors served beyond the Euphrates, or the gods of the Amorites, in whose land you are living. But as for me and my household, we will serve the L*ORD.

Israelites, if only we could say that we are better than you! If only we could shake our heads at your neglect of God's love and your haughty attitudes. Yet we can do no such thing. The years following graduation test every fiber of one's spiritual being. You choose where to worship, where to have a good time on Friday and Saturday nights, and what you will be like in your new place of employment. You choose who to marry and how to invest your money. You choose which friends to keep and those to "de-friend." Most important, you choose how you will honor your heavenly Father, who sustained you throughout your college walk.

It might be easy to commit your future to God today, especially if you are surrounded by believers who lift you up each day in prayer and positive conversations. You should be proud of the courage and conviction you have as Christ's servant, about to head into the world! You are totally equipped for every good deed God has planned for you to do. Armed with faith, you will stand firm in the Lord.

Pray continually. Serve the Lord unswervingly. Continue to feed your soul regularly at church. Marry a spouse who will encourage you in your walk with Jesus. Raise your children to know their Savior. Do not be swayed by the world's gods, as the Israelites were. As a fellow Christian and a fellow sinner, I am praying for you. Go out there and choose to serve the Lord.

PRAYER Father, you have chosen me to be your light in the world. Strengthen my faith's foundation through your Word and equip me with all I need to serve you fearlessly. Amen.

SERVE OTHERS

1 Peter 5:2,3 *Be shepherds of God's flock that is under your care, watching over them—not because you must, but because you are willing, as God wants you to be; not pursuing dishonest gain, but eager to serve; not lording it over those entrusted to you, but being examples to the flock.*

I go to a college that has a statue of Christ washing one of his disciple's feet. It's located in a central location where it serves as a daily reminder to everyone of their earthly mission: to serve others. Now, this is easier said than done because of our sinful nature. We are self-centered and want to bring ourselves glory.

Even though Peter is writing to the elders in the passage above, the advice is still applicable for all of us because we may someday serve as leaders. What is your motive when serving your fellow classmates, teammates, business associates, the elderly, and your family? Are you looking to gain favor and a pat on the back, or are you doing it with a humble and willing heart? Does your willingness change depending on the circumstance? Do you do it because you are getting paid or because you have to accumulate hours of service or to simply make a better name for yourself? Or do you do it willingly, eager to serve Christ by serving those around you?

True servants are not always noticed for what they do. Jesus once told a man, after healing him, not to tell others about what he had done for him but to keep it a secret. This reveals the servant heart of Jesus. What do your actions say about you?

PRAYER Help me serve others with a joyful spirit. Please take away the desire to bring myself glory and allow my thoughts and actions to glorify you always. Amen.

LET ME SHOW GOD'S LOVE

Philippians 2:5-7 *In your relationships with one another, have the same mindset as Christ Jesus: Who, being in very nature God, did not consider equality with God something to be used to his own advantage; rather, he made himself nothing by taking the very nature of a servant, being made in human likeness.*

Have you ever made a vow to be perfect, to be kind to everyone, or to not judge others? After making this vow, you come across two or three people that you know, and you are kind to them, not judging them for anything. This isn't so bad! Then a third person walks past and you cannot help but think, "What an ugly outfit!" How quick we are to judge others.

Serving others is easier said than done. Yes, we ideally want to put others before ourselves. Yes, we ideally want to treat others in the best possible way. But we quickly fall short of perfection. Thankfully, there was one who did not fall short of perfection: Jesus, the Son of God, who came to earth and entered into a state of humility. He came to earth to love you and that person who wears weird outfits.

We cannot comprehend what it must be like to be God, and to then assume humanity. Jesus loved me so much that he did this, and took all my sin, and everyone's sin in the whole world by dying on a cross. What amazing love this is!

How could Jesus do that? How could he humble himself and become a servant, just for me? Am I that special to him? Yes, you are. He created you, he saved you, and he sanctified you. Praise God for his amazing grace!

PRAYER Dear Jesus, thank you for humiliating yourself for a hopeless sinner like me. Help me never forget this fact. I confess that I often fall short of perfection. Make me a servant, Lord. Let me show your love to other people. Amen.

PUT GOD FIRST

Acts 4:19,20 *Peter and John replied, "Which is right in God's eyes: to listen to you, or to him? You be the judges! As for us, we cannot help speaking about what we have seen and heard."*

Life is no longer filled with playing house, shooting Nerf guns, or making forts. Growing up opens your eyes to a complex world. We learn about the necessities of life that consume all our time. We need money to survive; therefore, we need a job. Along the way we must make the right decisions to guide our path. Coming to the right decision may be the hardest part of it all.

What guides your decisions? Do you follow the crowd? The heart of your decisions can tell you who you are serving first and what you truly value.

In the verses in this devotion, the Pharisees had come up to Peter and John to tell them to stop telling others about Jesus. They immediately stated that they would not stop speaking about this news. Their decision was based on what God says is right. Their motivation came out of thanks to their Savior, who they witnessed die for every single sin.

When you are asked to act against God in order to progress at your job, what will you do? Will you stand up for the truth or sacrifice your beliefs for earthly success?

When God is put first in every decision, he promises that he will provide for you. Would not your father give you anything that you needed? God is our Father who holds more riches than anyone. Can you not trust him by serving him at all times?

Remember that God is faithful. He cannot fail us.

PRAYER Dear Father, help me make decisions that are pleasing to you even when they are counterculture. Enable me to share my faith and witness in my relationships. Amen.

HOPE IN THE LORD

Isaiah 40:31 *Those who hope in the* LORD *will renew their strength. They will soar on wings like eagles; they will run and not grow weary, they will walk and not be faint.*

Just a year ago, I was applying for jobs, looking for apartments, searching for a new car, and worrying about everything in between. Worry was a hot topic among my friends during our senior year. Thinking about the future is stressful and scary, but as I worried, applied for jobs, and worried some more, I remembered God's promises.

Isaiah 40:31 is one such promise. When I was so worried and so upset, just the thought of God's plan for me brought a new strength and joy that I did not have when I was focused on my plan for me. Since God provided for my greatest need by sending a Savior from sin, I live with confidence that he will supply my lesser needs as well.

Just the other day I was talking to my friend who has yet to hear any good news from any of her graduate school applications. She was wondering if she should reapply or start looking for jobs. I told her the same words that comforted me. No matter what you're doing, it's part of God's plan. So then the question is, Why worry? It's in God's hands.

PRAYER Dear Lord, you know that I am sinful and forget to put all my worries in your hands. Comfort me by reminding me that you are in control and that if I hope in your name, I will be strengthened. Amen.

THE UNKNOWNS

Luke 12:32 *Do not be afraid, little flock, for your Father has been pleased to give you the kingdom.*

Have you ever wondered about your future after college? What career will you have? Where will you live? Will you be able to pay your student loans? There are so many unknowns you face as you prepare for graduation. For me, it was scary to know I had to start a new chapter outside of the comfort of my college walls. I didn't know what the future would bring. Commencement was just around the corner, and I still didn't have a job lined up. The fear of the unknown overwhelmed me.

Our heavenly Father tells us not to be afraid. He calls us his little flock because he loves and watches out for us. He is pleased to provide us with the greatest gift—his heavenly kingdom. We have heaven as a sure thing in our future even when we have to face earthly scary unknowns. What a comfort to know that our future is secured in Christ alone!

God certainly had a plan for me after graduation. An unexpected job opportunity presented itself right out of college. Furthermore, my next two jobs since have fallen into my lap, so to speak. God has tremendously blessed me and directed my path. I never need to worry or be afraid because God always has a plan for me, just like he has a plan for you. We just need to trust in him and keep our eyes fixed on heaven. He is our Good Shepherd who will show us the way. Therefore, do not fear for your future; God is in control.

PRAYER Dearest heavenly Father, thank you so much for giving me the gift of heaven. Please be with me when I'm faced with unknowns. Help me lean on you instead of being afraid. Amen.

DON'T PLAY IT SAFE

1 Peter 2:11,12 *Dear friends, I urge you, as foreigners and exiles, to abstain from sinful desires, which wage war against your soul. Live such good lives among the pagans that, though they accuse you of doing wrong, they may see your good deeds and glorify God on the day he visits us.*

"Something is wrong when our lives make sense to unbelievers." That sentence from the book *Crazy Love* by Francis Chan really struck me as I read it. What a great point. Why are we surprised when people don't understand our actions as Christians? If we are truly living to glorify God and not ourselves or the world, shouldn't we expect weird looks or remarks?

I have one major regret from my college years: I chose to live a safe, watered-down version of Christianity. I went to church and never blatantly turned away from God, but I lowered my standards so I was just unchristian enough to fit in with my friends. Through my words and actions—or lack thereof—I made sure to tiptoe around the things I knew were wrong because I didn't want to stir things up or offend people.

Don't do what I did. Whether you're coming back for another year of school in fall or you're heading off to the real world at the end of this school year, don't live a safe Christian life. There's a God who deserves obedience and glory—not just because he is God but because he hid his glory for our sakes under his humanity and became obedient to death, even death on a cross. And there's a world of people all around you who need salvation and the truth more than they need your acceptance of or participation in their Christless living.

Here's to living a life that *doesn't* make sense to unbelievers, in the very best way.

PRAYER Dear Lord, help me live a Christian life with no regrets—one where I put you first and don't play it safe. Amen.

RUN THE RACE OF FAITH

Acts 20:24 *I consider my life worth nothing to me; my only aim is to finish the race and complete the task the Lord Jesus has given me—the task of testifying to the good news of God's grace.*

In Paul's final words to the leaders of the church of Ephesus, he likens the follower of Jesus to five different pursuits: a runner in a race, a steward, a witness, a herald, and a watchman. Which one resonates the most with you?

Reread today's passage. The key word in this passage is "given," which reminds us that we are stewards. We own nothing; rather, we have received the gift of faith and everything else we have as a trust from God. This includes our careers, our ministry, and our very lives. We are servants to God's will through baptism into his family. And he has given us a task: run the race of faith.

Our whole lives are meant to be a testimony of our faith, which we are to share with others. Still wondering about which of those pursuits you are? Here's a hint. You are all five. As a runner in the race of faith, you are a steward to everything God has given to you. Since you have been given this task to run, you are a witness who calls out the message of the gospel like a herald. Finally, be constantly watching for Christ's return, and by being in the Word, you will be ready for that final day. As you fulfill your task, remember that God is beside you the whole race.

PRAYER Dear Father, forgive me when I feel the race of life is too difficult. Help me keep my faith strong as I focus on the finish. In Jesus' name, I pray. Amen.

May 31

DEPART IN PEACE

Numbers 6:24-26 *The Lord bless you and keep you; the Lord make his face shine on you and be gracious to you; the Lord turn his face toward you and give you peace.*

These words are known as the Aaronic benediction and are often used to close worship services. It's only fitting, then, that we use these words as an ending to this devotion book.

It's the last day of May, which means that you are most likely done with another year of college. You might have graduated and are now entering the "real world," or you may be heading home to work your summer job to pay for another year of college. Whatever the situation, the blessing in this passage is comforting.

There is much meaning in these words. There are three phrases that begin with "the Lord"; three phrases that bring to mind the three persons of our God. While the Trinity is unfathomable to our human minds, we can appreciate the fact that our triune God lovingly acts on our behalf. Our Lord, the Father, blesses us through the material things he provides for us and by preventing dangers from overwhelming us. Our Lord, the Son, died for our sins on a cross and now looks upon us as his family. Our Lord, the Holy Spirit, miraculously brings us to faith.

Depart in peace, knowing that God's divine power and endless love back every word of the Aaronic benediction.

PRAYER Dear Lord, thank you for all the blessings that you have showered upon me. I ask that you be with me as I continue my journey and enter the unknown of the future. When I hear the Aaronic benediction, help me think about these words and know that they are true. Amen.

CONTRIBUTING AUTHORS

Jack Albert
Stephen Apt
Hannah Bartels
Emily Baxter
Christina Bender
Anna Biedenbender
Alan Bitter
Aaron Boehm
Mark Braun
Julius Buelow
Titus Buelow
Sarah Burk
Peter Buschkopf
Kai Tai (Stanley) Chan
Michael Cherney
Rebecca Christensen
Stefanie Cox
Michael Cyr
Brian Davison
Jenny Ebeling
Judy Eggers
Erica Ellington
Emily Elmquist
Raenell Engel
Brian Enter
Julie Favorite
Jonathan Fricke
Amanda Frier
Margaret Gartner
Lisa Gerlach
Courtney Giovinazzo
Sydney Giovinazzo
Lachrisa Grandberry
Jeremiah Harbach
Lydia Harbach
Mary Heins
Sarah Helwig
Abigail Himm
Caleb Hintz

Stacy Hoehl
Jim Holmen
Kate Jaeger
Ethan Jahns
Caroline Jensen
Diana Kerr
Marah Kiecker
William King
Allee Klug
Kristen Koepsell
Paul Koester
John Kolander
Melanie Laete
Sarah Lambrecht
Morgan Ledermann
Kathryn Leistekow
Katie Lorig
Greg Lyon
Charisse Miller
Troy Moench
Daniel Moldenhauer
Audrey Oppermann
Jimmy Pautz
Amanda Pearson
Brittany Peterson
Quinten Petersen
Kristen Plessinger
Emma Poetter
Jennifer Polzin
Emma Prost
Gary Pufahl
Josiah Ricke
Aaron Roeseler
Mitchell Rollefson
David Scharf
Elizabeth Scheibl
Ashley Schmidt
Brian Schmidt
Eric Schroeder

Alyssa Schwartz
Hailey Schwartz
Rachel Sebald
Michelle Shambeau
Wayne Shevey
Bethany Shiels
Hannah Shiels
Zach Shiels
Katie Slattengren
Katie Sloan
Brad Snyder
Bethany Soderlund
Erica Spiegelberg
Marta Stahlfeld
Angela Stern
Nathan Strobel
Kasey Struck
Amanda Swiontek
Craig Swiontek
Cameron Teske
Evan Teske
Luke Thompson
Emily Treichel
Eric Treske
Eric Ulm
Bethany Unkefer
Adam Volbrecht
Coltyn VonDeylen
Philip Warnecke
Michael Werni
Jacob Werre
Katelyn Werre
Samuel Wessel
Barb Westness
Nicole Westra
Meredith Wilson
Rhoda Wolle
Nathan Wordell

ABOUT TIME OF GRACE

Time of Grace is for people who want more growth and less struggle in their spiritual walk. Through the timeless truth of God's Word, we connect people to God's grace so they know they are loved and forgiven and so they can start living in the freedom they've always wanted.

To discover more, please visit timeofgrace.org or call 800.661.3311.

HELP SHARE GOD'S MESSAGE OF GRACE!

Every gift you give helps Time of Grace reach people around the world with the good news of Jesus. Your generosity and prayer support take the gospel of grace to others through our ministry outreach and help them find the restart with Jesus they need.

Give today at timeofgrace.org/give or by calling 800.661.3311.

Thank you!

50634691R00179

Made in the USA
Middletown, DE
26 June 2019